Praise for *A Spanner in the Works*

This unexpected and beautifully written story of the pioneer woman driver, Alice Anderson, enthralled me. I relished the realisation of Alice's dreams set against the development of feminism in 1920s Australia. And Alice's tragic death provides a powerful end to a thrilling book . . . I LOVED this story.

—Miriam Margolyes OBE, actor

[This] biography is fascinating.

—Kerry Greenwood, author of the *Phryne Fisher* series

I sat up until after midnight and read *A Spanner in the Works* in one sitting. I loved it. Totally. [Loretta has] wonderfully told a complicated story of a woman, her friends and family, a business, a city, a fascinating time. All the threads weave together in a way that made it impossible for me to put it down.

—Georgine Clarsen, Associate Professor and Discipline Leader for History, School of Humanities and Social Inquiry, University of Wollongong, author of *Eat my Dust: Early Women Motorists*

Loretta Smith has followed many career paths over the years, including teacher, youth arts worker, research consultant, case manager and life coach. She is also an accomplished musician, environmental activist, feisty feminist, dog lover and avid reader, with a penchant for writing. She first read of Alice Anderson in *The Unusual Life of Edna Walling* (Allen & Unwin, 2005). Then one of her aged clients, who had Alzheimer's, dropped a bombshell when she mentioned her mother worked as a driver and mechanic for Alice Anderson. So began Loretta's amazing journey researching, studying, writing and promoting Alice Anderson's exceptional legacy.

A SPANNER IN THE WORKS

THE EXTRAORDINARY STORY OF ALICE ANDERSON AND AUSTRALIA'S FIRST ALL-GIRL GARAGE

LORETTA SMITH

hachette
AUSTRALIA

Editorial note: To uphold the historical veracity of *A Spanner in the Works*, the author has made the decision to retain the original spelling and grammar of source material within the text. In doing so, errors in spelling and grammar have been reproduced. The author and publisher have refrained from using '[sic]' repeatedly to highlight any of these intentional errors as these instances are obvious to the reader and such an insertion would hinder the reading experience.

Published in Australia and New Zealand in 2019
by Hachette Australia
(an imprint of Hachette Australia Pty Limited)
Level 17, 207 Kent Street, Sydney NSW 2000
www.hachette.com.au

A catalogue record for this
book is available from the
National Library of Australia

ISBN: 978 0 7336 4210 4 (paperback)

Cover design by Luke Causby, Blue Cork
Front cover photograph first published in *The Home* magazine, 1 December 1920 (author's collection)
Back cover photograph in author's collection
Author photograph by Harriet Mantell
Text design by Bookhouse, Sydney
Typeset in 12.2/17 pt Bembo by Bookhouse, Sydney
Printed and bound in Australia by McPherson's Printing Group

*In memory of garage girl Nancy Houston's
daughter Mary Cohn (1918–2008) who told me
countless times, 'Oh, I adored Miss Anderson!'*

*And dedicated to all of Alice's garage girls – those who
appear within these pages and others whose identities,
despite my best efforts, could not be confirmed.*

CONTENTS

PROLOGUE

DESTINATION: ALICE SPRINGS

'Always see the Engine has plenty
of oil before setting out'

(1920s *Shell Motorists' Index*)

MELBOURNE, 6 AUGUST 1926

It is early evening and the ladies of the Lyceum Club are gathered for an extraordinary supper meeting in the members lounge. The view from the fifth floor of the English, Scottish and Australian Bank building on the corner of Queen and Collins Streets is an admirable one, especially at twilight when the sun shimmers on the Yarra across to Port Phillip Bay. However, at this moment, all eyes are focused on the motorcar that has just parked in the street below.

The tiny Austin 7 would not have merited a second glance except for the huge pile of luggage stuffed in the back seat and tied to its exterior. It has been stripped to its essentials; even its doors have been removed to make room for the hefty cargo. Behind the wheel sits its owner, the youthful Miss Alice Anderson. She kills the engine, legs it over the packing sacks and lands on the footpath, revealing driving leathers from head to thigh. Gloves off, Alice peels back her cap and goggles, and shakes out her short, shingled brown curls. She strides round the corner and enters the Gothic-style building, taking the stairs to the fifth floor.

Inside, the club boasts newly refurbished rooms of muted oriental tones and parquet floors covered with plush rose and ruby red Persian rugs.[1] Women in elegant gowns move to greet Alice. They are the crème de la crème of female accomplishment: luminaries such as Frances Taylor, founding editor and business manager of the immensely popular Australian women's magazine *Woman's World*; Dr Janet Greig, the first woman anaesthetist in Victoria; and Georgina Sweet, pre-eminent zoologist, current club president and Australia's first female acting professor in biology.

Alice removes the leather jacket and bulky coat, revealing her petite figure and, instead of frock, shoes and stockings, a masculine-style shirt, tie and breeches. A few of the older ladies seated in a corner chortle as they recall the impression Alice made when she first presented as a new club member almost eight years before. 'She strode into the dressing room looking like a boy, in her breeches, leggings and tweed cap pulled down over her eyes. Some of the conservatives looked at her askance, but others were intrigued!'[2], says a large woman wearing a pale peach drop-waisted gown with matching shawl round her copious arms. 'Oh yes!' cried a small-waisted woman in a red satin coatdress. 'I remember someone asking Alice for her qualifications and she responded, "Oh, I got through as the pioneer of women in the motoring industry," her face all wreathed in smiles.'[3] The ladies laugh and nod in recognition as they sip their tea and nibble on freshly made sandwiches. Meanwhile, Alice engages in lively conversation with those gathered round her.

Not all Lyceum Club members approve of Alice's dress code but she is nevertheless a popular young woman even though, unlike most other members, Alice has never completed secondary school, let alone university. Her '2B' membership, denoting women without academic qualifications 'who have otherwise rendered distinguished public service'[4], is well deserved, for Alice is an exceptional young woman. Not only is she the first woman in Australia to own and operate a motor garage, hers is the only garage in the country to employ all-women staff, be they 'chauffeuses', tour conductors, mechanics or driving instructors.

Alice's Lyceum Club membership application was helped along by many University of Melbourne women who frequent Alice's garage in Cotham Road, Kew, just a few miles from the university, including Florence Young and Margery Herring, who proposed and seconded Alice's membership. They are single, waged and among the first women able to afford the purchase and maintenance of cars in their own right. Margery's sister-in-law, Nancy, is even on Alice's payroll as a driver and mechanic.

The press affectionately call Alice and her employees 'garage girls'. Fitted out in masculine chauffeur uniforms or overalls, the public often mistake them for boys or men, and rumours of transgressions of all sorts are rife. But they wear the most practical clothing for the job and, thanks to Alice's excellent training and firm guidance, are widely recognised for their professionalism. Alice also wears mannish clothes because it is her sartorial preference. She only ever has a couple of frocks in her wardrobe for those special occasions when nothing else will do. Otherwise she finds dresses a nuisance. However, according to Alice's younger sister Claire, who works at the garage on weekends, Alice always impresses upon her employees that it is not necessary to ape men or to lose their femininity.

Another who stands out from the fashionable crowd this evening is Miss Jessie Webb, founding member, previous president, and the University of Melbourne's first female lecturer in the history department. She looks far from elegant in her sensible frock, woollen hat and stout shoes but she is dressed not so much for this evening as for the occasion to follow. Tonight, the ladies of the Lyceum Club are here to farewell Alice and Jessie, her driving companion, on their imminent departure to Central Australia. They will be taking the little Austin 7 on a return trip of 3000 miles where few roads exist. The continent's interior is populated by Aboriginal peoples, many of whom still survive on their traditional lands, with only a handful of Europeans living in homesteads on vast sheep and cattle stations. Throughout their journey the two women will sit, cramped side by side, with barely enough room for a gear stick between them. It will be a feat of challenging proportions.

Both women are well prepared for the trip and Jessie is particularly experienced in unorthodox travel. In 1922, for instance, she ventured from the Cape Peninsula to Cairo with Georgina Sweet, whose friends were so horrified at the whole trip that they refused to see her off. The two survived the journey with the help of porters who carried them in chairs over the roughest terrain and a collapsible rubber bath that Jessie insisted on bringing to keep them both 'presentable'.

Alice has no such tale to tell. At twenty-nine she is seventeen years younger than Jessie, and her overseas experiences have been limited to a childhood trip to England and Ireland. One could say the two are odd travelling companions but they are both pioneers in their fields and both believe in the advancement of women. As spinsters with no husbands to obey and no children to hinder them, they also share the freedom to take on such an adventure. Though Alice's travelling experience is not worldly, her trip through the outback with a lone companion suggests, particularly to her female customers, that the great-unknown highway belongs to anyone who dares take it.

Alice and Jessie's expedition, however, will be far from the first to have attempted long-distance travel in Australia. With most of Australia's settler population clinging to the eastern coastline, individuals are testing the limits of motorcars and their own endurance, departing from cities all round the continent and driving into uncharted motoring territory over rugged tracks, parched deserts, rocky outcrops, treacherous rivers and creeks. As early as 1912, the celebrated motor overlander Francis Birtles drove the first motorcar from the west coast to the east – a 2600-mile trip managed in twenty-eight days. The car was a ten horsepower British runabout with only one cylinder loaded with a full ton of equipment.

What better way to explore the vast continent than by motorcar? Automobile and motor oil companies are quick to promote the idea and choose to single out women motorists in particular as symbols of progress. After all, Australian women have won the vote, taken on men's roles throughout the Great War, and are proving resilient in tackling the back-of-beyond as well as any man, especially behind the wheel of a motorcar. The *Perth Mirror*, reporting on Alice and Jessie's trip, writes, 'long distance motor trips are becoming common to women drivers of late. Only a week or two ago a young lady from

Geelong drove her mother to Port Darwin and back home again without mishap.'[5] Meanwhile, a popular mother-and-daughter duo, both named Marion Bell, are attempting to circumnavigate the continent sponsored by two motor oil companies: 'Mrs. Marion Bell: The first woman motorist to attempt to encircle Australia reaches Adelaide on Plume and Mobil oil!' declares one newspaper advertisement.[6] Alice, too, has ensured publicity by linking up with South Australia's Butler Nicholson, a local Austin distributor, and Universal Oils, producers of Tydol Motor Spirit and Veedol Oils. The agreement is that Universal Oils will arrange for supplies to be delivered along the route from Adelaide to Alice Springs in the Northern Territory, and Butler Nicholson will publish updates of the trip in the South Australian newspapers in return for telegrams of her progress.

The Bells started out from Perth in October 1925 in a sturdy American Oldsmobile Six Overlander and are close to completing their goal just as Alice and Jessie prepare to depart from Melbourne to Alice Springs. However, Alice's trip is unique in that it will be the first time such a journey is attempted in the smallest vehicle to come off a production line. 'If successful, it will be a record trip for a car of its size,' says the *Adelaide Mail*.[7]

The Austin 7 is fondly known as the Baby Austin and for good reason: its wheelbase is only six foot three inches with a narrow forty-inch track and it weighs in at a mere 780 pounds – just over half the weight of a Model T Ford. Melbourne's Australian Light Cars Proprietary Ltd advertise the new Austin 7 as 'The Woman Driver's Ideal', being 'easy to drive, easy to enter and easy to maintain' and offering 'untold joys and pleasures'. The accompanying illustration shows ladies in fancy frocks and hats delicately stepping into the car with a pretty driver behind the wheel.[8] A trip by women who dress practically and load their Austin with supplies for a strenuous overland adventure is probably not what the company originally had in mind, but it is nevertheless eager to accept an opportunity to prove the dainty little car's reliability and endurance.

While the mother-and-daughter team have allowed six months to complete their journey, Alice and Jessie are taking just six weeks to drive to the centre and back. Alice has a business to run and Jessie must return to continue her associate professorship as well as additional duties as acting head of the university's history department. The tight timeline leaves little room for error.

Alice and Jessie's departure from the Lyceum Club at 7 p.m. is noted in the social pages of *The Herald* as well as many interstate papers. The decision to make an evening departure from the city shows Alice's sense of occasion and her savvy approach to publicity. An early-morning start from her Kew Garage might have been more practical, but fewer people would have witnessed the send-off and the social pages would have been less likely to report it. Among the ladies hovering around Alice and Jessie is a reporter from the *Adelaide News.* She asks about the route the women plan to take. 'There is only one main route from Adelaide to Darwin, and that is only a camel track,' says Alice. 'I believe that eleven cars have been through up to date.' There are a few murmurs and exclamations. 'We are not going to stick to the beaten track,' Alice continues. 'According to the map of the Northern Territory land has been taken up by settlers. We are going to try and find them . . . we want to make friends. We are going to talk to everybody we meet and tell them about our things down here.'[9] The reporter asks about possible encounters with Aboriginal people along the way and Alice explains she has packed a supply of sweets and tobacco. One assumes Alice has chosen such things as possible gifts, or perhaps for trade.

A friend ceremoniously hands the two women a farewell present. Alice unwraps the delicate packaging and they all break into laughter when she holds up two potato mascots wearing curly red wigs. The reporter smiles and scribbles in her notebook that the lady 'has sensed the possibility of a food shortage!'[10]

The ongoing jollity and speeches delay the scheduled departure until approximately 9 p.m., when the party finally heads downstairs into the cool evening air. Alice and Jessie take charge, double-checking their luggage is secure: the shovel and axe are still strapped to the back, the sleeping bags and other camping gear in the rear seat, the four gallons of water roped to the running boards and, hidden well away but easily accessible, the shotgun and rifle borrowed from friend and solicitor Mr Geoff Gair, who stands in the crowd with his wife. He has lent the guns to Alice in case the women need protection or extra food to cook over the campfire.

Alice slips back into her leather jacket and overcoat. She places a foot on the running board, manoeuvres herself into the driver's seat and pulls on the driving cap that fits snugly over her ears, protecting her from wind and noise. Jessie lifts her coat hem and dress, steps awkwardly over luggage and squeezes in beside her. Then, 'a shake of the hand all round, a cheer, a little purring sound, and off the little car sets' on its journey.[11]

Once the car is out of view, the Lyceum ladies re-enter the club. They pass Jessie's former club president photograph on the wall. On the hall table sits a neat pile of business cards, which read in Gothic copperplate: *Miss Anderson's Motor Service 'Qui n'a risque rien, n'a rien'* (nothing ventured, nothing gained).

Alice and Jessie head north along Spencer Street. Under normal conditions the Austin can travel as fast as 48 miles per hour but with the extra weight, speed restrictions and variable road conditions its average speed is significantly slower. They pass Spencer Street Station (now Southern Cross Railway Station), where trains link the city with Victoria's country towns, and the railway sheds and cattle yards beyond. At the end of Spencer Street the little Austin turns left into Adderley Street and continues west onto Dynon Road, just south of Flemington Racecourse, where every year on the first Tuesday in November the city stands still for the Melbourne Cup – the most famous horse race in the Southern Hemisphere. Then, over the Maribyrnong River and away from the city into the inky, crisp night air.

1

FAMILY PORTRAIT

'A well balanced spirit . . .'

(1920s *Shell Motorists' Index*)

Alice Elizabeth Foley Anderson was born to Irish Protestant parentage in the well-to-do Melbourne suburb of Malvern, Victoria, on 8 June 1897. Gemini, the twin star, aligned her arrival with both the groundswell of first-wave feminism and the commercial success of the motorcar, both of which would set her on a unique path of discovery and achievement. Western society was on the brink of modernisation and Australia, a pioneer colony still shaking off its convict shackles, was its latest frontier.

The horseless carriage race had begun just a little over a decade before Alice's birth. Carl Benz in Mannheim, Germany, built the first petrol car in 1885. Other 'firsts' quickly followed, including the first three-wheel steam car by Ransom E. Olds in America (1886) and the first English car built by brothers Frederick and George Lanchester (1890). The famous Henry Ford was not far behind, building his first vehicle, the 'Quadricycle', in 1896 near Detroit. In Australia, the first successful automobile was built on the eve of Alice's arrival, though historians argue over one of two possible contenders: either the homemade Thomson Steamer, which allegedly chugged down Melbourne's New Street, Armadale, in May 1896, or the Ridge-Austin kerosene-powered vehicle developed for the Australasian Horseless Carriage Syndicate that lumbered round Fitzroy at a top speed of 10 miles per hour in February 1897.

Despite early local inventions, Australia's population was too small to sustain its own car industry and had to rely on imports. The first imported motorcar reportedly arrived from Chicago on 8 November 1897, when Alice was just five months old. It was typical of most early-model cars: a spindly open carriage with four bicycle tyres and a motor. Built by Max Hertel, it had a 3.5 horsepower, twin-cylinder, internal combustion engine that sat underneath a wheeled platform. The central control lever made the crankshaft revolve, which filled the fuel tank and compressed it for ignition. On its first trip, the proud owner, a horseshoe manufacturer from suburban Brunswick, recorded the motorcar travelling an impressive 9 miles on one gallon of stove naphtha.

Alice arrived without complication to mother Ellen Mary (née White-Spunner) and father Joshua Thomas Noble Anderson (JT) just as brother Stewart had done in 1893 and sister Frances (Frankie) in 1894. All three children appeared healthy enough, though the fear of accident or illness, or even a failure to thrive, was a constant concern at a time when even a common cold could result in death. This apprehension was exacerbated by the approximate six weeks it took for letters to arrive from and be received by loved ones living on the other side of the world. From Ireland, JT's mother, Eliza, wrote an anxious letter to Ellen

Mary concerning Stewart's health and the impending birth of her third child.

May 6th 1897   Rosemount
                                                         Dunmurry
                                                         Co. Antrim

My dearest Ellen Mary,
Yours of March 23rd reached me on Sunday May 2nd and was
very welcome as I had been two posts without news and would
not have been uneasy knowing how busy you must be, were it
not for a haunting fear that dear Yoortie [Stewart] may not
have been well, I trust he has got over his Chill and that you
have got a satisfactory maid. I shall not feel quite easy about
the household until I hear that June is safely over and all well,
as I trust I may in due time . . . When you get this I shall if
living be constantly thinking of you,
       Ever your loving Mater.[1]

In another letter Eliza posted four months after Alice's birth there
was talk of health concerns for the baby and a problem or accident concerning her arm. Eliza wrote:

I hope little Alice did not suffer much from her arm. I am
glad you are trying additional feeding for her, but greatly
prefer spoon to the bottle, the latter is such a risky business.
Everything connected with it needs such constant care, very
slight neglect often bringing on gastric irritation.

She was also sorry to hear from Ellen Mary 'of the dark rings
under the poor wee woman's eyes, they are not usual in babies . . .'[2]

3

Those 'poor wee woman's eyes' would quickly turn into cheeky browns while every other Anderson child was destined to have eyes of blue.[3]

Alice's first public appearance arrived early in October 1897, when she was taken along with the rest of the family to a Melbourne photographic studio. Here, another family by the name of Monash greeted the Andersons. It was unusual for two separate families to be photographed together but this was an exceptional occasion: not only had Alice come into the world but JT and his business partner, John Monash, were finally poised to prosper in a decade that had seen the property market go from boom to bust.

The company of Monash & Anderson had just become the first Victorian agent for Australian civil engineering company Carter Gummow & Co and had consequently obtained the all-important patent rights to the new Monier concrete process. The process, a combination of ordinary cement mortar with a grid or latticework of iron rods, had originally been applied to the manufacture of flowerpots, though it soon became apparent there was potential for such material in the construction of fireproof floors, pipes and arches of all descriptions. For bridges, especially, reinforced concrete was cheaper, more flexible and just as strong as iron or steel. As Monash told architects the 'fine plastic substance could be moulded to any form of beauty'.[4]

In the photography studio, the two families assembled into position. Ellen Mary sat to the far left of the photographer, holding three-month-old Alice on her lap. The rest of the party gathered around a small wicker table on which teacups were set. The scene created a fine balance between Victorian austerity and familial camaraderie. This would be the picture posted to loved ones back home. The photographer then set about creating a more formal configuration for a second picture. The wicker table was removed and everyone jostled into various standing and sitting positions until again a pleasing tableau had been established. JT and John Monash, both in their prime at thirty-two years of age, stood self-assuredly at the rear of the party. The two men sported fashionably long moustaches and smart three-piece suits. JT's brother, 28-year-old Jack, sat at the far left of the scene, legs crossed with one hand on his knee and the other pressed into his seat as if he had just sat down or was about to jump up. He looked a carbon copy of JT: lean, narrow-faced and handsome.

Thirty-year-old Ellen Mary and Monash's wife, 28-year-old Victoria, sat round the children. They wore long dark dresses cinched tightly at the waist, their hair upswept into soft buns. Victoria, elegant and straight backed, her curly dark hair framing her slim features, looked straight at the camera. Ellen Mary, also dark haired and very pretty, sat to the right, leaning in with baby Alice on her knee. In the two child-sized wicker chairs sat Alice's sister, three-year-old Frances, and Bertha Monash, the only child of Victoria and John Monash, also three. Frances was covered from head to foot in white lace, her hands clasped in her lap, her face serious and self-possessed as if she were a little adult and Bertha looked like a fancy doll in her satin dress. Perched on a little stool between Ellen Mary and JT, Alice's brother, four-year-old Stewart, wore a sailor suit. He looked thin and pinched, as if he had already absorbed the term 'delicate'.

It was difficult, especially for the little ones, to remain still long enough for each picture to be taken. By the time everyone had been repositioned, Alice was kicking about in her lace gown. The photographer moved from under his cloth and grabbed a cushion, which he put on the floor between little Frances and Bertha. Ellen Mary placed Alice gently on the cushion then resumed her position. Now at the bottom of the frame, Alice formed an inverted apex to which the eye was drawn. She threw her little arms above her head and was only momentarily startled into stillness by the bulb's flash. Baby Alice had been captured, along with the people who would most influence her early life and help to shape the person she would become.

Relatives from England and Ireland eagerly anticipated the arrival of the portraits. They were keen to see the latest Anderson child and the rest of the family's progress. Ellen Mary's sister Katie put pen to paper as soon as she received her copy.

> 133 Acre Lane
> Brixton, London

1.11.97

Dearest Nellie,

Got the photo this morn. My dear — you are quite a big woman to look at now and the three wee ones — how like Jos [JT] Stewart is — and yet like you — the wee girlie we don't quite see which of you she is like — what nice hair she has as for the doll on your knee — well of course she is like herself so far. Jack does not seem to have changed much, no more than Jos, but photos only make one long to see the reality. That folk with you we know not . . .

> *Ever yours,*
> *Kitty.*[5]

The year the studio portraits were taken, life was a series of pleasant routines for the Andersons. JT regularly took the train to the Melbourne office of Monash & Anderson, and lectured in engineering at the University of Melbourne. Ellen Mary took up horticulture at Burnley Gardens Horticultural College, where she learnt to prune roses. The family also bought a pony and phaeton, in which Ellen Mary took the children picnicking every Saturday to nearby Brighton beach.

The regular beachside outings came about after Alice was diagnosed late in 1897 with a mild case of rickets. The condition indicated a Vitamin D deficiency caused by a poor diet in infancy and/or a lack of exposure to sunlight. When a doctor recommended that Alice should be given a different diet and have salt baths, Ellen Mary took his advice. The beach was a tonic for Alice's condition and all three children enjoyed learning to swim in the gentle waves of Port Phillip Bay. JT and Ellen Mary thrived in their adopted country full of warm, bright sunny days, of abundance and laughter, friendship and family. But this was not the world in which Alice's parents had grown up.

JT and Ellen Mary were born to Protestant families in Ireland where upper-middle-class values rubbed shoulders with financial uncertainty. Born in 1865 and 1864 respectively, both had strict clergymen fathers. JT's father, Reverend Samuel Anderson, Vicar of Upper Fals, refused to accept the disestablishment of the Church of England in Ireland in 1869 and as a result continued working in his parish on the small stipend of a curate. Nevertheless, Reverend Anderson ensured all his seven children – both girls and boys – received a good academic education. Young Joshua was the third child and very much his father's son. He was blessed with a fierce intellect and a questioning mind as well as a strong sense of principle, stirred with a dash of puritanism. Joshua was educated at the Royal Belfast Academical Institution and Queen's College Belfast, finally graduating at the Royal University of Dublin in engineering and arts, the perfect combination for his temperament and intellect.

Joshua's eldest sister, Alice (after whom he named his own daughter), was equally intelligent, if not more so. She was the first woman to study and graduate from Belfast University. Alice not only passed but gained first place in both mathematics and astronomy. However, as with most women in the 1800s, Alice was unable to take full advantage of her achievement. Despite her qualifications, the only employment she was ever able to secure was primary school teaching. One can only imagine what else the first Alice Anderson could have accomplished had prospects for women at the time been less restricted.

While the Reverend Anderson was Low Church, Ellen Mary's father, Reverend White-Spunner, followed High Church traditions to the letter. He took the rituals and ceremonies very seriously, even fasting every Friday. But with eleven children and a sickly wife, resources were scarce and bedlam often reigned. Ellen Mary told her children that the White-Spunners were an 'emotional, passionate, musical and uneducated' lot.[6] She said the house was bare except for 'four or five cats and dogs' and 'an organ and two pianos'. They were all musical and they were always fighting. 'You'd get a great fight start up and then everybody would rush off and you'd suddenly hear the organ and the two pianos all at once!'[7]

Ellen Mary was unwell as a child but she was fortunate enough to possess wealthy childless godparents who were prepared to give her a privileged upbringing away from the family chaos. She lived with her godparents from age three to fifteen. In that time she learnt French and to sing and play the piano beautifully, as well as master the game of chess. But she was never involved in day-to-day domestic concerns and therefore had no idea how to cook, clean or manage any general household tasks. When she was suddenly returned to the vicarage after her godmother died unexpectedly, Ellen Mary was completely unprepared for the shock of becoming one of many children in a house of mayhem and confusion.

When Ellen Mary and JT fell in love, Reverend White-Spunner was wary of their plan to marry and move to Australia. Despite, or because of, the chaotic situation in which his family had lived, he wanted only the best for his children. The Reverend advised JT that he would only approve of the union if his potential son-in-law could secure a position earning at least £400 a year in Australia, or if he were to remain in Ireland and take up a respectable position such as a county surveyor, a salary of £200 a year would suffice.

It was brother Jack who had inspired JT to seek his fortune beyond Ireland, having already emigrated to Australia himself on account of his 'weak lungs', probably due to tuberculosis. JT followed his brother to Australia in 1883 and was struck by its natural beauty and economic prospects, particularly for a newly qualified engineer. By 1889 he had established a private engineering practice in Melbourne and his success finally convinced Reverend White-Spunner of JT's ability to provide for his daughter. Only then did JT write to Ellen Mary, officially asking for her hand in marriage. By this time Ellen Mary was engaged to another man, but her heart wasn't in it, and as soon as she received JT's marriage proposal she broke off the engagement and happily accepted JT as her husband-to-be. It would be another three years before Ellen Mary arrived in Melbourne.

During that time, JT was back in Ireland briefly, receiving commissions for sewerage and water works in Holland. Then he relocated to Melbourne again, where he had secured a respectable part-time position as lecturer in mechanical engineering at the University of Melbourne. Here he met John Monash, who was struggling to secure an engineering qualification. JT's extra guidance and intensive tutoring helped Monash pass the supply engineer's exam with distinction, ensuring a lifelong friendship between the two men.

On 20 April 1892 Ellen Mary finally arrived. The only luggage she had brought was her trousseau and linen. She stepped off the ship to see JT eagerly waiting in frockcoat and top hat and wearing his muddy and torn surveying trousers. Her first thoughts were, 'the sooner I'm married and mend that, the better!'[8] Accompanying Ellen Mary was JT's childhood nurse, Bessie, who had come to the Anderson family when he was first born. He had always been her baby and she had missed him so badly she was prepared to travel to be with the couple and assist with the children they were sure to be blessed with.

On the following day, 21 April 1892, JT and Ellen Mary were married at Saint Margaret's Church of England in Caulfield. Bessie didn't have to wait long for a young charge to come along: the first of six children, Stewart, was born only eleven months later.

———

In 1894, with the toss of a coin to determine whose name would appear first in the company title, JT and Monash established the firm Monash & Anderson. The office was based at 49 Elizabeth Street, Melbourne, and offered civil, mining and mechanical engineering consulting services to the state of Victoria. When Ellen Mary first visited the office, the apparent differences between her husband's and Mr Monash's working styles amused her. Everything on Monash's desk was exactly right, neat almost to the point of obsession, while JT's was chaotic, evidence of what she understood to be his creative fervour. The two men were an attraction of opposites. Monash was Jewish, Anderson Irish Protestant. Monash was establishing a secondary career in soldiering and enjoyed the control of men in a disciplined structure; Anderson was a Fabian socialist who mistrusted authority. Anderson was an ideas man, the enthusiastic one who charmed people into signing on the dotted line, while Monash held everything together – especially once it dawned on him that Anderson had absolutely no head for business!

Fortunately, JT gambled on the idea that reinforced concrete would transform construction methods and propel Australia into the twentieth century, and Monash, in this instance, agreed. As agents for the new concrete technology, Monash & Anderson secured contracts for bridges in Melbourne, Geelong and Bendigo. Their bridges joined roads over creeks, rivers and railway lines, connecting the arteries and veins of the state for traffic driven firstly by horse, then by horsepower. In doing so JT was literally laying the path for his daughter Alice's future success.

Monash & Anderson completed their first bridge in 1899. A tri-arched structure with fine decorative detail, it crossed Melbourne's Yarra River in South Yarra at the end of Anderson Street, which bordered the Royal Botanic Gardens. It caused a stir within the profession, being the first reinforced concrete bridge in Victoria and the largest attempted in Australia. Would the three slender arches spanning ninety-five feet bear the weight? The bridge was put to the test with a fifteen-ton roller and hundreds of tons of dead weight. Its failure to buckle under such stress successfully confirmed its strength. The Anderson Street Bridge (now the Morell Bridge) became coincidentally connected by name with the man who was largely responsible for its design.

The Anderson and Monash families, immortalised in a Melbourne photographic studio in 1897, had every reason to hope for a bright future. When John Monash and JT first tossed a coin, it was to determine whose name would appear first in the company title. Their second coin toss created more far-reaching consequences, especially for the Andersons.

2

LAND OF THE LONG WHITE CLOUD

'Safety first and always'

(1920s *Shell Motorists' Index*)

The year 1899 was a good one for the Andersons. Monash & Anderson won contracts to build reinforced concrete bridges all over Victoria and Ellen Mary became pregnant with her fourth child. JT decided to move his growing family from Fraser Street, Malvern, to a larger house round the corner in Stanhope Street. Unlike their previous residence this place boasted not one but two reception rooms as well as a vestibule, which was quite an unusual feature and wonderful for children to play in on wet days.

The Andersons family life was typical of the upper middle classes: they had a cook, a governess and 'a boy for the garden'.[1] On 1 November 1899 their third daughter, Katrine, was born. JT's beloved childhood nurse, Bessie, had passed away the year before, and although Ellen Mary always chose to look after the youngest baby herself, she hired another nursery governess,

Muriel Umphelby, to care for the other children. So fond did the Andersons become of Miss Umphelby that they asked her to be Katrine's godmother and she graciously accepted.

Two-year-old Alice was particularly captivated by the latest addition to the family. Far from being jealous, she was happy to no longer be the baby and gave Katrine her full attention. As soon as Katrine could crawl, Alice had a devoted follower. They did everything together and, over time, became each other's closest confidante.

JT was elected as President of the Victorian Institute of Engineers in 1900. With a new decade and century upon them, JT was ever more optimistic. Reinforced concrete was the material of the future and Monash & Anderson had sole rights to the Monier method in Victoria.

In spite of such a bright outlook, things took a swift downturn during the second half of 1900 when a series of unforeseen events suddenly threatened the firm's very existence. The first occurred when King's Bridge in Weeroona Avenue, Bendigo, collapsed under testing and had to be rebuilt at the firm's own cost. This was just one of eight bridges the firm had successfully erected in the gold mining town, but it put a large dent in the profits. By October 1900 Monash & Anderson was seriously overextended when the shires of Corio and Bannockburn refused to pay the full cost of the successfully completed Fyansford Bridge. The two councils sought court action to delay, and then avoid, the large final payment for the Fyansford Bridge; to the disbelief of John Monash and JT, the action was upheld in the Supreme Court of Victoria in 1902.

As a result, all of Monash & Anderson's capital was depleted. After some serious discussion the two men concluded there was only one solution to save the business: one partner would stay and work off the debt and the other would leave. In a fitting end to the partnership, the two again relied on the toss of a coin to determine their futures. Providentially it fell to Monash, the more astute businessman, to stay and Anderson, the visionary, to find his fortune elsewhere. The agreement gave John Monash sole control of the Monier rights and released JT from the firm's debts.

By all accounts, JT had been a difficult man to work with. Although the two men admired each other's abilities – Monash even admitting JT had the more brilliant mind – JT was erratic and easily got people offside if they didn't go along with his ideas. Monash was frequently worried by what he considered to be JT's tendency to finesse, to be over-clever and create complications where none existed. The Fyansford Bridge debacle was a blow to both men but, while JT had wanted to fight it out to the bitter end, Monash took it upon himself to face the music and rebuild his shattered fortunes – though he did avoid crossing the Fyansford Bridge for the rest of his life.

JT searched for work and on 23 April 1902 was appointed engineer in chief to the Drainage Board in Dunedin, New Zealand. In accepting this position, JT had agreed to the mammoth challenge of designing and developing Dunedin's sewerage system. The following month he sailed on the *Westralia* via Hobart, leaving a wintry Australia for an even colder, windy Dunedin 1500 miles across the Tasman Sea. The family would follow once arrangements had been put in place.

JT soon discovered that such mountainous terrain, indicative of much of the country, resulted in supreme challenges regarding transport of any kind. For the first motorcars imported by its wealthier citizens, most of New Zealand's main roads were poorly formed and few arterial roads existed before the 1920s. Those who did drive were considered 'thrill seekers', travelling as they did with blocks and tackles to manage the precipitous slopes. It did not help that cars imported at the time were mainly British and European models not well suited to rough terrain. JT's generous £900 per annum salary was certainly enough for him to indulge in a motorcar but his engineering nous probably told him it wasn't worth the expense. Even later, when wider American models with a higher ground clearance were imported, their engines were too low powered for steep grades and were only popular in flatter areas of the country. Had JT not been employed to develop Dunedin's sewerage system, he could well have made a success of constructing much-needed roads in the 'land of the long white cloud'.

Despite Dunedin's engineering challenges there was no doubt in JT's mind that he could give the town a world-class sewerage system. Whether the ultra-conservative town councillors and members of the newly constituted Drainage Board of New Zealand would go along with his technological vision, however, was another matter. Dunedin, named after the old Celtic name for Edinburgh, was settled by Scots who had their own vision of recreating a new, more ordered 'Edinburgh' based on sober Presbyterian values. Such principles underpinned the society on which JT was about to impose his unconventional, innovative brilliance.

Stuart Murray, who, as Chief Engineer of Water Supply for Victoria, had written a glowing reference for JT back in 1891, had also advised him in a private letter, 'just a friendly caution – be not too impetuous; and do not rub people up the wrong way; especially those who are sincerely your friends and well wishers.

And this, even when you are wholly right and the other fellow wholly wrong.'[2] Years later, a family member described JT's personality in unequivocal terms: 'He knew what he wanted and he'd get it and he'd stick by it . . . He didn't know the meaning of compromise. And if he thought a fellow was either a fool or a knave, he showed them up. A nice way of making friends isn't it!'[3] No longer tempered by John Monash's level thinking, the full force of JT's personality was unleashed on his new colleagues; the stage was set for him to clash with the council and the Drainage Board as well as the local population.

From August 1902 onward the local *Evening Star* newspaper reported strained relations. One example read:

> Mr Sidey asked if, had the engineer had more money at his disposal, he could have put forward a better scheme, to which Mr Anderson replied that the scheme had really been designed irrespective of available capital. He had not restricted expenses otherwise than he would have done had he unlimited money at his disposal . . .
>
> Mr Moloney . . . moved – 'That an expert engineer of Australian experience be appointed to report as to the merits of Mr Anderson's scheme.'
>
> Mr Anderson said he felt slighted by the motion. He was appointed to carry out the scheme. If they wanted to appoint another engineer it must be by way of consultation with him. In no other way could he submit to it.
>
> . . . Mr Scott remarked that the interests of the ratepayers must be considered as well as those of Mr Anderson.
>
> Mr Anderson said he felt very much insulted by that remark . . . If the Board had not sufficient confidence in him to

consult with another engineer, the sooner they got rid of him the better . . .[4]

The Evening Star was not the only local press picking up on JT's apparent bull-headedness. Comments from a *Bruce Herald* journalist were particularly scathing.

'It is sport to see the engineer hoist with his own petar' must have been the thought of most citizens when they read at breakfast in the morning journal the report of the Drainage Board meeting on Wednesday. For there they read that Mr. Noble Anderson, the Board's engineer, loftily deprecated anyone criticising his work as an engineer, and objected very strongly to any interference with his work. This was no doubt quite professional, but Mr. Anderson showed quite a different spirit when he went out of his way to attack Mr. Rogers', the city Engineer's report on the Lee Stream water scheme. If he is such a thorough believer in professional etiquette he certainly did not go out of his way to show it, in connection with Mr. Rogers. Now, however, that the Board is treating him in the same way as the City Council treated Mr. Rogers, Mr. Anderson thinks his professional reputation is in danger![5]

JT never played by the rules. The authorities expected him to wait three weeks for the marine surveyors to study maps of the ocean currents before deciding where the outfall would go. But JT thought it might work if he took the piping across to a little rocky island about half a mile off the shore where there were no inhabitants except for birds. So he stripped off, swam across and round the island observing the flotsam, jetsam and seaweeds to ascertain the currents for that time of the year. The exercise had JT conclude his initial idea was not practicable. Additionally, the local farmers objected strongly to effluent being discharged into the ocean from their land. He decided therefore that the outfall needed to go two and a half miles further out. JT thought the best option to achieve this was to use diesel engines from Holland, which he ordered without council authority. Frankie explained:

> That meant either tunnelling through a steep hill or pumping it. My father decided pumping was the only alternative and feasible financially, and he recommended the then new diesel engines, which work on oil . . . No diesel engine had been across the equator and the . . . Scottish town council, they were aghast at the thought of being guinea pigs and trying out something new, so they refused. And my father headached for quite a while – some weeks – and then he ordered them on his own. They came, they were installed, and there was a terrific row, but they went for fifty years until the whole thing was electrified.[6]

The authorities must have been furious both because of and despite JT's success in designing and building one of the most successful drainage systems of its time.

———

Meanwhile, the Anderson family settled in their expansive new home, 'The Mount' in St Clair, little Alice floating, as all the family did, on JT's unwavering optimism and supreme self-confidence. He appeared larger than life, immensely capable and apt to get his own way through the sheer force of his intelligence. His extremely healthy salary afforded them a very amenable lifestyle and Ellen Mary kept the household running smoothly, hosting 'at home' days when ladies of the district would call. Between Mother and Father, the Anderson children were growing up surrounded by civility laced with conversations and actions that questioned, if not criticised, the status quo. Such dichotomies were not lost on Alice, who absorbed them into her growing understanding of the world.

The Mount sat atop a cliff so steep the road zigzagged up to it. Half a mile below, the ocean slept and woke with the wind and tides. For the Anderson children it was a fairytale place. A lavish garden ran down the slope from the family house to an orchard full of apples and plums. In between the apple trees were currant bushes of red, white and black berries. The children had permission to eat as much as they liked from the orchard, and they spent most of their afternoons in the nearby summerhouse. Eight-year-old Frankie and five-year-old Alice especially made use of the dozens of kerosene tins and wooden planks stored in the summerhouse to build a table fit for feasting.

Shortly after the family's arrival, JT's brother Henry visited The Mount. He was a well-travelled British Army doctor who had served in the Boer War. 'He gave us some Zulu ornaments and talked about Africa and he was our idol,' Frankie recalled.[7] Uncle Henry told the children exotic stories, which they reinvented as games. One of the most popular games was the 'cannibal feasts' they acted out in the summerhouse with little jelly baby sweets.[8] One can imagine Alice and her sisters taking great delight in dancing on the mats woven by Frankie from fallen fronds of the cabbage tree palm, biting the heads off the babies, and squealing until they were all gobbled up.

At The Mount, everything was writ large, a wild, thrilling playground. At the base of the cliff concrete baths had been built out from the rocks so that one could swim without being taken out to sea. Unfortunately, the town council allowed mixed bathing only before 7 a.m., which meant JT had to take Alice, Stewart and Frankie down to the baths in their obligatory neck-to-knee costumes just before the sun peeked over the horizon. There he taught the children to duck dive through the enormous, freezing breakers. Frankie said, 'even in summer the water was very cold, but my father encouraged us into it, by saying, "a coward dies a thousand times, a brave man only once."'[9]

As for the girls' formal schooling, however, JT appeared to take an even more conservative view than his own father. While he decided Stewart would board at the local high school as soon as he was of age, he believed, according to Katrine, that educating girls was not only a waste of time but possibly detrimental. 'Father used to say that education destroyed the combination of [female] hand and brain. And he really believed this,' she said.[10] This was despite his own sisters receiving a proper education, including obtaining degrees at Belfast University. Thankfully, JT put the girls' schooling in the hands of his wife. Ellen Mary took the task very seriously. She was determined her daughters would have an education more rounded than the limited one she had received through her godmother.

Social standing was of utmost importance to Ellen Mary. The children, who saw their mother as 'charming and aristocratic', knew she did not generally approve of them associating with others, especially if they were not of the same class.[11] They understood from a young age that class consciousness called for certain obligations and privileges that were upheld by associating with the class to which one belonged. Ellen Mary's Irish parents may not have been financially well off, but the clergy nevertheless possessed a high standing in the community and providence had given her wealthy godparents, along with a genteel upbringing. Ellen Mary visited various schools in and around Dunedin. She observed what each school was teaching and how, and who her daughters would be associating with. Ellen Mary came away underwhelmed by each and every school on her list. The better option, she decided, was for her daughters to be home schooled by a governess.

Unfortunately Muriel Umphelby, who had travelled to New Zealand with the family, stayed on only a month or two before deciding to return to Melbourne. Ellen Mary immediately advertised for a replacement governess and was delighted to appoint a Miss Cuthbertson, daughter of the Bishop of Christchurch. Being the Bishop's daughter meant Ellen Mary held her in high esteem and was more than happy to accept the governess on written application alone. As it turned out, this was a grave mistake. The few months Miss Cuthbertson lasted were a misery for the children. Frankie said she had no sense of humour whatsoever and no real understanding of children at all. 'She was the only one, bar one in Melbourne, when I was about four, when my brother and I decided we could not bear this woman my mother had engaged and he turned the hose on her and enjoined on me to help him. She left the next day.'[12]

While she sought a more suitable governess, Ellen Mary began to teach her daughters the fundamentals of music just as she had been taught as a child. She also took every opportunity to instill the correct use of English by having Frankie and Alice read newspaper editorials aloud. She said to the girls, 'Now, I've given you this to read because it won't mean a thing to you but you must make it understandable to me.'[13] The family went to Dunedin Symphony Orchestra concerts and to performances of Gilbert and Sullivan. Moreover, there was never a shortage of reading material: fourteen crates of books had travelled with them, including all the classics, the Encyclopaedia Britannica and JT's professional books. Ellen Mary encouraged the girls to read them all.

It wasn't until the third governess was appointed that the girls' situation finally improved. Miss Vyner not only stood up to Alice and Frankie with good humour, she developed a solid curriculum and demanded high standards. Every morning she gave lessons in reading, writing and sewing. On Wednesday mornings she taught darning, a particularly important skill to master in chilly New Zealand where everyone wore woollen undergarments. If the results weren't square enough she cut a larger hole in the garment and had the girls darn bigger squares until they got it right. On Saturday mornings Alice and Frankie were invited into the large kitchen warmed by the wood-fired stove, and under Cook's clear and firm directions were taught how to make cakes, scones and biscuits. The girls read each recipe aloud, put everything out and, when they had finished, put everything away properly. Afternoons were set aside for walks on the cliffs or the beach.

The two sisters thrived in this environment, though for different reasons. Frankie was a serious, sensitive young girl with a need for structure and adult reassurance. She was shy, awkward and self-conscious, and possessed unconventional looks. One family member rudely described Frankie as, 'very plain . . . she had a big mouth and rather a piggish nose',[14] though photographs of Frankie as a young girl show a rather unusually beautiful child with striking features. Being the eldest girl, she knew her place was in the home by her mother's side. Alice, on the other hand, had no such expectations put upon her. Even if she had, it was doubtful she would have complied. Though she was described as not having very good features, Alice 'sparkled and she was so bright and her face was so expressive',[15] with a mop of unruly curls, flashing brown eyes, and a very cheeky, crooked-toothed grin. She was forward, charming, clever and bossy, and was always getting into strife − a little like her father. Hardly ever indoors, except to pinch treats from Cook, her sisters experienced Alice as 'quick tempered and a bit greedy . . . [She] used to go and stick her fingers into the milk that was settling for cream and you'd see little holes'.[16] Alice constantly tore her dresses, and was almost always late for family meals. She was a wild child who benefited from being reined in by a teacher who commanded respect. An undated letter from Alice to her uncle Jack, probably towards the end of 1903 when she would have been six and a half (with spelling corrections from an adult at the time) confirmed the positive educational structure Miss Vyner was successfully applying to her charges.

The Mount
December 20

My Dear Uncle Jack
We had a break up, drill, and I riced (recited), and I plade the panow and Frankie plade the panow. I got a pries for reading.

24

Frankie got a prise for music, and Baby got a prise for writeing. Miss Viner got too frams, wone (one) the shape of a heart, and the other obe long (oblong). I caunt find eny thing mor to say, so, good bye from
Alice Anderson.[17]

On 11 September 1904 Ellen Mary gave birth to her fifth child, Claire. As soon as Claire could crawl, she was desperate to follow Katrine and Alice around. And it didn't take long for Claire to recognise Alice as the ringleader who made everything fun.

Both JT and Stewart had especially hoped the baby would be a boy. For JT, two sons were better than one and Stewart increasingly felt the loneliness of being the only boy in a family of girls. More than that, it was obvious to Stewart he was not turning out to be the son JT desired. He was a pale, thin, unhappy boy who, even at ten years old, preferred taking photographs and developing them in his darkroom to playing team sports and thinking like an engineer. JT was a man's man; Stewart was more akin to his emotionally delicate Uncle Jack, whose favourite pastime was making and playing his own violins.

To all the children's delight, Uncle Jack eventually came to live in New Zealand to work under JT, just as he had done in Australia. Jack missed his big brother's family terribly and likewise, the family adored his company. Initially, Jack had stayed in Melbourne and, possibly with JT's encouragement and assistance, secured a job constructing reinforced concrete pipes with John Monash's company. Jack was a quiet bachelor who worked hard and led a simple life. However, 1902 to 1904 had seen him struggling both physically and mentally with the work and the isolation of being away from his brother and family.

He wrote to Ellen Mary, 'I will not be sorry when something else than pipe making turns up.'[18] JT invited him to come to New Zealand there and then but Jack replied he was not sure about accepting the invitation: 'I have such a dread of being again out of work & feel that if I returned here I would come back at a disadvantage.'[19] But it was brother Henry's visit to Jack in early 1904 that alerted the family to what had become a worrying situation. Among other issues, Henry's letter indicated a problem between Jack and John Monash:

> I have been very unhappy about Jack's silence & felt that my visit had done little to help him, but it is a relief to find that you realise how serious his position is . . . I do hope you do not fall out with Monash, unless you have come to dislike him. He told me before I saw Jack how heavily he felt the responsibility, and the reason, and how he did not wish to annoy Jack by writing to you until he was sure his own influence had no effect . . . I am quite convinced that Monash was not at heart unfriendly towards Jack, and think that Jack knew this. The thing that grieved me most was how very carefully Jack concealed the weakness from me, so that I could never make direct reference to it, and our time together was so short that I had no heart to 'have it out with him'.[20]

Whatever the details of Jack's 'weakness' it was clear he was not coping on his own, and when JT again invited him to New Zealand later that year, Jack finally agreed to come. With JT's help, he secured work as a labourer at the Dunedin Cement Works and settled into a house close by.

Stewart turned eleven the year his favourite uncle arrived in Dunedin. It was then that JT took his son aside and, much to Ellen Mary's horror, taught him how to shoot the Colt revolver JT kept for the family's protection. It was an initiation that ostensibly made Stewart in charge of the house in JT's absence. This went some way to making the young boy feel like a man, especially as he proved to be a good shot. Alice was most impressed. She couldn't wait to be old enough to learn to shoot just like her brother. Katrine may have been her little playmate but it was Stewart whom Alice increasingly looked up to. However, Alice's beloved brother was about to be sent abroad.

The ocean that constantly crashed and sprayed against the cliffs below the Andersons' home at The Mount so impressed Stewart that at twelve years old he told his father that he would like to be in the Navy. JT was delighted. He had already considered sending his son to the old country to increase his chances at a respectable profession, and none was more respectable than the Royal Navy. JT contacted his brother William, then Secretary of Education for Berkshire County, England. William agreed to sponsor Stewart and arrange his enrolment in the local school that prepared boys for the Royal Navy entrance exams.

Early in September 1905, just as the spring buds began to appear, JT and young Stewart left New Zealand for Australia, where JT would put his son on a ship to England. Frankie, now ten, was distraught at seeing him go. She idolised Stewart, just as she did her father. As for eight-year-old Alice, the tomboy in her loved nothing more than getting up to mischief with her brother. His departure was her first experience of loss and it grieved her deeply. For Ellen Mary, having her only son leave without knowing when she might see him again, and her husband gone, however briefly, when baby Claire was not yet twelve months old, left her anxious and bereft. She had Alice write to Jack the following day requesting he visit them that week.

The Mount
September 4th Monday

My dear Uncle Jack,
Stweart wenl away on Sunday the 3rd. We are having haladays but we are very lonly. & mother wants to know could you come over any day this week. The mise have bitten the nik in the paper.
Goodbe from Alice e F. A.[21]

Stewart kept a stiff upper lip but he was in for choppy waters. When the ship stopped at Hobart, Tasmania, he wrote to Ellen Mary.

Post Office, Hobart

8 Sep
My dear Mother,
We arrived here about midnight last night, after a fairly rough passage, in 2 waves going a clean over the ship. Father and I spent 2 days in bed & he was very seedy but not as seasick as I. One night we slowed down to half speed as it was so rough & twice we slowed down to fix the engines . . .
We shall arrive in Melbourne at 12pm Saturday night.
From your loving boy,
Stewart Anderson[22]

Father and son had a few memorable days in Melbourne before departing on FMS *Dumbea*, which would take Stewart to Adelaide then Fremantle before sailing on to London via Colombo and Paris. Between Melbourne and Adelaide, JT found a professor of French on board who agreed to take charge of Stewart on the long trip to London. JT then disembarked and made for the return trip home, leaving his only boy, who had never been away from family, to sail to the other side of the world into the arms of relatives he had never met.

JT's brother William was a bachelor who lived with the brothers' two unmarried and university-educated sisters, horticulturalist Katie and English teacher Letitia (Lettie). All three of JT's siblings were somewhat taken aback at the hastiness of the decision to send Stewart to them, and the ensuing responsibility this entailed. As Stewart made his way to 'Hermit's Hill', their home in Berkshire, a flurry of letters was sent between family members. The most telling correspondence came from Katie, who wrote to brother Jack:

> We got a great surprise this week, when we heard from Jos [JT] that he was starting Stewart home here at once. It seems hard on Ellen Mary & the boy to send him off by himself so young but I suppose it is the best thing for him. Willie is rather put out at the responsibility being thrust so suddenly on him, he hates any kind of responsibility & is too apt to thrust as much as he can on Lettie's shoulders . . .[23]

Torn between the excitement of the journey and homesickness, Stewart filled his journal and wrote letters home. The letter he posted to his parents describing a brief stop in Colombo highlighted just how vulnerable young Stewart was travelling on his own. As it turned out, the professor was not so interested in looking out for the boy and pretty much left him to his own devices. While Ellen Mary missed him terribly and worried for his safety, Alice envied his freedom. *Oh, to be a boy and have such adventures!*

F.M.S. Dumbea
Friday 13/10/05

My dear Father & Mother,
I am getting back the £s from Mr Nalaghin . . . I taught
myself French as he complained that he came away for a
holiday . . . Also I learnt a lot at Colombo. After buying about
15/- worth of things, a vendor offered to show me the town.
(I think he said 'At my own price') He took me to the native
market where he bought me a bag of mixed fruit about 7 ft by
1ft x 2 ft 6 (made of flax-like grass) for 1 rupee 75 cents (2/4)
which would cost about 12/- . . .
*   The natives squat on the ground & yell, & chew betlenut.*
Then we went back as we came by elec. tram & saw the
cinnamon gardens in the distance from it, had lunch at a
hotel & returned to boat, having purchased at guide vendors
shop . . . When I was returning to the boat the guide <u>asked</u> me
to pay him 2 rupees for his services, 2 rup 70 cents for dinner
& 1 rup 25 cents for the fruit plus a former rupee I had given
him and forgotten about. On the boat a man said he would tell
my fortune for 25 cents took me along by myself & rubbed my
hand & made a pretty near guess at a little of my past . . .[24]

The fortune teller told Stewart that his father was at the peak of his career, that he had four sisters and there would be another.

However, according to Stewart, the man refused to predict anything of his own future.

It was not long after Stewart had settled into his new life in England, and JT had largely completed the Dunedin sewerage works, that the family was devastated by a horrific accident. On 26 April 1906, Uncle Jack and another worker, Archibald McKay, were de-galvanising iron in a confined space at the cement works, unaware that the process would produce poisonous chlorine gas. Inhaling chlorine fumes creates hydrochloric and hypochlorous acid in the body, damaging all the organs. There was no chance of cure. The gas caused a painfully swollen throat, their lungs filled with fluid, and they endured severe pain and burning in the nose, lips, eyes and tongue. Holes burnt into the skin as their heart and blood vessels collapsed. They vomited up stomach contents and blood, causing a rapid drop in blood pressure until their wretched bodies could take no more. McKay died the next day but Jack took an agonising four days to succumb.

JT felt overwhelmingly responsible for his brother's death and was utterly inconsolable. To have invited Jack to Dunedin, arranged work for him and kept him close, then to lose him in an avoidable accident that brought on an excruciatingly cruel death was almost more than JT could bear.

Only a few days before the accident the two brothers had agreed that once JT had completed his Dunedin contract, they would try their fortunes in America. Prompted by the devastating earthquake that had recently flattened San Francisco, they had seen an opening for engineers to rebuild the city in reinforced concrete and steel. Any dream of making it in America dissolved with Jack's death and JT could not stomach staying in New Zealand one moment longer. He promptly resigned from the Drainage Board, announced to his family that 'the colonies were no place to bring up children' and made plans to return to the old country.[25]

On 5 July 1906, under the cloak of grief, nine-year-old Alice and her family departed from Lyttleton on the *Turakina*, setting sail to a whole new world known to her parents as Home.

3

TO THE MOTHERLAND

'Keep your eyes on the road'

(1920s *Shell Motorists' Index*)

Ellen Mary and JT had regaled the children with so many stories of Home that Alice, Frankie and Katrine were eager to step into their parents' world and finally meet the many aunts, uncles and cousins for the first time. Everyone's greatest anticipation centred round the imminent reunion with Stewart, whom they had not seen in over twelve months. *Had he missed them as much as they had missed him? Would he be the same? Would he be all grown up?*

For Ellen Mary, the trip soothed intense feelings of homesickness. She had not returned to Ireland nor seen any immediate family since her departure for Australia fourteen years earlier. For JT, travelling back was a way to start life afresh despite being broken with anguish and sorrow. He took time to relax with his daughters, often lying with them on deck of the *Turakina* at sunset as the darkening skies revealed the stars of the hemispheres, pointing out the constellations, explaining the shape and meaning of each. There was also time for intimate moments with his wife, resulting in Ellen Mary becoming pregnant with their sixth child during the six-week voyage.

The Andersons arrived in London on 17 August 1906. The capital of the world's largest empire was almost unrecognisable compared to the last time Ellen Mary had visited. There was a fresh vibrancy about the place. The inner city alone was buzzing with over four and a half million people, more than the total settler population of Australia. Accompanying the crowds was an array of fancy department stores, such as the domed Harrods building in Knightsbridge. The Ritz was one of many glamorous new hotels and there were theatres too numerous to count. One was transported through this exciting metropolis via the new motorbus service and underground electric trains. Motorcars were still outnumbered by horse-drawn cabs, bicycles and pedestrian traffic but there were many different models on offer and they worked up quite a speed.

The burst of British motor vehicle manufacturing witnessed by the Andersons represented hundreds of general engineering companies and cycle manufacturers, such as Rover and Humber, entering the market simultaneously. The four-mile-an-hour driving limit (with the law requiring a man with a red flag to lead the motor vehicle) had been rescinded and automobiles were now free to drive with other road traffic. A general knowledge of engineering techniques and a modest amount of capital was all it took to compete in the automobile trade. Despite such prospects, there was a fundamental flaw in British business practices that saw many companies collapse within a few years of starting out. Rather than developing a sub-industry of streamlined, interchangeable parts such as occurred in the United States, British companies manufactured individual components for each car model. Each company, therefore, was compelled to build small numbers of vehicles at high prices. Had the Andersons arrived a few years later they would have observed far fewer models on the roads as the burgeoning British car industry temporarily struggled to expand.

The Anderson girls' most memorable time in London was their all-day motorbus tour round the city. The motorbus was more than likely the first opportunity Alice, Katrine and Frankie had to travel in an automobile. The vehicle was similar to a horse-drawn bus but considerably larger, with its driver sitting out front. A rear staircase wound from the enclosed lower level to the open upper deck – the best place to take in sights the Anderson children had previously seen only in photographs and picture books: Buckingham Palace, the Tower of London, Big Ben, the Thames and London Bridge.

The reunion with Stewart, who was boarding 16 miles from his uncle and aunts at Newbury College, Berkshire, was a teary one. Despite Lettie's letters to Ellen Mary assuring her they would do all they could 'to help Stewart and to make him happy',[1] he was a lonely, homesick boy who was visibly overcome at seeing his family. The girls had never seen Stewart looking so sad. Lettie had foreshadowed Stewart's emotional challenges when she wrote that he would 'have no temptations to take him away from work here as there are no boys about'.[2] For Stewart, Hermit's Hill was aptly named. Outside of boarding school he lived an isolated existence in a household of three adults with no parenting experience and no real understanding of a child's needs. It hadn't helped that Lettie and Katie had been horrified at the poor education Stewart had received in Australia and New Zealand. Lettie had coached Stewart as far as she could prior to his Royal Navy entrance exams but, despite this, and the presumption that the exams counted for less than 'coming from the Colonies', he failed. Stewart was demoralised, and being told he had to continue on at Newbury College as a boarder to at least achieve an all-round education did nothing to lift his spirits.

Uncle William was well meaning but was not an affectionate man and could be quite self centred – so much so that he chose to leave for Europe on his annual six-week holiday the day before Alice and her family arrived. Consequently, William never caught up with JT, whom he had not seen in years, and the girls didn't get to meet him at all. JT's sisters were similarly self absorbed. Lettie lost herself in literature and Katie spent most of her time in the garden. The Anderson children perceived them, tellingly, as the type of aunties 'you didn't kiss good night'.[3]

England, at the time in the grip of an unusually severe drought, carried an air of loss for the Andersons. Birds fell from the sky dead due to heat exhaustion and lack of water, and gardens shrivelled unless they were hand watered. Frankie, Alice and Katrine could not save the feathery creatures but they took it upon themselves to honour their deaths. The girls set up a bird cemetery in their uncle and aunts' expansive garden, making headstones and holding burial services in their honour. This simple act resonated with Uncle Jack's passing and JT's inconsolable grief, and must have gone some way to soothing the young girls' hearts, as well as their elders'.

The family finally left Stewart to his studies and went on to Cheltenham to stay for six weeks with Ellen Mary's sister Kate Smith and her three children. Here the Anderson girls had a truly wonderful time. They worked up an appetite swimming with their cousins at the Cheltenham Baths and feasting on bowls of junket and cream sprinkled with cinnamon. They also learnt very quickly to tell a white lie when strangers asked, 'Where are you from?' To admit one was Australian, they soon realised, was a shameful thing, as it was the equivalent of saying one was the descendant of convicts. So the girls learnt to chirp, 'Yes, we've just come from New Zealand!'[4]

Next visit was to another sister of Ellen Mary's, Isabel O'Rourke, in Holywood, Belfast. Isabel had defied the Protestant family tradition by marrying a Roman Catholic solicitor. This may well have isolated Isabel from some family members but her husband had recently died and Ellen Mary, now well into her sixth pregnancy, was anxious to see how Isabel and her two young children were coping.

Aunt Isabel lived in a large, semi-detached house surrounded by what was practically a park. It was here on 18 April 1907 that Joan, the final Anderson child, was born. While Ellen Mary took care of the baby and toddler Claire with Isabel's, and often Frankie's, help, Alice and Katrine shared the children's governess. Alice, however, lived up to her reputation of doing what suited her. 'She shared my aunt's governess with her cousins for a while but otherwise she just sort of ran wild, probably,' reported Frankie nonchalantly.[5] No one, it seemed, was keeping enough of an eye on Alice or Katrine to know exactly what either was getting up to.

One of the greatest objects to attract the Anderson girls at this time was Aunt Isabel's bicycle. It had a modern low-rise frame with sprocket and chain, and pneumatic tyres. Such bicycles, built for more than a Sunday ride in the park, had been around for a decade or more. Though it was still seen as unladylike for a woman to be mounting one in 1907, low-rise, otherwise known as step-through, frames had been fashioned with the female sex in mind. Long skirts made stepping over a frame terribly awkward. In 1897 JT's mother, Eliza, had written twice to Ellen Mary of her own cycling attempts on one of the new contraptions.

Katie had one dry week with their hired bike and enjoyed it greatly. I felt quite inspired watching them flying along, and had a couple of mounts in the lane when dusk but I never got a chance to stay up long enough to get my balance. When I saw anyone in the distance I was off in a moment, none of the young folk can come up to one in speed getting off – I wish I could ride but I feel ashamed to be seen on the machine, so out of place, a grandmother with grey hair and worst of all, a bonnet . . .[6]

. . . I wish they had been invented in my time. I should have enjoyed them so much.[7]

'Mater' Anderson felt too old to learn but she would have felt even more ashamed to wear bloomers – those loose, full-cut pantaloons worn under a short skirt, the most practical attire for women determined to properly ride a bicycle. It was a difficult dilemma: if a lady did not hitch her skirts she found herself tangled in the mechanism; if she did hitch, it made steering awkward and revealed her ankles, which was almost as daring in Victorian times as a woman attempting to ride a bicycle at all. Riding outfits with slightly shorter hems and skirts bifurcated at the rear for easier movement did appear but they were still restrictive. It didn't take much for one's shoes to get caught in the skirt while pedalling or for hems to get caught in the chain.

Skirt length had changed little for women in the Edwardian era but for female children, frocks generally finished halfway between the knee and the ankle even if they were covered in buttons and lace. This made bike riding for children of both sexes relatively easy. Isabel was happy to teach Alice and Frankie to ride, although much to Alice's chagrin, she chose the eldest, twelve-year-old Frankie, to learn first. Seven-year-old Katrine was too young and small to attempt riding a woman's bicycle but Alice was about to turn ten and was right on Frankie's tail. Frankie started off a little wobbly, but not so Alice. Barely tall enough to reach the seat, Alice was off and pedalling first chance, racing round the park, her long, curly hair flying about in the wind as poor Frankie ran breathlessly behind, calling for Alice to stop being so unfair about sharing.

The children enjoyed their time in Holywood but they were also aware of growing tensions between their parents, both of whom were mired in grief as well as being stressed about JT's lack of employment opportunities. His old firm had invited him to return to Belfast, but on doing so he fought with them, immediately ending his re-employment prospects. JT had assumed steady work would eventually come his way, that he was at an employment advantage, having literally paved the way for colonial progress in bridges and sewerage, but nothing could have been further from the truth. JT's contacts had dried up and he was no longer in favour for prominent engineering positions. Moreover, his bullish personality and unswerving opinion that he was worthy of nothing less than a wage in line with his Dunedin salary did not weigh in JT's favour. His career, it seemed, was in decline. Ellen Mary had to wonder whether the clairvoyant who had told Stewart his father had reached the peak of his career in 1905 had been correct.

Clearly, JT's decision to pack his family off to the motherland was not providing the new start he so desperately sought. In fact, the family's troubles were escalating. Letters sent back and forth within JT's side of the family revealed the widening rift between JT and his brother William. One of the main issues centred round the financial implications of Stewart's continued schooling in England. JT believed William had offered to cover the costs of Stewart's schooling but William denied ever agreeing to such an arrangement. JT vehemently held his ground, even going so far as to threaten a lawsuit against his brother. Moreover, spats between the Anderson brothers over the family estate made for even greater tension. The whole mess eventually resulted in JT becoming estranged not only from brother William but also Henry, with whom he had previously been on good terms.

Ellen Mary felt powerless and despaired over where the family would end up. With Ellen Mary preoccupied and JT away in Mexico for an American Society of Engineers congress, where he also planned to explore further business opportunities, the children were largely left to amuse themselves. Before JT's return, Ellen Mary also took off, leaving the children with Isabel and her two servants while she travelled to Jersey, the largest of the Channel Islands between England and France, to explore the idea of living there tax free. JT was determined to earn a good wage while Ellen Mary was desperate to find a way the family could save money. It didn't take her long to realise the prices there were

'very high because too many people had had the same idea –
to escape income tax'.[8] Unfortunately, JT's business attempts in
Mexico also came to nothing.

On her return to Ireland, Ellen Mary sought out another
sister, Zoe, whose clergyman husband, Richard Merrin, had been
managing Ellen Mary's small annuity of about £150 granted
her from her grandfather's estate. Merrin had made bad invest-
ments over the years, so much so that Ellen Mary was never sure
how much or when the money would arrive. As early as 1902,
JT's mother had advised Ellen Mary to acquit Merrin of this
responsibility, but it wasn't until Ellen Mary was back in Ireland
and needing every financial resource available that she had the
motive and the opportunity to finally take her mother-in-law's
advice. The issue wasn't as straightforward or easily resolved as
Ellen Mary had hoped. Unfortunately the White-Spunner side
of the family was also in a fiscal mess. Not only had there been
ongoing problems with Ellen Mary's annuity, she and all her siblings had been constantly embroiled in financial bickering over
their family estate. Family trust had broken down. Her brother
Harry, for example, had lived beyond his means for years and
owed them all money.

Despite tensions between the Anderson brothers, Henry, who
happened to be very responsible with finances, finally agreed to
manage Ellen Mary's annuity on her behalf. It was then that Ellen
Mary made a promise to herself that the money would not be used
to prop up her own family's financial shortfalls but would be put
aside for her daughters' further education. She did not have a head
for business but, at forty-two years old and after fifteen years of
marriage, she knew her husband, despite his optimistic perception of his own fiscal aptitude, was too impulsive and erratic to

ever be a good manager of money. Of course, Ellen Mary had little experience of managing money herself. In fact, neither had the least idea of living on a budget, or of budgeting at all.

When the school holidays came around Stewart was allowed to leave boarding school and spend time with the family at Aunt Isabel's. For the occasion JT bought two bicycles, one for himself and one for his son, with little thought to the sizeable dent such a purchase put in the dwindling family coffers. With Isabel's bicycle also at hand, JT took his two eldest children, Stewart and Frankie, off to experience the Ireland he had known as a boy. The three took in several counties, sometimes cycling over 40 miles a day up and down the gentle hills and back lanes of JT's youth. Meanwhile Alice, sorely disappointed to have missed out on such an adventure, had to be content with getting up to tricks with Katrine and her cousins.

The family stayed on in Ireland after JT finally, though reluctantly, accepted part-time work as an acting professor in engineering at Belfast University. The income it provided was far from what the family was used to, so they rented a cheap but picturesque house at 'Silverstream' that belonged to the city engineer, who happened to be in a mental hospital at the time. Apparently his wife felt too alone in the large house with its big garden, and was glad of tenants. Before the husband was committed he had left a project in the garden that the children were delighted to discover. In what may have been attributed to his deteriorating mental state, the man had built two tree houses, one at least twenty-five feet high.

JT struggled to keep the family going on his part-time university wage, so once a two-storey house became available in University Street, the row of houses let cheaply to university personnel, the family moved out of Silverstream and resettled there. Shortly after, a box arrived by post from Reading. Inside was a note from Ellen Mary's sister Kate and a pile of beautiful clothes. Kate's children had outgrown the clothes said the note, and she hoped her nieces might find a use for them. It was true the girls were quickly outgrowing their New Zealand attire, and Ellen Mary had hardly been in a position to be dressmaking. The girls huddled round the box, excited to see what was inside. JT walked in just as Ellen Mary was lifting the clothes out. 'What are those?' he asked. Ellen Mary handed him the note. To JT, this was the final blow. Had his wife let on to her sister that they were struggling? He stormed over to the box and slammed it shut. 'I am not going to bring my children up to be charity children!' he roared. 'We are going back to Australia.'[9] And that was that.

It was September 1907. After more than twelve months in the home country and with few reserves left to sustain his wife and six children, JT had to concede that the plan for his family to stay and create a new life for themselves was futile. He resigned from his poorly paid position at the university and arranged their voyage back to Australia. The family were going full circle, from a green and misty Ireland to a scorching antipodean summer, with far less than when they had first arrived.

4

A BUSH RETREAT

'Never trust to luck'

(1920s *Shell Motorists' Index*)

On 21 September 1907 the Anderson family, including Stewart, travelled to Plymouth and boarded the *Ophir* bound for Australia. It was not a pleasant voyage. Unable to afford an upper deck cabin, they were forced to tolerate steerage class, situated in the bowels of the ship close to engine noise and vibration. On top of these less-than-ideal circumstances, Ellen Mary became seasick, causing her milk to dry up, which in turn caused baby Joan to cry constantly from malnutrition. Then all the other Anderson children developed a nasty case of nits. Later, while the ship was in the Bay of Biscay, tragedy struck.

Ellen Mary had brought a pair of castanets on board and, according to Frankie, this prompted one of the passengers to ask her about Spanish dances. The question inspired Ellen Mary to deliver a spontaneous dancing demonstration, despite her weighing a hefty thirteen stone. She held the castanets above her head and threw up her heels just at the very moment the ship rolled. Ellen Mary heard a sound like a whip cracking and instantly went down in a heap. The pain was tremendous: she had torn her Achilles tendon, something early twentieth-century medicine could not repair. This single snap in a joyous moment would cripple her for life. For the rest of the voyage, much to her distress, Ellen Mary's voluminous body had to be physically carried by crew members from deck to deck. As awkward and humiliating as this was, Ellen Mary's great worry was the thought of how on earth she would cope getting about once on shore.

As the *Ophir* berthed at Port Melbourne on the morning of 30 October 1907, an unsettling gale blew from the north. After more than five years abroad, the Andersons disembarked with two additional children, two bicycles, their fourteen crates of books, a few other basic belongings and, according to Frankie, no more than £15 in their pockets. Just as Ellen Mary had lost her ability to walk unaided, the family had, in a few short months, completely lost the lifestyle to which they were accustomed.

JT sent his wife and children directly to their little country summer cottage that he had christened 'Springbank', after JT's mother's place in Ireland, while he tended to other business in town. In 1891, the year before his marriage to Ellen Mary, JT had fallen in love with and purchased a square mile of virgin bush at Narbethong, a small isolated village in Victoria's north central highlands, fulfilling his dream of owning his own country estate. On it, he had built a cottage situated between two creeks. Away from the old country, it was the only place the family could now call home.

Initially, two acres were cleared and the cottage was built from felled trees. Jack and JT, and JT's friends at the university including John Monash, turned up on weekends to build what was a roughly hewn shack intended for holiday stays only. Firstly, three rooms were built: a living room with a bedroom either side and an eight-foot-wide verandah out front. At the back there was the kitchen separated from the main cottage by a pathway of coarse planking for protection against fire. Cooking was done over an open fireplace with iron kettles and pots hung from chains. The floor was packed earth. There was no sink. Water came from nearby Fishers Creek, from which JT had built a channel and a well. Kerosene tins were used to carry water up to the cottage.

Alice, Stewart and Frankie were particularly excited to be returning to Springbank. The place had been the source of some of the children's best memories: bright sun casting shadows through towering mountain ash; the pungent smell of eucalypt and lush ferns; the raucous, warbling sounds of cockatoos, lorikeets and magpies; creeks for swimming; and bush as far as the eye could see.

To break the journey the family stayed overnight at Daly's Hotel (now the Healesville Hotel) in Healesville before taking a Cobb & Co. coach-and-four the 16 miles to Narbethong. Clip-clopping hooves sent up whirls of dust from the dry, unsealed road. Above, the sky was a dazzling blue, and all round the familiar greens and greys of the Australian bush were so different from the dazzling greens of Ireland's countryside. After five weeks in a cramped cabin, it was paradise. The fact that it was November 1, Katrine's eighth birthday, only added to the children's excitement. Once in Narbethong they had the coach stop at a local establishment, where they ate beautiful raspberries covered in thick, pure cream. From there it was a further 2 miles to the path that took them to Springbank.

Alice, Frankie, Stewart, Katrine and Claire may have been happy but it took all of Ellen Mary's strength just to keep up appearances. The pain of her injury, the constantly crying baby, her inability to walk and JT's absence had her on the verge of despair. How much more could she endure? The coach pulled up at the mile-long path leading from the main road to the cottage and the carriage driver disengaged a couple of his horses to assist them to the door. By the time they all came face to face with their new home, Ellen Mary was physically and emotionally spent, only to be confronted by the mess inside.

For the years the Andersons had been away, Miss Annie O'Neil, one of the children's former nursery governesses, had been invited by the family to stay at Springbank and keep an eye on it in their absence. Apparently 'Neily' had fallen in love with the place after accompanying the children there on their holidays and was most happy to take up the offer. In the years between the family leaving Australia and Jack joining them in New Zealand, Annie and Jack had both kept an eye on the property and were in close correspondence, their letters even hinting at a possible romance. However, after Jack died Annie found resident employment as assistant to the post mistress at the local Narbethong post office. Once she had vacated the cottage, unbeknownst to her, local woodcutters had taken to squatting there and in a very short time had almost destroyed the place. It was filthy, infested with fleas and bed bugs, and the roof leaked everywhere except Ellen Mary's bedroom. The family had no choice but to travel a further mile to the nearest boarding house, St Fillans, in the hope a vacancy would be available for one night at least.

St Fillans, an elegant place at the end of a long avenue of pine trees, had room for Ellen Mary and the three youngest girls, Katrine, Claire and Joan. In the meantime the eldest three, Stewart, Frankie, and ten-year-old Alice, returned to tackle the cottage. Between the three of them they washed the bedding and curtains in kerosene, blocked the external doors with newspaper and burnt sulphur in the old cast iron camp oven to kill the fleas. It wasn't until the cottage was free of parasites that Ellen Mary and the other children returned to begin a life so primitive they might have been early pioneers.

Narbethong itself consisted of no more than a stable, a pub and the post office. Families were spread far and wide across the district and the only other 'gentry' were the Crooks, who lived a mile from Springbank. Healesville was the closest town and Melbourne, the nation's capital, was a distant 40 miles southwest.

The ever-optimistic JT had plans for Springbank to include an orchard, a sawmill and a eucalyptus distillery, as a means of becoming somewhat self-sufficient. But no matter what he envisaged it didn't help or add a shine to Ellen Mary's daily struggles. Not only did she have difficulty walking, the family could no longer afford domestic help of any kind. Years ago, Ellen Mary had utilised Britain's most popular domestic guide, *Mrs Beeton's Book of Household Management,* to direct her staff in cooking and keeping house. Because her own cooking and cleaning experience was minimal at best, her changed circumstances now compelled her to learn firsthand from *Mrs Beeton's* while relying on Frankie to do many of the household chores.

Once settled, the next thing Ellen Mary put her mind to was the sensible and brave move to take her girls out of 'all those silly underclothes, bodices and stays, petticoats, lace trimmings and things dripping with buttons', and put them in simple navy blue bloomers and blouses. Locals from Marysville to Narbethong were horrified and henceforth the Andersons were viewed as being quite odd. Ellen Mary also let the girls wear their hair long rather than tie it in curling rags. Loopy curls made from twisting the hair with damp rags might have been the fashion of the day but Ellen Mary despised the artificiality of it all. Frankie, who had a natural gift for sewing, helped make the children new clothes from practical and hardwearing materials such as blue Galatea (a denim-like fabric) for summer and blue serge for winter. Sailor's blouses were made in the same material for 'best'. For the girls' feet Ellen Mary bought boys' boots, which were far sturdier than those made for girls and had buckles rather than rows of delicate buttons that tediously needed doing up with a buttonhook. Alice and Katrine were especially thrilled; for these two tomboy gad-abouts the clothes spelt freedom!

Despite Ellen Mary's efforts, she remained an emotional wreck. Even though there were occasional opportunities to travel, she felt she could never show her face in fashionable Melbourne again. *What would her 'at home' circle think?* Crippled and forced into isolation through poverty, her shame seemed complete. JT was sympathetic but he had to leave Narbethong to seek work for weeks at a time, and when he did come home it was often so late at night that there was little time for moral support.

Transport was a challenge. At one point JT chose to lodge in East Melbourne while he worked as a drafter for a large Melbourne firm, something far below his training and experience. Unable to afford a horse, let alone a buggy, JT relied on the train and his own two feet to get home. Claire recalled that:

49

When he was able, he would catch the train from Melbourne to Healesville, arriving around seven or eight in the evening. Then he would walk, in his town clothes, over the Black Spur by the old road and then two miles past Narbethong [to the cottage] and arrive about midnight. Mother would have been waiting up for him.[1]

Alice was not deterred by their change in circumstances but she did avoid some of the domestic tensions by finding things to do outdoors, where she felt most comfortable. She was quite happy for her older sister to continue to take on the inside jobs. In the bush Alice could pretend she was the hero of her own adventures. She especially loved reading the boys adventure stories such as Rudyard Kipling's *The Jungle Book*, Robert Louis Stevenson's *Treasure Island* and Mark Twain's *Huckleberry Finn*. Even the books themselves lived outdoors: there was no space to house them inside so all fourteen crates of them, along with crates for linen, stayed on the verandah covered in sacks to protect them from the weather. (JT eventually built a 'library' that contained all the classics, including *Seven Little Australians*, but he could never afford enough timber to line or finish it, so it was the hottest place possible in summer and the coldest in winter.)

Frankie, who was old enough to have experienced the best of governesses and other hired help, identified far more with her mother and the weight of the family's slide into relative poverty. As for the other girls, Alice was in her element and Katrine was happiest following Alice around like a lapdog. Claire and Joan, who knew no other life in Australia, had no reason to yearn for something they'd never had. With JT's frequent absences Stewart found his place as the man of the house. He took on the heavier outdoor tasks such as chopping wood and building fences, and, as with Alice, found solace in the bush.

JT continued traipsing the countryside, picking up various surveying jobs with district shires. True to his desire for self-determination, JT deliberately chose to promote himself as a consultant engineer rather than applying for shire positions. After his Dunedin experience he was keen to stay an arm's length away from the machinations of shire politics and felt he was best served by working outside an institution rather than within. However, in making this choice, he limited his prospects. Victoria was still recovering from the 1890s crash and local governments were reluctant to hire external consultants. Ellen Mary, being physically isolated, was no longer in a position to lubricate the social wheel with the wives of men of influence. Criticisms of JT's work were also appearing in the press. The editor of the *Mildura Cultivator* did not mince words when he criticised the boiler JT had ordered for a local irrigation project. Whether the editor was accurate in his assessment or not, the overall impression was disparaging and served JT no favours:

> ten years ago . . . I ventured to criticise the recommendations and designs of Mr. J. T. Noble Anderson, at whose insistence the boiler and the Otis plant were procured, in rather disparaging terms. I had not a very high opinion of that cocksure but calamitous young man's ability to teach Geo. Chaffey how to raise water for irrigation, and from what I know now my admiration has not yet been excited so far as his work at Mildura is concerned. The boiler was unsuitable to local conditions. It never had the steaming capacity required, which is proved by the fact that it has to be assisted by steam from the old boiler . . . It is

safe to predict that no more boilers or pumping plans similar to these will be obtained by the Trust . . .[2]

While away, JT kept in touch with his family through letters. He wrote to Ellen Mary daily, jotting down his thoughts and doling out advice and recriminations, always opening with the endearingly affectionate 'My Dear Life'. In the first, most difficult couple of years at Springbank, his letters revealed a man who wavered between self-satisfaction and despondency. As early as mid January 1908 JT's buoyant optimism had all but evaporated, such was his financial burden. He wrote to his wife:

> I am too poor to go where I can attract attention, and I cannot afford an office. So what good can I possibly do? The sooner you and I realise that the labourer's lot, with the help of the farm is all that is left us, the sooner we will be happy . . .[3]

Later that year he wrote to Ellen Mary regarding his reconnection with friend and former business partner John Monash. In the time JT had been away, Monash had become very successful in business as well as forging his military career. Monash was clearly in a situation to assist JT, which he did by passing on odd jobs that JT accepted with mixed feelings. 'Monash was asked to write an article on a new steel process – he put it on to me,' JT wrote to Ellen Mary. 'I ought to be thankful, but I have the conviction that he would have taken it himself as he could.'[4] JT found dealing with Monash's success so difficult he convinced himself he was better off without the man, writing to his wife a couple of days later that:

*Everything makes me satisfied that my career has been 'for
the best' so far, and in nothing more so than in parting with
Monash. Seeing all I now do, and looking on things with my
present experience what I wonder at is how I ever came to
remain so long with him & having left how I ever could have
entertained for one minute any thoughts of returning.*[5]

This was despite JT having no steady employment and being
unsure where his next job would come from. The truth, more
likely, was that JT knew Monash had no need or desire to ever
work with him again.

Although neither excelled in money management, JT encouraged Ellen Mary to keep a budget, and was relieved when
she finally produced one in writing. He replied with a letter,
addressing her lovingly as always, but in regards to her actual
handling of household finances, he was scathing.

*My dearest life . . . you need not count on my bringing up
cabbages nor much else because my postage & trams have
made a big hole in my pocket money & I have only 15/- left –
you are very foolish to talk of paying Mrs. J. Nichols from your
ready cash & so on – You ought never to have less than £10
in cash but you seem to have no more foresight than a small
child . . .*[6]

Despite their lack of resources, the cottage had to be extended
and improved to accommodate the family of eight. With Jack
gone and JT unavailable to do much more than the basics, the
family had to rely on the only available carpenter in the district.

He was an old German called Passek who, by all accounts, was not a nice person. Passek had a son who was even rumoured to have murdered his mother, 'very bloodily with an axe', though he was never charged. The old man's carpentry skills were questionable and he made some bad mistakes that the family just had to put up with. His first extension was a verandah at the back of the cottage, which was 'very badly built and [with] very unfinished timber'.[7] Nothing he did was ever level.

The very least Ellen Mary felt she deserved was a decent bathroom from which she could attend to her ablutions with some care. JT made an attempt to build one but, due to the plumbing devised to access water from the nearest creek, the room had to be accessed by a ladder. The kitchen also had access to the water through a newly installed tap but that was the only improvement. *How on earth was she going to manage to clamber up a ladder in her state?* Ellen Mary flatly refused to have 'a bush bathroom with a bush shower!'[8] JT tried to convince her the set up was temporary but Ellen Mary knew better than to accept the arrangement as it was. She wasn't going to have a bathroom 'until she had a proper one, not something temporary, because temporary would become permanent'.[9] Consequently, the family was left without a functional bathroom altogether and instead washed in the sandy bathing pool JT had dug out close to the cottage.

Although a bedroom was added to the cottage for Katrine and Alice to share, Alice preferred to rough it on the back verandah in the swing bed. The bed:

> hung by four ropes on the rafters, with pulleys. It was made with two saplings cut from the bush, with two chaff bags put across from one to the other, so making a nice bed, and

a stretcher to keep it from collapsing towards itself at each end, made out of a piece of 3 by 1, and the poles that supported the bed itself went through the holes in those two stretching pieces of timber. And that was supported by four ropes from the rafters, and could be pulled up to the roof out of the way in the daytime if you wanted . . .[10]

Alice loved lying there out in the elements, where she could gaze at the stars, listen to the nocturnal sounds of the bush, and dream her dreams.

5

AN EDUCATION OF SORTS

(1920s *Shell Motorists' Index*)

Each family member was caught up in their own challenges brought about by their dramatic change of circumstance. For Alice, it meant taking control and learning to push and create new boundaries. JT understood this about his precociously clever daughter. He attempted to guide and encourage her even from afar, as demonstrated in the letter he wrote to her from his Melbourne lodgings in November 1908, addressing Alice affectionately by her family nickname:

My dearest Lol,
I hope you have buried those gohannas (or ought they to be
called iguanas?) before now. On no account might reptiles like
them ought to be skinned except just when killed, because there
is great danger of getting blood poisoning from them. I saw a

large one when I was walking over the Spur — and pretended I
was going to strike it — when it turned and opened its mouth
at me. It would have bitten me if it could and the bite is
dangerous since it festers.

I am writing to you because I want you to be very good and
not to quarrel with Katrine while Mother is away — and I want
you to do all you can to help Frankie with baby & by milking
& looking after the fowls in turn & watering the seeds,
Your own loving Father[1]

Alice often found things to do that took her miles away from home. She was not disrespectful to Mother or Father but circumstances in those first few months at Springbank allowed both Alice and Katrine freedom. Ellen Mary attended to Joan while Frankie helped indoors and took on the main responsibility of caring for four-year-old Claire. Meanwhile, JT was off looking for work in Melbourne and Stewart was caught up doing the outside chores. The only time everyone gathered together was at mealtimes, when Ellen Mary took Stewart's Boy Scout bugle and bellowed tunelessly for her wayward children to come home.

At the beginning of 1908 the three older girls were sent to the local half-time state school. Ellen Mary was distressed that this meant her girls would be mixing with working-class children. In fact, she wouldn't ever let the girls stay and play with the other children: 'You might get nits in the hair . . . and you might pick up the Australian accent.'[2] But she had no choice. A governess was beyond the family's means, as was a private denominational education, even with Ellen Mary's annuity. Public education was not only free: education was compulsory for boys and girls up to the age of fourteen.

State primary school subjects consisted of reading, writing, arithmetic, grammar, geography, history, drill, singing, drawing, elementary science, manual training and gymnastics. Health and temperance were reserved for children over nine years old. Girls' education included sewing, cooking and domestic economy. However, the curriculum the Anderson girls were exposed to at the Healesville half-time school was of a very questionable standard.

Any teacher assigned to the remote area moved the 20 miles between the Healesville and Marysville schools, alternating three days at one school and two at the next. This arrangement ensured the children in each small town had a total of five days' schooling per fortnight, hence the term 'half-time'. The teacher was billeted centrally, usually with a poor family that needed the extra income, and had to travel long distances to the schools. Not surprisingly, the position was not a popular one – children were either saddled with very young teachers just out of training or old ones who were almost ready to be pensioned off.

The Healesville School swelled from ten students to thirteen when Frankie, Alice and Katrine were enrolled. Teachers came and went, and few were satisfactory. Often the students would arrive to find there was no teacher present at all. Hoorah! Those were the days the children headed for the bush to play cowboys and 'injuns', or they went to St Fillans and swung on the branches of the pine trees flanking the avenue to the boarding house. Ellen Mary worried so much about the school that she continually wrote to the Education Department demanding better teachers. One teacher she heartily disapproved of was a former classics master at Wesley College who had been sacked due to his alcoholism. At school he would put up the lid of his desk so the children couldn't see him drinking out of his whisky bottle. By eleven o'clock he would be red in the face and ready to hit students with a stick.

The Anderson girls took such incidents in their stride. Once the school day was over they put it out of their minds and went home to play. In the hot summer months Alice led the charge, running past her mother's japonicas, through the orchard, stripping off clothes as they raced each other to the creek to throw themselves into the cool, fresh water.

Although the girls' education might have been patchy, the school routine gave Alice structure and encouraged her furtive mind to apply learning and teaching outside the classroom. At eleven years old Alice was full of ideas, determination and self-righteousness, not unlike her father. And the family's changed circumstances appeared to provide early opportunities for Alice to unleash her natural tendency to initiate and act on her ideas without hindrance.

Soon after commencing school Alice decided it was important to learn how to milk a cow, since baby Joan was still suffering the effects of malnutrition and required fresh milk every day. So Alice began heading off to school fifteen minutes early every morning and stopping in at Miller's farm, where the children walked more than a mile every few days for the family's billy of milk, to get in a bit of milking practice before she continued on to class. Once she had mastered the skill she went to Ellen Mary and said, 'Mother, we have to get a cow so that Joan can have fresh milk and we don't have to go down to Miller's for it.'

'Well, who's going to milk the cow?'

'I will.'

'You can't milk!'

'Oh, yes I can!'[3]

Alice's initiative so impressed (or amused) Ellen Mary that she later wrote of the incident to a friend in New Zealand. By this time the Andersons had acquired three milking cows and Alice was in charge of them. The friend replied, 'fancy Alice milking 3 cows night and morning, I can tell you there are heaps of girls [who] would not have the courage to tackle work like that'.[4] Ironically, what the family didn't know at the time was that cow's milk was not good for Joan's digestion – but it was good for Alice. She was caught more than once with her fingers in the milk bottles, taking off the cream. When Katrine helped her with the milking, Alice would sneak a tin with a little sweetened condensed milk into the cowshed to which they'd add the fresh milk, straight from the teat, and sometimes a little cocoa Alice had stolen from the kitchen.

One of the cows had a bull calf they named Jockey, which Alice trained to become a working bullock just like those she'd seen hauling local timber to town. 'She had it so it would pull logs and all sorts of things,' recalled Claire. 'She made the pulling gear for it, and we used to have calf races down the steep slope into the valley.'[5]

Despite the poor quality of instruction at school the Anderson girls generally loved what they were taught and, unsurprisingly, did well. However, for Alice, the curriculum lacked one important subject: religion. The Andersons, true to their background, kept up the traditions of daily prayers and Bible readings at home, but they no longer attended services or Sunday school because the closest Anglican Church was in Marysville, 8 miles from Springbank. Religion was connected to one's standing in the community, being threaded with class, politics and dedication to the British Crown. Irish Protestants were the cream. Irish Catholics, the majority of working-class Australians, were the rabble. It was not only a matter of faith – there was the pride of keeping up one's traditions.

Despite her cheekiness, though true to her sense of righteousness, Alice became the most religious of the children. She thrived on tales of punishment and redemption, where stakes were high and outcomes dramatic. The stories of the Old Testament particularly captured her imagination, as they did JT's, and she was determined her younger sisters would be captured by them too. Alice established her own Sunday school in the paddock at Springbank, gathering four saplings about six feet high and five feet apart as a base for her pulpit, accessed by a ladder she built. On high she delivered lessons, reading out loud from *Line Upon Line*, the Andersons' book of Old Testament Bible stories for children, and initiated discussions from her readings.

Katrine and Claire were the main attendees and Alice had a hard time keeping her charges in order. Katrine had become an instant atheist when her favourite cow had fallen into a wombat hole and broken her back. Counting on the belief that 'if you asked anything in the name of Jesus Christ it would be granted to you',[6] Katrine had climbed to the top of a hill and prayed and prayed. But when the cow died she concluded God wasn't much use. It was only four-year-old Claire whom Alice managed to impress. Claire loved having stories read to her, especially by her big sister!

When she wasn't mucking about with Katrine, Alice loved to spend time with Stewart, getting dirty and helping out with chores her other sisters were not interested in or were too young to tackle. Alice the tomboy was little, but physically strong for an eleven-year-old girl and Stewart, being four years her senior, had become nothing less than her hero. A big brother didn't quite fill the shoes of an absent father but it was possible he could teach her things Father might not have even allowed. What thrilled her most was the prospect of Stewart teaching her how to use a gun. It didn't take too much begging from her before Stewart agreed. Alice was the closest thing to a brother Stewart could have and he was happy for a protégée he could teach and tease in equal measure.

Stewart turned fifteen in 1908 with no clear idea of his future. Tall, with well-defined features and large blue–grey eyes, he was developing into a handsome young man. Still, he remained a stoic and a loner, his failure to pass the Royal Navy exams an unspoken disappointment. At Springbank Stewart had quickly fallen into the role of general handyman. When the meat became rancid or they had run up too much of a tab at the local butcher, he shot rabbits and caught trout from the nearby creeks. Being a farm-hand was no great career prospect but he loved the physicality of it and the quietude of the bush. He took over the little unlined hut his uncle Jack had built two hundred yards away from the main cottage and made it his own sleeping quarters and sanc-tuary. He found comfort in Uncle Jack's simple bush bed and mattress made out of two chaff bags stuffed with green bracken.

Stewart had access to two 16-bore double-barrel shotguns. One was his and the other had been Jack's. Alice observed her big brother making his own bullets by stuffing casings with lead shot and gunpowder. After a few lessons she learnt to shoot rabbits with accuracy, wring their necks in case the bullet didn't bring instant death, and clean them for Mother and Frankie to cook. With Alice able to supplement the dinner table, Stewart was free to concentrate on other outdoor tasks. He taught her to fish for trout but she didn't have the patience for a rod, so she passed that responsibility on to Katrine.

Soon Alice had the skills to survive away from the comforts of city living as well as any man living out in the bush. Since the family couldn't afford a horse, every week Alice, Frankie and Katrine took it in turns to bounce the bicycles along the mile track, over the rickety wooden bridges spanning the two creeks, and onto the main road. There they met the coach that brought the weekly mail and supplies from Healesville in a sack containing five four-pound loaves and a standard order from the butcher, which usually included a forequarter of lamb, some sausages and sometimes rump steak as a treat. There was usually half a case of lemons as well, which JT ordered believing lemons had tremendous blood-purifying qualities. It was a challenging task taking it all back to the house. Frankie remembered 'balancing a whole fruit case of lemons and things' on one bicycle and having to negotiate the track with great care so everything arrived intact.[7]

While Stewart, Alice and the younger girls found bush life stimulating, thirteen-year-old Frankie was torn between relating to her siblings and supporting Mother, who continued to struggle physically and emotionally. Frankie often felt the pressure of responsibilities beyond her years, especially since Ellen Mary confided in her when the loneliness became too much to bear. No wonder Frankie, a secondary mother figure to the younger girls, came across as 'over responsible and serious-minded'. She was always the 'peacemaker', Claire said. 'She never bullied, never teased. She was never cruel. She was a lovely little mother.'[8]

Frankie tried so hard to be the good little girl but often, it seemed, without much reward or even acknowledgement. In contrast, Alice continued to do just as she pleased and almost always got away with it. Alice was incredibly capable but she was no saint. She often bullied the other girls and even Claire, who had Alice on a pedestal, said she was a 'disrupter, was wicked, a tease – and she had a temper'.[9] Alice demanded attention and expected to get her own way if not by charm, then by persistence and insistence, even force. The world had better look out.

Despite Frankie's support, Ellen Mary was barely coping. JT's priorities, however, were far more pragmatic than Ellen Mary's perceived fall from grace and respectability: he was trying to secure a decent living for his family. One letter from JT to Ellen Mary in 1909 revealed such exasperation that his words read as a veritable slap in the face.

> *And I fear if you cannot reconcile your mind to let a lot of things slide that you now strive after – you will collapse entirely – and then where would we be –*
>
> *To some extent living so much away – I can look at your life as if I were an outsider – and I am amazed at the way you spend your energy on things of the least consequence . . . The greatest wisdom is contained in the teaching of 'consider the lilies' – Martha and Mary and above all 'is not the life more than the meat' . . . About every page of the Gospels are full of condemnation of this immature striving after respectability . . .*[10]

Ellen Mary had little choice but to pick herself up and carry on.

The year 1909 did see one material improvement: JT finally brought home a horse. It was called Winnie and the girls were ecstatic. Even little Claire had been longing for a rocking horse so much that she had taken Ellen Mary's old sidesaddle and, dragging it over the verandah rail, galloped on the spot. Winnie was officially a pony, 'but at fourteen and two' had more than a little thoroughbred in her. When Winnie arrived at Springbank she was three years old, 'not very well broken in and quite naughty'.[11]

One major concern became Winnie's terror of the cars and motorcycles that would pass on the roads. The noise and the dust they blew up always sent her shying. Automobiles were alien to her. She had been bred in remote Howqua Shire, in Victoria's high country, where they were still a rare sight. The Anderson girls learnt to ride Winnie by trial and error, which meant falling off and getting back on again. But when automobiles were involved, the stakes were higher. Once Frankie was sent flying when Winnie ran high up an embankment and threw her back onto the gravel road to avoid a motorcar. Luckily for Frankie, her schoolteacher came by not long after and revived Frankie with water. Apart from shock and a few grazes, she was fortunately unhurt. On another occasion, however, a motorcycle and sidecar caused Winnie to bolt when Katrine was in the saddle. The poor girl 'went right over her head on to her face and was terribly injured. She was quite unrecognisable,' Frankie recalled. In fact, Katrine's scalp had been split so badly it required stitches.[12]

Once Alice mounted Winnie there was no getting her off. If she experienced any falls or accidents, they weren't worth noting. Alice refused to ride sidesaddle, as ladylike Frankie had done, and proudly rode on Winnie legs astride, like a boy. Alice took the pony for long, fast rides through the bush, away from the roads and automobiles. In some ways this was more dangerous: Winnie had only to clip over a fallen log, land in a dip or have

Alice clobbered by a low-hanging branch for the two to come unstuck. The only consequence of these adventures, however, was a scolding for regularly returning late for dinner. As usual, Alice paid little heed. In Winnie she had discovered something faster than herself and this thrilled her to the core.

———

In the cities and towns, automobiles were taking to roads with increasing familiarity, and the area around Narbethong was close enough to other small towns to attract some automobile traffic, as well as being a weekend attraction for daytrippers from Melbourne. Alice and her family were bearing witness to the private automobile becoming the early twentieth century's greatest new hobby. Whether powered by petrol, steam or electricity, it offered 'sporting excitement and touring exhilaration' for those wealthy enough to afford one.[13]

From the earliest American Model T Fords to the more luxurious European models of Benz and Daimler, the first decade of the twentieth century saw motorcars steer away from the style of a horse carriage to become more recognisable as automobiles in their own right. There were custom-built tyres, comfortable seating and room for more passengers. Steering wheels replaced tillers, and retractable cloth hoods provided protection against the elements.

In the six years the Andersons had spent abroad, Australia's motoring enthusiasts had established car clubs, reliability trials and motoring journals, just as their counterparts were doing across the developed world. The Automobile Club of Australia and the Automobile Club of Victoria both came about in 1903, and other states quickly followed suit. The country's first reliability trial took place from Melbourne to Sydney in 1905 and 1908 was the year the *Australian Motorist* monthly journal came into being. This magazine, almost singlehandedly, heralded the era of motoring across the nation and informed enthusiasts of developments overseas. When a Mr Wallace of the Wallace Tyre Company in Windsor, Victoria, returned from a worldwide tour exploring global rubber and tyre manufacture in 1908, the *Australian Motorist* reported on his observations of 'automobilism'.

> [Mr Wallace] readily admitted that in motor matters generally Australia does not lag far behind the European vanguard. 'Australian motoring is but a small side eddy', he remarked, 'but it lacks little in freshness of ideas for all that. Very little time elapses before the latest improvements in cars or tyres reach us.' The only real difference Mr. Wallace observed was that, 'the great cities are alive with self-propelling vehicles. Australian cities seem to be asleep compared with the hum of automobilism that haunts the streets of Paris, Berlin and London. Motors are everywhere and the tireless German is pushing his interests in this enormous development of human activity and trade. In London you see strings of motor cabs and buses panting through the great avenues of traffic.'[14]

Australia was yet to establish automobile motor cab or bus services, though the 'speed and versatility' of self-propelled vehicles meant their commercial prospects were slowly coming to fruition.[15] Doctors began to consider motorcars for home visits, and businesses for the delivery of goods and services.

This was not to say everyone was happy with the idea of increased automobile traffic. As early as 1900 there was a fearful backlash against 'automobilism'. An article in Melbourne's *Argus* went so far as to predict what could be viewed today as a dark yet somewhat accurate premonition.

> The real truth is that when the motor comes into universal use life will not be worth living . . . to live in a city when motors have superseded horses will be like living in a cotton mill, with a boiler factory on one side and a merry-go-round with a steam organ on the other . . . A horse does not like to run a man down if he can help it, but a machine of steel and brass will delight in killing people.[16]

Despite such fears, the horseless carriage had bolted and there was no turning back. Towards the end of the first decade of the twentieth century there were enough automobiles to require laws to control their use, and the first motorcar and traffic acts began to appear throughout the various Australian states. The acts created laws for the provision of numberplates, licence registration, warning bells and speed – though speed limits were left to common sense. It was a matter of driver judgement, police perception and circumstance as to whether one drove safely or in a manner that endangered life or property. Specific regulations were self-evident: drive on the left side of the road unless overtaking; don't drive on footpaths; don't drive backwards for longer than is necessary; use lights after dark; stop in case of an accident. However, it would take years before traffic signs, traffic lights and well-made roads became part of the motoring landscape.

Once Alice and her younger sisters had developed some confidence with Winnie, the girls began riding her to school. Alice sat on the saddle and Katrine held on behind while young Claire was propped in front. It was 1909 and Claire, now five, was the newest school member, replacing fourteen-year-old Frankie. The girls took the dusty road to Healesville carefully, hoping to trot all the way to school and back without passing a motorcar or bike. Protective of her younger sisters, Alice kept Winnie calm and steady as she went. Still, motorcars held Alice in thrall and she was always torn between avoiding Winnie going into a panic and hoping an automobile would pass their way.

6

COMING OF AGE

'Every car must be fitted with a horn,
bell or other warning device'

(1920s *Shell Motorists' Index*)

Alice wasn't the only family member who was developing an interest in automobiles. Towards the end of 1908 JT took up an engineer consultancy position in the Shire of Towong, a large grazing and squatting district covering approximately 2600 miles on the Victoria–New South Wales border. The job, based in Tallangatta, entailed travelling throughout the shire, which he described to his wife as being 'as big as one of the largest Irish counties'. Locals travelled on horseback or by horse and buggy as they had always done, but as JT justified to his wife:

> I think I must someway or other manage to get a motorcar to
> work this district — even if it be dearer than a horse, as I think
> it will. It will give me a distinction in a district where that sort

*of thing is unknown, and it would be a start of mechanical
training for Stewart.*[1]

However, the arguments against purchasing a motorcar at this time
were significant, not withstanding JT's inability to afford one.

It was around 1908 when JT also convinced his wife they
should invest in the goldmines of northern Victoria. He told her
he 'knew the insides of the mines at Warren and Dufney's Creek'
and they were a sure bet. As usual, he was dismally wrong. As
Katrine said, 'If he had kept his money rather than investing in
goldmines and things, he would [have been] a very rich man.
But we were always in penury or luxury.'[2]

Motorcars manufactured in the first years of the twentieth
century were not built for remote Australia and remote Australia
was not prepared for motorcars. Many locals still viewed horseless carriages as a passing fad. They were cumbersome machines
that regularly broke down and had to be filled with petroleum
at a time when fuel stops and garages were almost non-existent.
Macadam – crushed-rock-based roads – existed in cities and some
towns for regular road traffic but even these roads were often in
such poor condition they were only accessible on horseback. They
had been built for horse and carriage, not motorcars. Under rough
conditions it was common for bolts to be wrested loose, car parts
to break or fall off, and engines to overheat. Motor garages and
car mechanics were still in their infancy so blacksmiths quickly
became specialists in forging replacement parts.

Despite his failure to predict a good investment, and his eager-
ness to purchase a motorcar at the wrong time and in the wrong
place, JT was clearly correct in seeing a future for automobiles
right across the country. Ironically, it was his more successful

former business partner and friend, John Monash, who wrongly envisioned their future as limited. Monash, the pragmatist, appeared to underestimate people's thirst for adventure, speed and steering off the beaten track. In 1904 his money had been on fixed-line trains and tramcars replacing horse and buggy.

> From city and town streets the horse must undoubtedly go. Some, and some only, of its function will in the future, be performed by the automobile, but its principal and larger functions have already been wholly taken up by the electric street tramway . . . the motorcar . . . has excessive vibration and noise, and there is little protection from dust, smoke and weather . . . The necessity for 'steering' an automobile is one of its most serious objections, as it has no fixed route like a tramcar. This necessarily reduces its safe speed, and greatly increases the liability to accident . . . The automobile must travel upon ordinary macadam roads, often in very indifferent condition . . . a shilling's worth of steel rail will last 25 years, while a shilling's worth of macadam road will not last 5 years . . .[3]

One could understand Monash's views at the time. The vibration, noise and dust he wrote of made long-distance travel in a motorcar uncomfortable at the very least. The extent and quality of roads also differed wildly between municipalities. There was no governing body overseeing road development, either federally or statewide. One would have to wait until 1913 for the Country Roads Board to establish control of the care and management of main roads in Victoria. Monash was also right to predict trams (first cable, then electric) would expand to become a major mode of public transport in Australian cities and towns. However, he did fail to mention major issues facing long-distance travel on Australia's railway systems. Begun in the 1860s, all Australian states were linked by rail within the first decade of the twentieth century, except for far-flung Western Australia. It was a marvellous achievement – aside from the fact that individual colonial governments prior to the Federation of states in 1901 did not plan beyond their noses. Not only were operating practices and equipment incompatible between states, line gauges were different widths. The lack of forethought meant all trains had to stop at each border to transfer passengers and goods. It is not surprising, then, that many chose coastal shipping services over rail in the first few decades of the twentieth century.

Four months after his decision to purchase a motorcar, JT was cursing himself for doing so. It continually broke down, leaving him stranded and at the mercy of passersby. 'My motorcar experience has been a sorry one . . . the whole thing is like a nightmare at present, and I want to forget it and get on with my work,' he wrote to Ellen Mary in April 1909. However, he was still optimistic that the situation would right itself: 'In the meantime as you see I am not paying anything – but sooner or later they will get the car right or else get me another so that I will not be stranded, only temporarily hindered in getting about.'[4]

JT had in mind that Stewart would also come to Tallangatta, some 190 miles (307 kilometres) from Narbethong, as his 'lieutenant'.[5] If the boy was not suited to the armed forces, JT surmised, then maybe he needed to follow in his father's footsteps and become an engineer. Despite Stewart's lack of interest in his father's profession, JT was determined to have his only son motivated and skilled up for a career of merit. He not only wanted Stewart to get himself sorted, he needed another earner in the family. The motorcar, JT argued, gave Stewart an opportunity to learn mechanics, which was a good, practical entrée into engineering. However, he was directing his energy towards the wrong offspring: it was Alice, not Stewart, who was craving such attention from JT.

JT held out for a reliable motorcar but it was not forthcoming. He finally settled on purchasing a horse called Rowdy who was part Arab, big and gentle, and far from the temperament his name suggested. He drove Rowdy strapped to a jinker, and once the horse knew the way, he would go on for miles in the right direction, even when JT fell asleep.[6]

Once JT had developed a solid work routine from his office in Tallangatta he sent for sixteen-year-old Stewart, despite not having a motorcar. With the two Anderson men away for weeks at a time, Alice completely took over the role of handyman at home. She was only twelve years old and heading up all the hard outdoor work for which Stewart had previously been in charge: bucketing water from the well, collecting and chopping wood, fixing fences, shooting and skinning rabbits, milking cows, and warding off wombats and other creatures threatening their vegetable garden and the orchard. Alice may have been a short, skinny kid but what she lacked in brawn she compensated for in brain. Claire watched her sister, for instance, chop wood with a wonderful coordination that had Alice 'swing the axe so that it did most of the cutting'.[7]

The winter of 1909 saw Alice turn thirteen but any presents she received were homemade affairs tailored from bits and pieces found in and around the cottage. Snow fell so heavily that winter that the bridge over Fishers Creek collapsed, making the only path from the cottage to the main road inaccessible. Ellen Mary, Alice,

Katrine, Claire and Joan were suddenly housebound, completely separated from the outside world and their weekly supplies from Healesville. There was no telephone connection and no electricity, only wood for the fire and kerosene for the lamps. To survive, Alice braved the weather with Katrine and killed game for the table. The two sisters, bound up in every bit of warm clothing they owned, took the rifles and fishing rods, and between them shot enough rabbits and caught enough trout from the icy creeks to keep them all from starving. If Ellen Mary ever had concerns about Alice taking up bush skills fit for a man, she was certainly grateful in this instance. Left to her own devices, she and her two youngest might well have perished. Not only had Ellen Mary refused to learn how to shoot, her torn Achilles tendon meant walking in deep snow was utterly impossible.

While Alice had learnt outdoor skills from Stewart, it was JT who taught her inadvertently how to get ahead in life. Both father and daughter were unshakable optimists and dreamers, and through JT's poor decision-making and difficult behaviours Alice learnt what it was also best not to do. True to form, JT continued to have merely a passing acquaintanceship with the words 'tact' and 'compromise' when dealing with associates; and he lost money time and again on what the family perceived as hare-brained schemes and crackpot ideas. Behind closed doors the family tiptoed around his moods. Living with JT was like 'living on the edge of an active volcano', especially when he was in a financial mess, which was much of the time.[8] One minute he was telling Ellen Mary they would have to remortgage Springbank, the next he was considering making money by converting the cottage into tearooms! Alice quickly learnt to adapt and make the most of each situation. Importantly, she didn't make the mistake

of putting JT offside in the way Stewart appeared to. JT was continually frustrated with what he perceived as Stewart's insolence
and lack of respect. His son was not interested in engineering nor
did he care for shire work. JT despaired and, after one particularly rude confrontation, was so disgusted with his son's behavior
he wrote to Ellen Mary, 'Things like that convince me that he
will end his days as a tramp and an outcast.'[9] By this time Alice
had, in a sense, become the favoured de facto son.

By 1911, JT was consultant engineer and surveyor to several
shires across Victoria, including the Shire of Alexandra close to
Narbethong. At the time, Stewart was indentured to Austral Otis,
an engineering and manufacturing firm in South Melbourne. JT
had arranged the apprenticeship for Stewart after yet another failed
business scheme in which he had Stewart extracting eucalyptus
oil from the leaves of the surrounding blue gums at Springbank.
JT had purchased two steel tanks for the distillation process that
required round-the-clock operation. He ordered Stewart to keep
the fire going throughout the night but naturally the boy kept
falling asleep. Only a few gallons of oil were produced before
JT gave up and converted the distillation tanks into water tanks
for the cottage.

Once in Melbourne and away from his father, Stewart began
to blossom. While working at Austral Otis he studied for his
matriculation with Miss Jessie Webb, principal of the coaching
college at 6 The Block, Collins Street. Miss Webb was a brilliant University of Melbourne graduate who had helped establish
the college in 1905. It was purported to be the first such college
run entirely by women and the atmosphere suited Stewart well.
With Miss Webb's firm yet gentle persistence he remained

focused and passed all of his exams. Between work and study, Stewart also found time to join the junior cadets. It was then he finally decided military life was far more attractive than trying to follow in his father's footsteps. He promptly left his job and took on extra study at the coaching college. By the end of 1912 Stewart was eligible to sit an entry examination for the Royal Australian Garrison Artillery (RAGA). Not only did he pass, his score topped all candidates across Australia. At nineteen, Stewart was on his way to becoming the successful son his father had always wanted. By the beginning of 1913 he was based at RAGA headquarters in Sydney, New South Wales, training to become a second lieutenant.

Frankie, who turned seventeen in 1912, won a scholarship to study art part time at the National Gallery of Victoria. JT had taught Frankie drafting after she completed state school. She became his assistant draftsman and had a propensity for drawing as well as clay sculpture. She complemented gallery studies with art-teacher training at Swinburne and took on additional academic classes at Jessie Webb's coaching college alongside Stewart. Miss Webb took an instant liking to both Anderson students and through this initial contact became great friends with Ellen Mary and Alice. Frankie fondly remembered teaching Jessie to ride a horse when she was first invited to Springbank.

She had beautiful golden hair in a bun at the back of her head. Of course she didn't know to rise to a trot so she suffered the next day! However, it was fun, and her hair came down and it floated right down her back. She could have been Lady Godiva if she had wanted to. [10]

It seemed the whole family had fallen in love with the beautiful, clever Miss Webb.

During their year of study in Melbourne, Stewart and Frankie lived in the inner suburbs, first boarding at a house in Richmond before moving to a flat in South Yarra. With the two eldest Anderson children away, Alice became the most senior child at home. It meant she could no longer escape indoor tasks such as cooking and ironing. Claire remembered Alice's cooking with horror, variously describing her attempts as 'adventurous', 'ghastly' and 'terrible'. Meals were unreliable and came at all sorts of hours because Alice still had responsibility for the outside work.[11]

Alice the tomboy was on the verge of womanhood. An incident in 1912, when she had just turned fifteen, cemented her legendary status as one of the most fearless, resourceful girls in the district. It was her coming of age: no one from this point on could ever call her a child.

On a cold, wet night the Andersons heard a frantic knocking on the cottage door and opened it to a man from the local sawmill. He was wild-eyed and drunk. There had been a terrible accident, he said. Up at the hut. He needed a telephone to call for help. The Andersons' recently acquired telephone was out of order and the nearest doctor was hours away. Without a further thought, Alice grabbed Katrine and they ran to get Winnie. The two girls doubled up on the pony and raced to the hut. There they found a man whose throat had been slashed from end to end with a broken beer bottle. He was shaking uncontrollably and blood was pouring from his neck. Alice took immediate control, instructing her sister to pull some horsehair from Winnie's tail. Katrine remembered:

> It was pouring with rain and fearfully dark, and we rode up to this hut where the men were. And I'll never forget it because it was only a sort of makeshift hut and this man had roaring DT's and I think it was three in the end, or four men, held him down while I went and got some horsehair out of Winnie's tail, [and] boiled it up in a billy on the open fire. On Alice's instruction one of the men produced a darning needle about 'that long' and while the men held him down Alice sewed it up – from 'there to there'. Had it not been for Alice's quick actions, the man would have almost certainly died that night. Well, the next day they took him to the doctor, of course, and he said she [Alice] made a pretty good job of it. [12]

This was not the only incident for Alice to display her bravery. As tea was being served one early evening in the summer of 1913, the Andersons all heard an awful scream from the far paddock. Diana, their much-loved black-and-white kangaroo hound (a cross between a staghound and a greyhound), came into view with one back leg almost fully severed from her body. It was unclear whether she had been attacked by a kangaroo or had torn her leg on fencing wire but Alice knew what had to be done. She immediately went for a rifle and shot the dog dead. For Claire, it was her first experience of the death of something she adored. She ran off to the end of the front paddock and cried inconsolably. Shooting the dog was no less a devastating experience for Alice. Her only consolation was that she had put the poor thing out of its pain and distress.

Alice's bush upbringing somewhat paralleled and even sur-
passed the fictional life of tomboy Norah Linton, a feisty character
created by favourite Australian children's author Mary Grant
Bruce. *A Little Bush Maid*, published in 1910, was the first
of Bruce's successful 'Billabong Series' that introduced young
readers all over the world to the girl who lived on a big station
in northern Victoria. Like Alice, Norah rode horses like a boy
and 'had grown just as the bush wild flowers grow – hardy,
unchecked, almost untended'.

Smart and restless, Alice became desperate for further stimula-
tion beyond home and family. She wanted to go back to school.
Although secondary education was not compulsory and was the
preserve of those whose families could afford the fees, by 1913
Ellen Mary had finally saved enough of her small annuity for
Alice to further her education. Ellen Mary studied the options
and finally chose Melbourne Church of England Girls' Grammar
School (MCEGGS) in Anderson Street, South Yarra, one of the
most progressive schools for girls in Victoria. It was known to
be 'part of an aristocracy of girls' schools' that 'espoused the
rights of women to a rigorous, academic education leading to the
University of Melbourne and the professions, and, more contro-
versially, the possibility of an autonomous life'.[13] The school was
established under the leadership of two strong women, Emily
Hensley and Alice Taylor, in 1893. By 1900 the main classroom
building, Merton Hall (by which the school is informally named),
was completed and in 1903 it became the first Anglican school
for girls in Victoria.

Alice began at Merton Hall in May 1913, the second term
of the school year and a month before her sixteenth birthday.
She was put into the B stream rather than the more advanced A

stream because she had not previously studied Latin, geometry or algebra. Alice may have had a broad and varied education living in the bush, but it was a fair social and academic handicap to be older than all the other girls in her class and starting halfway through the year with only a part-time state school education.

However, Alice was not on the outer. The Andersons might have been relatively poor financially but they weren't without connections. Alice became a day boarder, staying with former neighbours and family friends, the Brombys, in Malvern. Mr Bromby was the son of Dr Bromby, headmaster at Melbourne Grammar School, the boys' equivalent of Merton Hall. It was on Dr Bromby's advice that Ellen Mary had chosen the school.

Alice's confidence and natural charm meant she thrived socially and in a short time caught up to the academic standard of her classmates in languages, mathematics, geography, history and hygiene. Claire, who eventually followed in Alice's footsteps via a scholarship, noted that 'every teacher that taught her [Alice] remembered her with delight. Because she was a joy to teach, and because she was smart and because she was original and different.' Those 'sparkling brown eyes, curly brown hair' and her 'vitality' meant she was naturally a popular girl.[14]

Once Alice had discovered the pleasures of real academic learning she tended to bully and tease her younger sisters less. She was finally being challenged in ways that excited and fulfilled her intellectually.

Alice rarely spent time at Springbank during school terms. However, this didn't stop her feeling a sense of responsibility towards her mother, the running of the house – especially the outdoor jobs she had largely been responsible for –and the horses she loved dearly. Now Alice and Stewart were both away, the family took on a local orphan called Oscar to help with chores. Still, Alice wrote bossy letters to Katrine, demanding certain things be done and imparting her wisdom – just as JT often did in letters to home.

No 5 ~~Saturday~~
Sunday

My Dear Katrine,
Hurry up and write. We went to church this evening. Has Oscar rugged Taggerty [the family's third horse] yet?

. . . I hope you have helped Mother all you could with the washing before you get this & don't let her get too tired. Does Oscar get up & light the fire & does the new clock wake him every morning? Don't forget to make him barrow manure from the stable every <u>Saturday</u> & to give Rowdy Nitre <u>Weds</u> & <u>Sats</u> & Winnie none . . .

In the same letter Alice also wrote to her mother, seeking Ellen Mary's pity.

. . . for goodness sake write to me often it was horrid not to get a letter from Home yesterday. I got excruciating chilblains coming down on the coach & when I got here we bought a bottle of vinegar & I sat on my bed bathed my feet with it. My bed is <u>beastly</u> uncomfortable . . . <u>Do</u> send down a tin of cream biscuits or something as well as apples – milk even! I wonder when I shall see Father again? . . . Please give Claire & Isabel[15] [Joan] a hug for me & of course all of you . . . much love & kisses

from Alice.[16]

Alice was torn between adult feelings of responsibility and a girlish need to have her mother to soothe her pains and plump her pillow, albeit in a tongue-in-cheek sort of way. This was a letter written at a time when home was longed for and being away from home was a thrill.

Meanwhile, Frankie still saw herself as next in line to Mother. In June 1913 she wrote to Ellen Mary regarding Alice's schooling and the poor state of her teeth.

> My dear mother,
> . . . Alice's teeth are <u>dreadfully</u> crooked. They are all grown either right into the middle of the mouth or right on top of one another. [The dentist] took a cast of her mouth & I saw it today. There is a tooth covering as near the middle of the roof as a tooth could come. He says it will take some months to straighten them . . . There is one important thing I was nearly forgetting — Miss Hunt says Alice must have a seventh subject for Junior. On looking through the list of subs Algebra & Geometry seem to be the two best from every point of view. Since Latin, German, besides meaning too much work, would not be so useful — and geography clashes with Botany & Phys hours. And Miss Hunt wishes to know which subject you want Lol to take. <u>She</u> advises algebra. Alice is quite indifferent, knowing nothing of either . . .[17]

It seemed Alice took Frankie and her teacher's advice by taking up algebra, though it turned out to be her poorest subject. In August 1913 Alice wrote to Ellen Mary revealing her marks and, more importantly, what mattered most to her at this point in her life:

My dear Mother,   24th Sunday
This Sunday I went out to Miss Collison for the 3rd time. <u>She</u>
is preparing me for confirmation — Last Sunday she gave me 2
whole hours but this Sunday she had a bad cold & gave me
half an hour less. I feel that she is really teaching me what I
want. She lent me a little poem — 'The Hound of Heaven' by
Francis Thompson — do you know it? It is beautiful language.
She was looking at some books to lend me — but said she
thought she had better send them to you first as you might
not like me to read them! They were religious books. She is
disgusted with the way I've passed the Divinity exam

- I only got   50%
- I got for History   64%
       " "   Algebra   40%
       " "   Hygiene   71%
       " "   Geography   53%

And that's all the results I've got yet — 50% is a pass . . .
I hope Winnie is not still lame & that Oscar won't leave the
Barn door open the night before I come home! I expect to see
Father in Hville on my way up. I am looking to you to give me
some prep for confirmation. I've played in two of the School
District Cup Hockey matches now . . . Are you getting <u>any</u>
milk? & if so from which? Oh, please answer this letter quickly.
I'm getting so excited.
    Goodnight
    with love
    fr
    Alice[18]

Francis Thompson, the author of 'The Hound of Heaven' referred to in Alice's letter, was a tortured British poet addicted to opium and fits of depression. The poem is a wonderfully overwrought and overlong religious poem, and perfectly suited to capture Alice's adolescent heart.

> I fled Him, down the nights and down the days;
> I fled Him, down the arches of the years;
> I fled Him, down the labyrinthine ways
> Of my own mind; and in the mist of tears
> I hid from Him . . .[19]

Clearly, Alice had continued to take her religious beliefs seriously. Claire understood Alice and Stewart as being the only siblings who 'had any time for religion, and had faith. There was never any doubt in her [Alice] believing'.[20] Perhaps God the Father seemed more solid and reliable than her erratic father, who was rarely at home and who perpetually struggled to live up to his own hubris.

7

ANNUS HORRIBILIS

'"They Shall Not Pass" is the right idea on
the battle front, but not on the highway'

(1920s *Shell Motorists' Index*)

For the time Stewart was based at Sydney's RAGA headquarters,
he failed to communicate regularly with the family. JT, Ellen
Mary and the daughters corresponded through letters on a daily,
if not weekly, basis but Stewart had become an intermittent writer
at best. His lack of contact might have been due to finding his
feet away from family or perhaps, as had occurred with his uncle
Jack, he was struggling to cope on his own. By August 1913 the
family had become concerned. Alice wrote to Ellen Mary, 'Have
you heard from Stewart lately?'[1] More tellingly, JT wrote to Ellen
Mary that November saying, 'I wrote to Stewart a week ago,
I wonder if you have heard from him? I don't want him to drift
away from us more than can be helped, & impressed on him the
necessity to have no stone unturned so as to ensure getting home

at Xmas.'[2] A couple of weeks later a formal letter from Artillery District Headquarters arrived.

2nd December 1913

Dear Sir:-

I have to report for your information that your son Stuart O'Neill Noble Anderson left the officers' mess South Head, Sydney, at 4-p.m. yesterday afternoon for the purpose of fishing. He was dressed in an old Blue Serge Suit, White Shoes and Cap. He had been in the habit of descending a Wire rope to the foot of the cliff some 180 feet in height. He had been warned on several occasions not to do so. We have had men and boats out during most of last night and to-day, but no trace of him whatever have been found. I wired early to Derham this morning asking him to inform you of the fact, as I did not know then your address. We will keep you informed of any tidings we may get. We are all very distressed at the occurrence, we sympathise with you very much, as we fear the worst has happened, knowing how dangerous the spot is. No effort will be spared on our part to unravel the mystery of his disappearance.

Yours faithfully,

Major R.A.G.A.

For Lieut-Colonel. Commanding, R.A.G.A. 2nd Military District.[3]

But before the letter reached the family, they were informed of Stewart's disappearance via Colonel Frank Derham, who had been in charge of a military unit at Victoria Barracks at the time of Stewart's training there. He also happened to be the father of Frankie's friend Ruth Derham. It was through Ruth that Frankie first received the worrying news. Frankie later told it like this:

> you'll think I'm a superstitious person if I tell you the beginning of that terrible Monday morning. My mother had come to town and was staying with me at this flat. We were having breakfast, rather in a hurry and I spilt the salt, and she said – frankly, this was one of her pet superstitions – 'Oh, throw it over your shoulder.' I said, 'Nonsense, you're just so superstitious,' and as I swept it up it spilt again. As I went outside with the dustpan it spilt the third time. She said, 'Frankie, you still must throw that over your shoulder – with your right hand over your left shoulder.' I said, 'Nonsense,' and laughed. I went to the gallery as usual, my mother went I don't know where, but shopping, I suppose . . . Now my great dear friend at the National Gallery was Ruth Derham . . . Spilling salt is bad luck . . . and [I] refused to throw the salt over my left shoulder to placate the devil, a centuries-old superstition. I don't smile about it now, as I laughed about it at the moment, but in the middle of the morning Ruth Derham was called out of the drawing room to be told that her father wished to see her. She said, 'Father! Leaving his office to see me, there must be something terrible the matter.' She ran out and she came back looking very grave and brought me out to see her father, and I went to his office. He said, 'I have already managed to find your mother and your father is waiting at the office. Your brother is missing off South Head, Sydney.'[4]

Alice and Frankie dropped everything and returned to Springbank to look after their younger siblings while Ellen Mary took the train to Sydney, desperately hoping Stewart would be found alive. Frankie reminded her sisters that Stewart had survived the sea before:

> He had once before been fishing out in Sydney Harbour when his rowboat had capsized and he had been two hours in the water swimming with his heavy Army overcoat on which he wasn't going to take off because he hadn't paid for it and it had cost seven guineas – a lot of money, and it was two hours before himself and his boat were rescued.[5]

Frankie believed his main reason for being on the dangerous cliff side was fishing and that the rope trailing down the cliff had been fixed by adventurous fishermen for that purpose. 'A wave must have come, as they do, you know, that open ocean, and swept him off.'[6] But Claire recalled being told that Stewart

> had a long-standing debt or a dare with one of the men that you could go round the heads, from South Head via cliff climbing. You see, he [Stewart] was a marvellous rock climber. He used to go and look in eagles' nests and things. So he thought, oh well . . . I'll fulfil this dare . . .[7]

However, any possible explanation regarding his disappearance was theoretical: the RAGA authorities insisted Stewart had been on his own when he went missing.

When Ellen Mary arrived at South Head, the weather was hot and sultry with barely the whisper of a breeze. She stood staring at the great expanse of water beyond her reach. It was awful to imagine her son lost out there somewhere. The horizon seemed so far away, and the patrol boats searching for him looked like little toys bobbing in the middle-distance. *Father, I want to join the Navy.* She could see him at twelve years old earnestly looking up at JT with those soft, blue–grey eyes of his.

Only a few days before, 21-year-old Stewart had succeeded in receiving his commission as second lieutenant and was presented with a sword, wearing his smart navy-coloured uniform with red stripes down the trousers. A photograph taken on the day shows a neat, young-looking man with the beginnings of a moustache, staring back in full uniform, a mixture of pride and mild apprehension across his face.

After two days without finding any trace of Stewart, the Army conceded defeat. Ellen Mary attended the funeral service held on the cliffs where Stewart had allegedly disappeared. She then went straight home to Springbank. A few days later the dreadful news arrived that the search party had retrieved Stewart's body from the ocean. One leg was missing, probably taken by a shark, they were told. He was buried in South Head Cemetery with military honours but without those who loved him most present.

Alice was crushed. She had been Stewart's protégée and confidante. He had taught her how to fish and shoot and mend fences, and passed on to her the British public school code of conduct: remain stoic; never tell a lie; don't show your feelings; and, perhaps fatefully, learn to be physically daring.

Christmas 1913 was a close family affair. Many memories were shared round the dinner table, including Stewart's tale of the clairvoyant he had met in Colombo in 1905 who had correctly predicted that JT was at the peak of his career that year (he was never more successful than when he developed the Dunedin sewerage system) and that Stewart did have four sisters with one more to come (Joan in 1907). What troubled the family most was the clairvoyant's refusal to tell Stewart anything of his own future. They wondered if the soothsayer had truly sensed Stewart's fate, knowing he would only just achieve manhood.

At forty-nine, Ellen Mary took to her bed with profound grief, which coincided with menopause, and Frankie abandoned her studies in Melbourne to look after her. It was months before she was strong enough to get out of bed, or see anyone. For JT, losing his only son literally 'took the stuffing out of him.'[8] He returned to work but found it difficult to keep his emotions in check. A week after Stewart's death was confirmed he wrote to Ellen Mary:

> It has been a tremendous relief to get to Melbourne where
> no-one knows — or too few to count — and I now feel fit
> to stand anything without feeling it . . . there are things to
> live for, possibly if I get into politics, a whole country to live
> for . . . for myself I do not look forward with any zest nor much
> ambition . . . far better to spend my days and nights in my own
> home with you & the children — the one thing I regret most is
> that I had so little time to give to dear Stewart . . .[9]

Just seven months after Stewart's death, World War I was declared. Seventeen-year-old Alice stood by while boys – many her age and younger – passed themselves off as eighteen and volunteered to fight for King and country on the battlefields of Europe. Most eligible Australian men couldn't wait to serve. Glory and adventure awaited them across the seas and they would all be home by Christmas. Alice regretted she wasn't a man and able to go to war herself. She could have been the Australian boy from the bush perfectly prepared for soldiering, as described by Australia's official war correspondent Charles Bean:

> The bushman is the hero of the Australian boy; the arts of the bush are his ambition; his most cherished holidays are those spent with country relatives or in camping out. He learns something of half the arts of the soldier by the time he is ten years old – to sleep comfortably in any shelter, to cook meat or bake flour, to catch a horse, to find his way across country by day or by night, to ride, or, at the worst, to 'stick on' . . .[10]

Bean's musings reflected a nation brimming with patriotic fervour. People were spurred by powerful propaganda such as *The Empire's Call*: 'Men of Australia, it is your privilege to join this mighty resolute host and march triumphant on to victory. Coo-ee! The mother country's calling . . . Australia's sons will man the guns and prepare to do or die.'[11]

Alice's response to the 'Empire's Call' was a cry of patriotism mixed with grief for the brother who would never go to war and never come home. She purchased a copy of the *National Anthems of the Allies* and taught herself all the military calls on Stewart's Boy Scout bugle; she worked hard to produce melodies from the simple copper and brass instrument. She went out into the bush and practised the 'Reveille', 'Last Post and 'Come to the Cookhouse Door' with vigour and tears.

JT, meanwhile, embarked on yet another business venture. He leased a thousand acres at the back of Springbank and started a water-powered sawmill. A Pelton wheel that he designed generated the electricity. The land was covered in good hardwood and JT was certain this would bring the family a decent income, even though, much to Ellen Mary's despair, he had remortgaged Springbank to pay for hired staff and building materials. Unfortunately, the drought that had begun in 1913 continued into 1914 and the Pelton wheel rarely turned. Not only did this business venture collapse and put them at risk of losing their only home, the Andersons lost most of their cattle and horses through day after day of burning heat, bushfires and lack of water. The only stock feed left was in Roach's swamp, a large, mushy paddock that always had green feed in it, but the animals became bogged in the mud and were too weak to pull themselves out. Even gentle old Rowdy, who had faithfully trotted JT for miles and miles across the state, became stuck in the swamp. The family tried desperately to drag him out with ropes but he died from exhaustion. All the Andersons were overwhelmed by grief. Rowdy, too, had been family.

The last straw for the mill came when all thirteen men JT had employed downed tools and volunteered themselves to the war effort. Within a few months the mill lay rusting in the bush and the family was forced to live on credit. Ellen Mary felt humiliated having to ask suppliers to keep the family on a tab. 'You've got to give me some money to pay the butcher in Healesville,' she said to JT. 'It's six months since we paid him!'[12] The country was at war and the Andersons' world was in pieces.

Alice continued to study hard towards her Junior Public Certificate (or JP, the equivalent of today's Year Ten) though she had to leave school before she could sit the exam. While Alice would have loved to continue on to matriculation, she knew Ellen Mary's annuity was running out and JT could not afford to contribute to the fees. After only five terms at Merton Hall, Alice left the school in 1914. It was a great disappointment to have her studies cut short in this way, with her intelligence and enthusiasm for learning. Given the opportunity, Alice could have easily continued on to university, as many of her school chums would do.

This made her all the more determined to do well and pass on what she had learnt to her younger sisters. If she could prepare them to pass a MCEGGS scholarship entrance exam, they too could have an opportunity for further study. And although Alice could not attend classes, she made plans to sit and pass the JP exams. Thankfully, the teachers at Merton Hall had agreed to support her in any way they could.

Despite attempting to coach all three younger sisters, Alice decided that Katrine, at thirteen, was too old to sit for a scholarship and Joan, at seven, too young. In fact, Joan was yet to attend state school. Ellen Mary had been so lonely and bereft it seems she kept Joan home for company. While Alice included all three younger sisters in her 'classes', she set her sights on Claire to take on further study. Alice announced, 'I'm going to take the kids for school every morning for three hours, nine 'til twelve – and teach them French and the sort of things you don't do at state schools'.[13] She threw herself enthusiastically into the task, although the new home–school arrangement appeared to create domestic chaos. Ellen Mary wrote to Frankie, 'Alice is teaching vigorously and ironing at the same time. Biddy [Claire] is writing her hated English letter. Katrine raised the dickens on three consecutive days. Yesterday over exercise books. Today she was good. She was out.'[14]

Claire remembered almost every lesson taught out on the cottage verandah that Alice had set up as a makeshift school. She said Alice ran classes just as they were taught at MCEGGS. 'We had exercise books and textbooks. She wrote to the teachers at school [asking] "what's the best to get?" and so on, and they sent her up the books'.[15] Alice grounded them well in history, geography, French and English. 'I loved those lessons,' Claire recalled. 'There was always a travelling lightfoot on the table and the inkpots were put there and everything was laid out for us and Alice rang a bell when we had to come . . . she used to give us exams and correct them and give us A's & B's and things.'[16]

In September 1915 Alice boarded for a time with Frankie at 67 Cotham Road, Kew, owned by a Miss Marion Cattach. Ellen Mary had arranged for Alice to receive extra coaching with Jessie Webb so she could feel more confident sitting the JP exams. Frankie wrote to her friend Ruth's brother, Alfred Derham, who had been quietly courting her before leaving for the battlefield:

> I am not to be a lone bird for much longer. Alice will be arriving very soon I think . . . I should be very glad in many ways — it is horrid being by myself, & tho' it has its advantages at times — in the way of undisturbed work etc. I shall be very glad of my small & pugnacious sister.[17]

Alice included bookkeeping in her extra studies, which fortified her employment prospects. As much as Frankie was looking forward to boarding with her sister, Katrine was glad to have a break from Alice's incessant carrying on about the JP. Not long after Frankie wrote to her sweetheart, Katrine also wrote to Alfred, who had become a family friend.

> *I have not much time now Alice is gone . . . for a good while*
> *before Alice left, we heard a good deal about J.P. Mother got*
> *her to help her do the raspberries for the season, 'Oh, well if I*
> *don't pass J.P. I'll blame it on you for getting me to do this.'*
> *Then any extra at all – 'I won't pass J.P' I'm sick of the sound*
> *of J.P. Frankie has it now. I hope she is more sympathetic than*
> *we were. You see we couldn't be, not knowing anything about*
> *exams . . .*[18]

Alice remained in control of her younger sisters' schooling even when she was away from home and studying hard herself. She wrote to Ellen Mary, 'Please keep the children's noses to the grindstone in the matter of my lessons <u>&</u> [underlined several times] when you return me their written work – <u>I want the questions</u>.'[19]

The work paid off when eleven-year-old Claire sat the entrance exam in 1915 and was accepted into Merton Hall for the following year. Not only that, she succeeded in winning a three-year full boarding scholarship. Alice couldn't quite believe it. Frankie wrote home to Ellen Mary telling her the good news.

> *Dear mother,*
> *Alice heard . . . this afternoon when up for an exam, but*
> *thought it was only one of the minor (fees only) scholarships –*
> *and so it was father who broke this joyfuller news, this evening.*
> *It's just too good to be true – the family will <u>have</u> to manage it*
> *somehow . . . Claire seems to have created quite a sensation at*
> *school. Everyone crowded round Alice to remark on the 'sweet*
> *little sister.' I'm so pleased I can't write! She did look sweet that*
> *day – hair loose & shining – eyes bright – & I wasn't ashamed*
> *of my/your? dressmaking either . . . She came home in great*

delight — had thoroughly enjoyed herself — said it was such
a lovely paper. I must write to Lola [Alice] now . . . she took
Claire yesterday at 11am. The Capt., Cora & Claire squeezed
in their dear little car — Claire absolutely radiant . . .

  Tell Baby to hurry up & get a scholarship!
  Love to Katrine & you
  Frankie[20]

The Anderson girls were maturing towards a future beyond
Springbank and the fulfilment of Ellen Mary's dream for her
daughters to have the education and opportunities she had been
deprived of. Frankie's comment regarding dressmaking refers to
the clothes, including school outfits, she and Ellen Mary made.
According to Claire, their homemade clothes 'weren't quite
right'.[21] It might have been practical for the Anderson girls to
be rid of fancy frocks in the bush, but once through the portals
of Merton Hall they were unofficially judged by their dress.
Wearing homemade outfits probably didn't bother Alice – there
was never any suggestion that she felt self-conscious among her
school peers – but Claire remembered being teased, especially
about her mother when she visited in her outdated clothes. Ellen
Mary's outfits were always 'old fashioned – a blue serge skirt
with a belt and blouses . . . and her hat! She had a funny hat. It
was a very plain felt hat.'[22] Ellen Mary's clothing was testament
to the sacrifices she had made for her daughters and suggested
how far she had removed herself, through poverty and isolation,
from Melbourne society.

When Alice returned to Springbank after passing her Junior
Public Certificate exams in 1915, JT was heavily engaged in surveying work over several shires and was still away from home for

days and weeks at a time. Often he took Alice to work alongside him as his chainman. This was no mean task: lengths and parameters were calculated with a surveyor's chain measuring sixty-six feet divided into a hundred steel links. Seventeen-year-old Alice was only five foot three inches tall but she still managed to drag the chain into place and assist JT in his calculations for areas to be developed. Unlike Stewart, Alice enjoyed working and learning alongside her father. She loved being treated as the eager, capable, intelligent person she was. The physical outdoor work and mapping out Victoria's roads was fun. Surveying work was not the highly skilled, well-paid engineering job JT desired, but Alice's enthusiasm kept his natural optimism alive. On the road JT forgot the kid in breeches was his daughter; she became his mate.

It wasn't long before JT's inexhaustible enthusiasm had him off on another of his business ventures, but this time, perhaps with Alice's help, there would be a chance of success.

8

OVER THE SPUR

'If the ignition system is properly adjusted,
the car will start after a few revolutions'

(1920s *Shell Motorists' Index*)

In travelling between Narbethong and Healesville one is confronted by a steep, winding road that passes over the Black Spur – a wide ridge that protrudes from the Great Dividing Range and descends to the floor of the Yarra Valley. Today much of the road has disappeared beneath the smooth ribbon of the Maroondah Highway. The Black Spur itself has been bypassed and replaced with a safe stretch of bitumen known as Black Spur Drive. The most hazardous of hairpin bends have been subdued and the Spur's earlier history has all but been erased.

The Black Spur was originally known as Blacks' Spur. It was where the Woiworung people gathered, and it was where other Aboriginal groups from northern Victoria passed through on route to the Coranderrk mission settlement near Healesville in the 1800s. From Healesville the trail leads northeast through forests of towering mountain ash and giant ferns, on towards Narbethong and the creeks, hills and gullies of Marysville and Alexandra.

By the early 1900s the Spur had gained a reputation as one of the most treacherous stretches of road in the district. It was full of bends at dizzying heights with mud and ruts sometimes up to a foot deep. All manner of accidents occurred on this route, and there was at least one fatality per year. In 1915, when JT was contemplating his next business idea, people were travelling over the Spur by coach-and-four. The risk of horses slipping off the edge was high and the results disastrous.

JT saw it was time to offer a safer and more efficient transport service between Healesville and Alexandra. He envisioned the service utilising the newly available motorised char-à-bancs that could carry more passengers than a coach-and-four and would be affordable for every traveller. The motorised versions were similar to the horse-drawn variety comprising rows of hard seats running from front to rear with open sides. In addition, motorised char-à-bancs had side doors to accommodate the higher speeds, as well as a windscreen and a cape cart hood for when it rained. The chassis was akin to a two- or three-ton commercial vehicle but with a higher-powered engine and appropriate gear ratios. Motorised char-à-bancs had been around for some time but their tyres were solid, which made for a very rough ride. Prior to 1915 the pneumatic tyre construction designed for private vehicles was not strong enough to take a load over three thousand pounds. However, by 1915 stronger tyre fabrics allowed air-filled tyres to take these extra weights. Motorised char-à-bancs then became a favoured source of transport. They were sturdier than horse-drawn carriages and less likely to lose their grip on the road. It seemed JT was at last onto a timely, sound and potentially successful venture.

The char-à-bancs were as well equipped to handle the district's unsealed roads as any other motorised vehicle at the time. Properly sealed roads suitable for automobiles were slow to be built, particularly outside cities and major towns. It took time to experiment with materials for wear and durability – there was packed earth, wooden blocks based in concrete and sealed with tar, compressed asphalt, plain concrete, macadam and techniques with bitumen. It also took resources and expertise, which were lacking through the war years, particularly in Australia. An *Australian Motorist* article from 1918 bemoaned that 'due to lack of facilities and expertise', Australia had developed '"hit or miss" methods of road construction' compared with America's rigid scientific work on rocks and 'bituminous products'.[1] Even JT appeared not to be involved in methods of road construction until the early 1920s, when, as City Engineer to the City of Richmond, he trialled reinforced concrete roads in Bridge Road and Swan Street. (They endured well but were impractical to dig up when accessing services below the road.) In 1919 George Broadbent, a popular motor journalist, made a particular point of the 'pitiful state' of the Blacks' Spur Road in the hope that it would shame authorities into improving its condition, but his pleas fell on deaf ears and it would be more than a decade before the road was finally sealed.

JT decided he wanted to establish the transport service as a cooperative, with interested parties purchasing shares. This arrangement would have the communities of each hamlet working together. It was an admirable concept. As a member of the Fabian Society, JT held socialist-leaning views alongside his ideas of financial success. Despite his reckless entrepreneurial streak, he appeared fair and reasonable with those he felt responsible for, which, in this instance, included his own community. Claire commented that, although he was intolerant of people he saw as 'pretentious', he was 'extremely tolerant of people working on his jobs. They always thought he was wonderful. He got on with all people under him.'[2] The question remained, however, whether JT could be fair and reasonable with all stakeholders, and they with him.

Unfortunately, JT undermined his own vision even before the cooperative had been established. On a visit to Melbourne in early 1915 he was taken in by a large, shiny motorcar in a showroom window and was moved to pay a deposit on the spot. JT's justification at the time was that char-à-bancs would do well for the regular traffic but they couldn't offer a service for those in a hurry, who wanted a bit more comfort or who could afford something else.[3] JT put £240 on the 'Hup', the full, luxurious price being around £700. It was an expensive investment for even the most discerning motorist: the deposit alone was enough to buy a lesser motorcar outright.

The 1914 Hupmobile from the Hupp Motor Car Company in Detroit was promoted in Australia as 'The Comfort Car'. Classed as a tourer, it boasted 32 horsepower, four cylinders and two manual gears. The comfort lay in its broad dimensions, its beautiful finish, the padded leather upholstery and the two dickie-seats at the back that allowed the car to seat up to seven passengers. However, it flew in the face of JT's original concept of affordable community transport run by the cooperative's members, and the board he was in the process of forming did not want to underwrite its cost. JT could barely afford the deposit, let alone purchase the vehicle outright. Again, he had acted on a whim without considering the consequences. JT had to quickly find a solution to his predicament.

On 8 June 1915, Alice turned eighteen. Imagine her surprise when JT handed her the keys to the Hupmobile, saying, 'If you can manage to pay for the rest of this, that's your car and that's your eighteenth birthday present.'[4] JT had even put the family crest on the front of the bonnet: a stork (representing filial duty and an emblem of a grateful man) with the insignia 'We Stoop Not'.[5] The family crest could not have been more symbolic, nor ironic. He had given his motor-curious daughter the most extravagant present and, in the same magnanimous gesture, relieved himself of its £460 debt.

Alice was overjoyed. She would have been grateful had she received a book and a birthday cake! She slid into the driver's seat and was immediately swallowed up by the car's enormous dimensions: the wide, padded leather seat designed for a man of her father's proportions; the foot pedals she had to stretch to reach, and the top of the steering wheel planted at her eye level. The feel and smell of that fine-grained leather, the wood and freshly painted metal, the pungency of grease and gasoline set her heart racing. It was like climbing onto a pony that was the size of a horse. *She would tame it, and train the metal beast to respond to her commands. And of course she would find a way to pay it off*, though at this point she had no idea how.

First Alice needed to learn how to drive. If it had been 1908 and not 1915 she could have, after a few basic instructions, taken to the road alone. Prior to the introduction of the Victorian *Motor Car Act 1909* (around the same time as other Australian states) road rules were minimal and no one required a licence. But before Alice could hit the road she needed to obtain a driver's licence or at least be accompanied by a licensed driver. At eighteen, she was eligible to apply for a licence, but she needed to develop a degree of competence before taking the required driving test with a policeman. JT was the obvious person to teach her: he was the only driver in the family. Except he was busy running round the district attempting to convince people his transport cooperative was a good investment. For the time being, Alice was left to practise 'kangaroo-hopping' her luxury tourer round the lumpy paddocks and bumpy back roads of Narbethong.

Meanwhile, Christmas had come and gone with no end to the war in sight. The Andersons had no family member enlisted except for JT's brother Henry, the British Army doctor. Their initial experience of war came via the experiences of friends such as John Monash and Frankie's sweetheart, Alfred Derham, both of whom were present at that first fateful landing at Gallipoli.

As Commander of the Fourth Infantry Brigade, Australian Imperial Force, Monash's combination of tactical skill and determination in leading his men against the ridiculous odds has been well documented. When he was promoted to Brigadier-General and awarded military honours shortly after the Gallipoli debacle, JT wrote to Ellen Mary, requesting she 'write to Mrs Monash congratulating her on the general's new honour'. 'When he comes home,' JT rightly predicted, 'he will be a very big man.'[6]

As for Derham, he had suspended his medical degree to enlist and, as a private in the Fifth Battalion, was one of the first wounded onshore at Gallipoli. Although the wound was relatively minor, he became one of the first Australian soldiers to be awarded a Military Cross, a new honour for lower-ranking officers instituted in 1914 by King George V. Once healed,

Derham returned to the Front and, as with Monash, managed to survive his time there.

Far from the battlefield, JT ploughed on. By April 1916 he had set up meetings in each town to air his proposal for a transport cooperative and garner support. Local papers, such as the *Alexandra and Yea Standard*, kept the public updated:

Motor Service for Alexandra

Last week, Mr Noble Anderson, once engineer for the Shire of Alexandra visited the district for the purpose of forming a company, on the mutual principle with no private interests, to organise a system of motor services between Healesville and Alexandra, including Marysville, Thornton, The Weir, etc. The shares are £5 each, £2/10/ payable on allotment, £1/25/ in three months, and £1/25/ in six months . . .

After a public meeting had been held in Marysville to consider the subject, and the proposal approved, a meeting was held in Healesville, where a provisional board of directors was chosen, and Mr Anderson was appointed chairman. Mr Anderson's visit to the district was to secure capital for and interest in the undertaking, and we have been informed that on the journey from Narbethong to Alexandra, not one single inhabitant called on refused to take shares.

It is proposed to allot the shares equally between applicants on both sides of the Dividing Range, with an equal number of directors, and that directors meeting should be held alternately at Healesville and Alexandra. The Alexandra branch of the National Bank has been chosen by the company, as no doubt the bulk of the company's business will flow this way. This system should give a great impetus to the tourist traffic to Alexandra and neighbourhood.

A test of the Buick char-a-banc under offer to the company was made from Healesville to Marysville, carrying twelve passengers. It negotiated the well-known Black Spur, without dropping to the lower gear. As a matter of fact, at the most difficult pinch on the road, it was only for a few seconds on the middle gear; everywhere else it took the rises on the top gear, a performance unsurpassed by any car on the road.[7]

Despite JT selling a number of shares there were a few snags. According to Katrine, many people actually refused to buy into the cooperative because they saw JT as a 'ratbag'.[8] Apart from his involvement in a number of failed businesses, JT appeared to be either oblivious to, or unrealistically optimistic about, the district's Catholic and Protestant divides. As Claire pointed out, JT's idea went down well in Alexandra, a town 'full of hard-headed, good and honest Scotsmen', but Healesville 'was always a tourist place and tourist places tend to be rather corrupt, dishonest'. More to the point, Healesville had 'a big peasant Irish Catholic element' and JT was 'very Protestant.'[9]

Nevertheless a few weeks later the Blacks' Spur Motor Service Co., Ltd, had garnered enough support to be a going concern. The need for improved transport, it seemed, had prevailed over class and religious differences – though not without councillors, such as the Irish Catholic Mick Sheehan, 'playing dirty tricks'. According to JT, Sheehan was always out to get him. Claire remembered, 'the Shire meetings would end up "I'll see you outside after." It was Father and Mick Sheehan. Oh gosh!'[10]

The centre of operations was the Healesville garage in Harker Street, which was conveniently placed next to the Terminus Hotel, with the railway station only a few paces along. The building itself had been erected in 1889 to store the coaches of visitors next door. It was perfectly suited to the needs of twentieth-century coach travel and well placed to accommodate connecting rail commuters. Local papers advertised days and times of departures and arrivals in connection with the Melbourne train timetables. Single fares to and from Healesville and Alexandra were 12 shillings and sixpence. And, though the Hupmobile now belonged to Alice, JT formally requested the board take purchase of the vehicle for JT's original intended use. Not surprisingly, the board of directors refused.

Once the Blacks' Spur Motor Service had been established, JT needed someone to keep track of the paperwork. Alice was happy to be appointed office secretary and make use of the book-keeping skills she had learnt at Jessie Webb's coaching college. *Now she could start paying back the Hup!*

But, unsurprisingly, deskwork would not satisfy Alice for long. She was eager to be where the action really was, on the other side of the office door where the smell of oil and petrol, and the roar of a combustion engine, filled her world with possibility. She was desperate to obtain her driver's licence and take to the roads in earnest.

Alice was in good company when it came to being intoxicated by the idea of taking to the open road in a motorcar. The uptake of car ownership in Australia at this time was one of the highest in the world. By 1915, the year Alice received the Hup, Australia's motor vehicle population had reached 38 000, with 108 different brands competing in the market. Throughout the war

Australian Motorist continued to be a leading voice for all things motoring. It aligned driving with notions of freedom, independence and exploring the unknown. Such sentiment was the perfect antidote to the weaponry of purpose-built military tanks, trucks and planes savaging Europe. Conversely, there were also attempts to allay the feelings of vulnerability of many white Australians living in a vast country where so much land felt under-populated and exposed. The poem 'A Road that Leads to God Knows Where', published in *Australian Motorist* during the war, spoke to such desires and fears. It began:

> I like a road that leads a way to prospects white
> and fair,
> A road that is an ordered road, like a nun's evening
> prayer;
> But best of all I like a road that leads to God
> knows where
> You come upon it suddenly – you cannot seek it out;
> It's like a secret still unheard and never noised
> about;
> But when you see it gone at once is every lurking doubt . . .[11]

With the war seeing young men leave Australia's shores in droves, there was greater incentive by manufacturers to encourage women behind the wheel. *Australian Motorist* was a champion of this trend, with their 'Women Awheel' pages avidly read by women such as Alice, even though Alice's no-nonsense outlook would have recognised some of the writing as feminine drivel. Shortly after the outbreak of war, a soothing antidote to the 'Empire's Call' titled 'The Call of the Open Roads: One golden day' appeared full of idyllic, perfumed pleasantries. Its sentiment could not have been further from the theatre of war:

> A day's outing in a willing car in early December! An ordinary pleasure, available to many ordinary people – but is there any delight equal to that of a pleasant day's spin into the wildwood? A lady motorist, well known to readers of these pages, burnished up her motor, packed a dainty hamper cooked and prepared by her own fair fingers, cranked up her engine, and seated herself behind the wheel one fine day last month . . . It was 8 o'clock in the morning on a day of emerald, sapphire, gold and diamonds, when we set out from Brighton, through Elsternwick and Caulfield, into Burke-road. The sparkle of the summer day's brilliance was softened with a veil of morning haze, and the crisp freshness of these earlier hours in an atmosphere as exhilarating as wine made us catch our breath in a song of sheer joy at the goodness of life as we cut through the pearly morning . . .[12]

Alice planned to drive into that 'pearly morning' with gusto. She stood in the doorway between the Blacks' Spur Motor Service's office and the garage, and watched while the mechanics serviced the char-à-bancs and drove off to pick up passengers. She asked the men endless questions: *What's this? What's that? How does it work?* They would give her little jobs to do to assuage her curiosity, but of course that wasn't enough for Alice. Not only did she want a driver's licence to drive her Hup, she wanted to get behind the wheel of one of those big open buses!

The mechanics liked and respected Alice but they were reluctant to teach her too much. A diminutive eighteen-year-old female, they argued, should not be taking any motorcar out on dangerous local roads, let alone a char-à-banc! At any rate, a noisy, greasy garage was no place for a woman. Alice was not dissuaded. She persisted until the employees finally caved in. Perhaps JT encouraged them to take her under their wing; he owed Alice that much. The men agreed to teach her to drive, but 'not until [she] could take an engine down and put it together again'.[13] Not only did a driver need to be able to handle her vehicle, she needed to understand what was under the bonnet and be prepared to do on-the-road repairs. If the garage men thought such demands might act as a deterrent, they were clearly wrong.

Alice listened and tinkered and got her hands dirty until she was as familiar with the ins and outs of a motor engine as she was with the ins and outs of the enterprise itself. The men were quietly impressed with their eager student and ended up teaching her everything they knew. Claire said, 'She could not have had better tutors both in practical machinery and cars.'[14] Years later, in an article for *Woman's World*, Alice wrote, 'The writer was taught on the Blacks' Spur Road . . . by men who considered that women should never be allowed to drive over the Spur. Every time the query was put, "Do you think I will ever be able to drive over the Spur?" the answer was "Perhaps, some day, but it is no place for a woman to be driving." The consequence was that it was five months before she was taken up for her licence but during that time she had been through the boggiest tracks on the mountains, and learnt how to get out of them without damaging the car.'[15] Of course, Alice passed her driving test in 1916 without fuss, and an annual licence was granted her on the payment of 2 shillings and sixpence.

By June 1916 the new motor service was being hailed as a great success. Its popularity, according to one newspaper, was due largely to the convenience afforded to those interested in travelling to the district for health or pleasure at an affordable price. Motor tourism in Victoria was being put on the map:

> Here we have a town forming the railway and road centre of the most beautiful mountain and river district in Australia. But owing to the discomfort of the railway journey few, except those who are compelled for business to travel, are sufficiently spartan to brave the discomforts of leaving before daylight and dragging luggage from train to train and up down over head ways at suburban stations, then at Tallarook and afterwards at Cathkin, and latterly, on non-train days, having to drive the last 10 miles from Cathkin to Alexandra. Now, however, all that can be avoided and in its place a comfortable motor ride is offered by the new company through that most charming river and forest country from Alexandra to Healesville, leaving Alexandra at 3.35 p.m., giving travellers over an hour to enjoy their tea, the train leaving at 7.55 p.m. On the return journey the car meets the 8.7 a.m. train from Melbourne which arrives at Healesville at 10.13 a.m. The car leaves at 10.40 a.m. and stops at Nicholl's Buxton Hotel for lunch reaching Alexandra before 3 p.m. . . . . To bring the fares into as near an equality with the railways as possible and to tempt the public to patronise their own mutual company, the directors have made a specialty of a return fare at £1. This, for 90 miles motoring, is about the cheapest in Australia and compares favourably with its rival run through the Blue Mountains.[16]

Alice's first real break came later in 1916 when the motor service won the mail contract from Healesville to Marysville. She immediately put her hand up for the job. 'I got the opportunity to vacate the office stool for the wheel, and I took it,' she said.[17] However, difficulty for Alice lay in the route, which would take her over the Black Spur, and being alone behind the wheel of an enormous char-à-banc. Others may have doubted her but Alice knew she was well prepared. As she said to one journalist, 'my experience was gained in a hard school'.[18] JT must have had great faith in his employees' mechanical and driving training, and supreme confidence in his daughter for her to take on such a daunting task. As for Ellen Mary, driving a mail delivery bus was not quite the future she envisaged for the daughter who had studied at the prestigious Melbourne Church of England Girls' Grammar.

Alice was the first woman to drive an automobile over the Black Spur. Imagine the trip: the big open bus empty and ready for the mail bags to be picked up; Alice tiny behind the wheel in cap, overcoat and driving gloves, the men cranking while she gently pulls the choke and revs the engine. Alice pulls away, honking madly on the horn as she is waved off. Turning out of the garage at Harker Street and down Nicholson she drives to the Healesville Post Office, where the sound of the engine has the postal workers throwing sacks onto the bus. A few well wishers wave her off and onto the Spur. The char-à-banc struggles on the uphill pass but the tyres keep hold. Alice reaches the top and she can see the hills rolling down to the plains below. She keeps to the left, descending slowly with the brake on and the clutch thrown out. She changes gear and pulls the steering wheel hard right before taking the first of many sharp bends. The mailbags slide in the back. She grips the wheel hard and concentrates, quickly swinging to the centre for the downhill ride. She throws the clutch again, gently tipping the brake just the way the men have taught her. The engine quiets and Alice breathes in the damp air. Ancient ferns, almost the size of trees, edge the road and fill the valley creases. Towering mountain ash mask the sky. Approximately two hours later Alice pulls up to the Marysville Post Office, grinning with the achievement. Now all she has to do is make the return trip.

The locals didn't believe she could cope taking the mail route alone in all weather. *What if she broke down en route? How was a young girl expected to be able to get a large bus out of a bog? What if the lights failed after dark?* All this did happen and Alice found a way through each obstacle as it occurred. As she said, 'I learned to drive in a char-à-banc of the service, and any who know the track can guess that I had quickly to acquire a knowledge of repairing.'[19] When it rained and the bus became stuck in yellow mud she levered it free using bran sacks and branches. When it was dark and the lights failed she drove with a pocket torch in one hand and the steering wheel in the other. It wasn't long before many 'applauded this girl pioneer's initiative and pluck; the sceptics, and they were many, doubted whether she would last, and if she did, whether it were possible for a woman to be successful in the motoring world'.[20] But Alice not only lasted, she became crucial to the Blacks' Spur Motor Service's success. Her exceptional motoring achievements were noted in several newspapers and magazines including the Melbourne *Punch*, which reported in its motoring column, 'Several times she has run the Healesville–Marysville mails entirely alone . . . Those motorists who have climbed Blacks' Spur know the arduous journey this is for a girl to take in a big motor car'.[21] Alice was also honoured as the first woman to reach Matlock, the highest township in

Victoria, which lies past Healesville, over the Black Spur and beyond Woods Point.

When labour was short at the cooperative, Alice helped out in the garage as well as the office. The service also took on maintenance and repair work for other motorcars in the district, and in the busy periods she supplemented driving staff and frequently went out as a relief driver to tow in breakdowns. Alice later told a motoring journalist for *Australian Motorist*'s 'Women Awheel' page that 'her record as a solo breakdown gang [was] eleven "cripples" in fourteen days'. The journalist wrote, 'She rescued cars that had been "shot cross-wise" on the horse torn roads, made impassible by the untaxed timber jinkers and bullock teams.'[22] Alice must have been a sight for stranded passengers: a short, slim teenage girl standing with a mass of curly hair and welcome grin sticking out from under an oversized driver's cap and goggles, singularly coming to their rescue.

Alice kept working as secretary and Jill-of-all-trades as well as becoming the main tour operator for the cooperative. The char-à-banc mail runs had given her the skills to confidently drive her Hup around the district. She took on paying passengers under the auspices of the Blacks' Spur Motor Service and provided local tours, along with a running commentary based on her knowledge of the area while stopping at various points of interest. Alice was in her element. The more she was out on the road the less she wanted to be stuck behind a desk at the Healesville terminus.

By the second half of 1916 Alice decided she had learnt all she could from working at the cooperative. She had just turned nineteen and was ready to find a better paying job, relieve herself of the Hup's debt as quickly as possible, and become independent from JT. In September Alice placed an advertisement for a motor manager in *The Argus*. She signed off as 'Acting Secretary', indicating her intention to vacate the position once a suitable replacement was found:

MOTOR MANAGER
BLACK SPUR MOTOR SERVICE COMPANY LIMITED.

Applications are invited for the POST of WORKING MANAGER, from qualified drivers.

All applications to be addressed to me, at this office, not later than Thursday, 14th post., and accompanied by personal references, and address, with statement of age, experience, and condition of applicant, also salary required.

By order,

ALICE E.F. ANDERSON, Acting Secretary,

Black Spur Motor Service Co. Ltd., Grand Hotel, Healesville,

September 2, 1916. [23]

A month later, when Alice was still working in the role, Frankie wrote to a friend saying, 'Alice stays in Healesville most of the time being still the secretary of the "Black Spur Motor Services Co." and is a very fine young person – lately driving her own car (more or less) and taking out passengers for the company! Mother doesn't approve very much!'[24] Despite, or perhaps because of, Ellen Mary's disapproval and JT's reliance on her skills at the cooperative, Alice found a way to leave Healesville. By the end of 1916 she had taken her Hup and moved to Melbourne.

9

HUPMOBILE TOURING

'Rapid engine pick up is dependent upon its quality'

(1920s *Shell Motorists' Index*)

The secretarial and bookkeeping experience Alice had acquired at the Blacks' Spur Motor Service helped her secure a junior clerk position at the Caulfield Town Hall. The area was familiar to Alice, being close to Malvern, where she had spent her early childhood. She drove her Hup to work every day from Miss Cattach's at 67 Cotham Road, Kew, where she had joined Frankie as a boarder. Claire also spent some time there now she was boarding at Merton Hall. Claire remembered the cottage as a 'horrid little house [that was] very cramped'. She recalled Miss Cattach as:

> a funny old landlady who used to wear total black – bonnets and things – and who was very Scottish–Australian, strict and very economical, 'Oh, I wash me stockings when I had me bath,' and we knew she had her bath every Saturday night and she would wash her stockings in the bath. Oh, she was funny . . .[1]

Alice's salary at the Town Hall was quite good at '30 bob [shillings] a week'[2] when compared to the average weekly male wage in Victoria in 1915, which was 55 shillings and 3 pence, and the average female wage, 26 shillings and 11 pence. Alice was the only woman among a staff of thirty at Caulfield Town Hall. To her colleagues she was a charming novelty and her Hupmobile a shiny magnet. Not only was it unlikely that fellow employees could have afforded such a car, it was a rare thing to come across a young woman who owned a luxurious motorcar and who also needed to work for a living. According to Claire, 'She used to take the car over to Caulfield and from the moment she was there, she was the darling of the whole staff . . . they liked the look of the car, she kept it beautiful.'[3]

Where Alice's father had attempted and failed to promote motor tourism with the Hup, Alice was determined to succeed. Unlike JT, caught in a web of tensions and competing interests back in Healesville, Alice had a willing and ready audience in her Caulfield workmates. Admiration for the car and her anecdotes about life in the bush had them eating out of her hand long before she suggested, 'I could take your family up to the Dandenongs where there [are] lyrebirds and you can see them and I could make you a chop picnic!'[4] They were more than happy to take Alice up on her offer and were prepared to pay for the privilege. Once the first couple of families had taken a trip the word spread: 'Get Miss Anderson to take you up there!'[5] Almost overnight, Alice had every weekend booked out.

The Dandenong Ranges were the perfect destination. They were the closest ranges to the city and, at 24 miles from Melbourne, a good day's trip in a motorcar. The Dandenongs sat at the southernmost tip of the Yarra Valley Ranges, where Alice had learnt to drive. She was not so familiar with the Dandenongs as she was with the mountains further north, but the terrain was similar, with cool fern glades and lush mountain forests. What she didn't know she learnt along the way or simply made up. Katrine recalled with a laugh that 'she could tell you anything at all. They'd ask her how high was this hill? She wouldn't have a clue, but she'd have a good guess and say it was so many feet and inches.'[6] The passengers loved the trips as much for Alice's guiding commentary and lessons in bushcraft as the chance to get out into the fresh country air in a comfortable tourer. 'She would take them up and she'd show them how to [light a fire], make billy tea and cook chops and tell them "that's a lyrebird down there and if you sneak down you'll see it,"' said Claire.[7] Families would come back and say, 'we had the most wonderful day in the hills than we've ever had [sic]. Alice knows everything; she knows about all the birds, she knows all the names of the trees, and she's lovely and she knows how to light a fire and she produced beautiful food and a billy tea.'[8]

Despite Alice taking charge of the Hup, as late as 1917 JT was still attempting to employ it as a fancy commuter car with the cooperative. How this worked in with Alice is unclear, but it was causing rancour among locals who did not trust JT's motives. His letter to the editor in the *Healesville and Yarra Glen Guardian* in January 1917 was intended to appease his critics but neither its tone nor content would have helped his cause in the least:

TO THE EDITOR.

Sir, I ask publicity to this refutal of the statement that I am running a motorcar in opposition to the interests of Healesville's cab proprietors and the Mail Company, of which latter I am a director. My sole reason in helping to float the Company, and being at present the owner of a large touring car, is my desire to help the district by filling a want which neither the cab proprietors nor the above said company have as yet adequately catered for, namely, the provision of reliable and attractive touring cars, to meet the call of the class of visitors who frequent the more expensive boarding house; a class which is accustomed to this luxury, and which if served with unreliable or uncomfortable motors will cease to come. So soon as I am satisfied that others have established a service sufficient to adequately fill this want, it will give me great pleasure to withdraw my car. In the meantime I am doing all I can by increasing share holding and subscribing to purchase of a new car to help the Mail Company overtake the present strenuous demand. In none of my efforts have I looked for points – I have striven merely to get what I believe the district wants – and as soon as I am satisfied that the concerns are earning enough to warrant it, I will strive for lower fares rather than dividends.

J. T. NOBLE ANDERSON

'Springbank', Narbethong. [9]

True to JT's character, he said he believed he knew what the district wanted without consulting anyone before putting a deposit on the Hupmobile. By the time this letter was published, factional tensions were putting the whole cooperative at risk and the war, which had been dragging on for three years, was forcing local businesses to shrink rather than expand. Moreover, JT was prepared to dig his heels in and go broke on the principle that his views were correct.

In the meantime, demand for Alice's services as a capable woman driver was beginning to spill into after-hours and evenings. Husbands would say to her, 'Look, my wife has to go to hospital and she hates the idea of having to get a taxi with a man driver. Do you think you might take her when the time comes?'[10] Alice would agree, driving expecting women to various hospitals around Melbourne, quietly putting herself at the ready if she needed to help with the baby's delivery. 'Oh, well it can't be very different from a cow,' Alice said to her sisters.[11] As it happened, the occasion for comparison never arose.

By June 1917 Frankie, who was still boarding at Miss Cattach's cottage with Alice, was preparing for her marriage to Alfred Derham. After Alfred had survived the fighting at Gallipoli, the two had been in constant correspondence. In October 1916 he cabled Frankie that he had been given permission to return early from the war in order to complete his medical degree. The cable also included a marriage proposal. It was three days before Frankie finally cabled 'yes'.[12] Back in Australia, Alfred returned to 'Hindfell', his family home in Harcourt Street, Hawthorn, and studied hard so he could provide for his wife-to-be. By this time Frankie was enjoying employment as an art teacher at Swinburne Junior Technical School for Girls, but at the time a woman could not continue to work for the public service once married. After Frankie informed her employer of her plans, the Swinburne school recommended she be retained to teach until the end of the year only because they had no one to replace her. With Alfred focusing on medical books and hospital rounds, Frankie was left to make all the practical arrangements. She found a suitable flat for the two of them not far from Miss Cattach's in Wellington Street, Kew. The landlords, Mr and Mrs Menzies, had an empty upper floor with two sons fighting in France and another son, Robert (Australia's future prime minister), studying law at the University of Melbourne.

It was a wet winter's day in Melbourne on 10 July 1917 when Frankie and Alfred were married at St Mary's Church of England, Caulfield. JT gave away the bride and Claire was the only bridesmaid, though all family members were in attendance. The party of guests also included Miss Cattach, Ruth Derham, Jessie Webb and the Crooks from Narbethong.

After the wedding there was a simple reception at Miss Cattach's. Towards the end of the reception Alice retired to the back room. She pulled off her frumpy black felt hat, fur-collared coat and the dress she'd worn for the wedding, and replaced them with a freshly pressed outfit consisting of shirt, breeches, belted coat, cap and driving gloves. Suddenly she was transformed from an awkward-looking young woman in a dress to a smart, boyish chauffeuse ready to drive the two newlyweds to Springbank for a quiet honeymoon. Her Hupmobile was polished to perfection and its motor gently purred as Alice ceremoniously opened the car door for her sister and new brother-in-law. She dashed round to the driver's seat, tipped her cap to the bridal party standing on the footpath, and tooted the horn before taking off down Cotham Road and on to Narbethong. The remaining guests stood waving until the tourer was out of sight. Miss Cattach then ushered Ellen Mary, JT, Katrine, Claire and Joan inside as the rest of the party bid their goodbyes. The Andersons had been invited to stay a few days to give the newlyweds their privacy.

Alice and her tourer did not return to Miss Cattach's until 10 o'clock that evening. She had had no tea, and Ellen Mary found her daughter resting on the vestibule step, cold, shivering and hungry. 'I'm so tired I was nearly asleep from Lilydale, and at one point I found myself at the side of the road,' Alice said feebly. Ellen Mary helped her inside and made some hot milk, which Alice barely finished drinking before rolling herself into a ball and falling asleep.[13]

Despite being exhausted much of the time, Alice had never been busier or happier. Unlike Frankie, the idea of marriage could not have been further from her mind. She certainly had enough potential suitors willing to woo her, but Alice was more interested in the growing demand for her driving services. Moonlighting as a tour operator was overshadowing her work in Caulfield, though it meant the Hup was paying itself off very nicely. By September 1917 Alice had even stepped in on JT's territory by advertising motor trips from Healesville to Melbourne. Compared to JT's rambling 'publicity' letter of January 1917 in the *Healesville and Yarra Glen Guardian*, Alice's advertisement submitted to the same paper eight months later was attractively simple:

MOTOR TO MELBOURNE

Saturday and Sunday Evening

Special Cheap Single Fare

To Melbourne for party of Seven

persons or less

£4.00

Telephone, Hawthorn 1956

MISS A. ANDERSON,

67 Cotham Road, Kew[14]

There might have been the odd well-to-do person who would have appreciated JT's offer of a luxurious ride around the district, but it was far more sound to offer such a ride to passengers wanting to travel to and from Melbourne. This was the sort of drive Alice had already made with clients who, enticed by weekend trips to the countryside and back, also appreciated a driver who made the journey as enjoyable as it was informative. What Alice offered was an affordable extravagance for families or groups of friends, especially attractive in wartime when people conserved petrol and rubber, and were more likely to prefer day runs and family picnics over long weekend trips. For Alice, it was also an opportunity to drive home to see family.

It was on one of these day tours that Alice's motoring and public relation skills were put to the test in an incident that threatened to end her fledgling business. She was driving through Marysville to Keppel Falls, a popular destination with tourists. It had been raining heavily and the earth was sodden. The falls, full and cascading, rumbled in the distance, sending out sprays of mist. At a particular point on the road Alice pulled over and stilled the engine. Everyone took in the pungent ozone air and the lively birdsong that always occurs in the bush after cleansing rains. Suddenly, there was a collective cry as the embankment gave way. Alice's passengers dared not look out at the Hup's side wheels, which hung over the edge of a deep, heavily treed ravine. They sat white-faced, rightly terrified the Hup could tip off the edge at any moment, sending them into a cold, wet oblivion. Alice calmly, and oh-so-gently, slid out from behind the wheel, which was, thankfully, on the side of terra firma. She urged those seated away from the edge to remain still and act as human ballast while the others ever so slowly inched their way across their companions and out of the vehicle. At that moment

Alice's abilities and reputation, her passengers' safety and her Hupmobile were held in delicate balance.

'This is nothing, you know, this is part of being in the bush,' Alice chirped, pulling out bran bags packed for such circumstances.[15] The touring party could do nothing but watch on as Alice cranked up the jack and began to drag the bags under the Hup for stability. She was red-faced and mired in mud by the time two middle-aged women, out on their own motoring jaunt, pulled up to see what on earth was going on.

Jessie MacBeth, a hospital matron, and Kate Griffiths, her nurse companion, cut their engine and looked on. They could have offered help — as nurses it was their natural instinct — but the girl was doing so well they didn't want to risk further complicating an already precarious state of affairs. 'Miss MacBeth watched and thought, "goodness me, she's only a kid, young, and look at her in charge of the whole situation. And coping! And keeping the people's morale up and not having anything, how terrible, and managing it all".'[16] They could see Alice was furious at being caught in the predicament but determined not to lose face in front of her tour group. Alice grabbed a few branches and continued to impress her onlookers, manoeuvring the car with her careful manipulation of sticks and bags. Clearly there was nothing the two women could do but watch on as Alice admirably righted the situation.

Once it was clear that all passengers were safe and the car was not going to disappear over the cliff, the two women introduced themselves to Alice. Jessie commented on the impressive show Alice had put on for everyone. Alice was immediately taken with the two women and was particularly charmed by Jessie's soft Orcadian brogue that gave away her Orkney Islands roots.

In the short conversation that ensued, all three women were surprised to learn that Miss Cattach's cottage and Jessie's hospital were literally round the corner from each other. Jessie MacBeth was the matron and part owner of Lancewood Private Hospital in Glenferrie Road, Hawthorn. She and Miss Griffiths worked at the premises. Jessie was both a masculine and motherly figure who so admired Alice's pluck that she wanted to take Alice under her wing immediately. And Alice was happy to oblige.

As Alice's life in Melbourne took shape, JT's life in Healesville continued in a shambles. By 1918 the Blacks' Spur Motor Service had lost the lucrative mail contract. According to Katrine this came down to Jim Roach, another one of JT's 'enemies'. The Roachs owned a hotel along the passenger service's route but the hotel 'got cut out because passengers didn't stop for lunch at the pub. Roach bribed the drivers to miss the mail train three times so JT lost the mail licence and Roach took it on.'[17] With pressures mounting due to the war, the in-fighting and a growing loss of confidence from the board and the public, the whole business finally crashed, leaving JT in disgrace. It didn't help that a serious accident occurred on the Spur in one of the cooperative's char-à-bancs early in 1918. *The Argus* reported:

MOTOR SENSATIONS: BLACKS' SPUR COACH OVERTURNS. Remarkable Escapes.

A most sensational motor accident occurred in the Blacks' Spur at half-past 5 o'clock on Saturday evening, when the mail coach running between Healesville and Marysville overturned whilst travelling at a speed of about 30 miles per hour. The driver, Alfred Albright, employed by the Blacks' Spur Motor Co. Ltd., left Marysville at 10 minutes to 4, with six ladies, three men, and a boy, together with their luggage, calling at St Fillans and Narbethong for the mails.

The driver had safely negotiated the last turn but one of the Spur, and was preparing for one of the steepest grades and the final sharp turn leading into Fernshaw, when the motor slipped out of gear. The brakes were put on, but proved inadequate. A precipitous valley was on the right, an embankment on the left and a dangerous crossing ahead. In an instant the driver had to determine what to do, and with great presence of mind he swung the coach into the embankment. The two near side wheels mounted the embankment, and the car was thrown over on to the roadway with great force. The front three-ply wooden roof of the coach prevented the occupants from being thrown out, and nothing was to be seen but a heap of confused humanity and baggage, over which lay the heavy spring seats of the coach. The Misses Levi occupied the front seat with the driver. All three were flung over the shattered plate-glass shield, and they escaped most luckily with scratches and bruises only. Mr R J Whalley was the first of the inside passengers to emerge from the wreckage, and one by one the others were extricated. Wonderful to relate, all escaped without as much as a broken limb. Many, however, were badly hurt and shaken, and all suffered from shock . . .

On reaching Healesville two hours after the accident occurred, Mr Anderson, secretary of the Blacks' Spur Motor Co, on seeing the condition of Miss Crispe, Miss Peel, Mr Davey, and Mr Whalley, conveyed them to Dr Parker, who attended to their wounds, and later in the night Mr Anderson provided a car to take the travellers to Melbourne, and they reached their homes shortly before 1 a.m. yesterday, thanks to that nothing more serious had occurred. The other passengers were picked up by a passing privately owned car, and taken to the Healesville railway station in time to catch the last evening train to the city. In addition to other damage the front wheel of the coach was smashed to fragments, not even a spoke being left on the hub. Pending an inquiry, the driver, Albright has been suspended.[18]

While JT was caught up in the demise of the Blacks' Spur Motor Service, Alice was making other plans to pay off the Hup's debt. She could have easily continued enjoying her well-paid job in Caulfield and happily moonlighting as a chauffeuse-cum-tour-operator, but she envisioned something far greater for herself. JT had given Alice great incentive to succeed in a motoring career but there was always the possibility that he might find a way to justify wresting the Hup from her for his own purposes. She had no time to waste. The best way for her to move forward was to take the plunge and get the Hup working for her full time.

Late in 1917, as the days became longer and the nights warmer, and the war continued in a northern winter far away, twenty-year-old Alice resigned from the Caulfield position she had held for twelve months to set up shop in the old shed in the backyard of Miss Cattach's at number 67.

10

MISS ANDERSON'S
MOTOR SERVICE

'Test the battery by switching on the lights'

(1920s *Shell Motorists' Index*)

For me the hills – no winding valley ways
Hemming me in and sheltering my days;
For me the effort, the vast, far flung goal,
Great draughts of beauty for my thirsting soul.

From far above, the mists that drift below
Drown the soft azure beauty sin and woe;
And oh the joy of conquest, looking back to say:
'My feet are bruised, but I have climbed today!'[1]

One can imagine the twinkle in Alice's eye when she went to
Miss Cattach to persuade her of the benefits of making the
cottage's rundown backyard shed the garage headquarters for 'Miss
Anderson's Motor Service'. Not only would Alice's glamorous
motorcar be officially attached to the residence, it came with a live-in
chauffeuse who could drive Miss Cattach to town free of charge!

By the time she had talked the quirky old Scotswoman round, Alice had not only secured use of the shed but also the use of the cottage telephone. Alice's power of persuasion was such that Miss Cattach even agreed to become the motor service's assistant secretary, fielding enquiries and taking bookings when Alice was out on a job. The landlady who rented out rooms in her weatherboard home due to necessity could not help but be uplifted by Alice's enterprising enthusiasm. Number 67 Cotham Road, Kew, one of the most humble houses in the street, could finally hold its shabby head a little higher with the shingle 'Miss Anderson's Motor Service' out front. Alice's full-time business would attract nearby residents of the lavish nineteenth-century mansions such as 'South Esk', 'Madford', 'Wimba' and 'Charleville' that collectively housed families of pastoralists, merchants, doctors, lawyers, politicians, artists and newspaper magnates.

Alice took short trips to the city and suburbs, and daytrips to the country and the seaside. She was a chauffeuse and tour guide who could answer any question put to her and could pull together a pretty good picnic. She also continued to offer a door-to-hospital service for pregnant women, ensuring they were well cared for beyond the hospital entrance. And there were the stock-and-station agents who relied on Alice to take them all over Victoria and sometimes beyond.

Alice's popularity and reputation had quickly grown. Over Christmas 1917 she was reported to have taken as many as '253 people in her big touring car'.[2] With room for seven passengers at a time, this amounted to at least thirty-six excursions.

Of course, the idea of a private motorised service was not new. Wealthy households often employed a chauffeur to drive their own motorcars, as driving was seen as an activity for servants.

Motor garages also commonly offered chauffeur services along with petrol sales, mechanical repairs and driving tuition. Then there were fleets of taxicabs that had serviced Melbourne as early as 1909. The original fleet was made up of Renaults fitted with meters for passengers to observe the charges for every mile driven, just as taxis are today. For a time people had the dual option of hiring a motorised taxicab or one of the horse-drawn hansom cabs that still transported city dwellers, as they had done since Melbourne was first established. Many of these cab drivers were ex-chauffeurs and all were male. That was until Jollie Smith, the first registered woman taxi driver in Melbourne, began driving in 1918 under the trade name Pamela Brown.

Alice was unique in that she was the first woman in Australia to provide a private motorised service to the public. Also, her working situation was rather different to most. The fledgling service Alice began in 1916 via her Caulfield colleagues, which she formalised in 1917 at 67 Cotham Road, could not be described as a taxi or even a chauffeur service as was understood at the time. She did not work out of an established motor garage, she did not wait along main streets to pick up clients, nor was she indentured to a wealthy family as their driver. What made Alice's situation unusual was the rare combination of a young woman owning an expensive car who also had to pay her own way. As the first woman in Australia to create her own motoring enterprise, Alice was in a position to control all her operations and tailor services to the needs of her clientele.

With Alice's confidence, charm and networking abilities it wasn't long before she became the darling of wealthy families with young daughters who wanted to have fun but, of course, required a chaperone to keep them from 'mischief'. As one news-paper reported:

> when parties of young girls set out on an all-day tour in one
> of Miss Anderson's cars arrangements are often made by their
> parents by which the certificated chauffeur acts also as a chap-
> erone, so that the mothers are secure in the knowledge that their
> daughters are in the care of a responsible woman.[3]

Never mind that Alice, at barely twenty years of age, was hardly older than many of her charges and no stranger to mischief herself. Young women flocked from the city, suburbs and country towns – all to spend thrilling times touring, shopping or going to dances and the theatre with Alice.

In town, Alice offered her charges an array of shopping adventures. Basing the concept on her weekend tours, she often suggested which shops they may find interesting and led them to their purchases. When Alice drove to Melbourne's city centre she aimed for Bourke Street, where large department stores such as Myer's Emporium and Buckley and Nunn's offered the latest local and imported clothing and shoes, perfumes, velvets, laces and silk stockings. Nearby, fancy boutique shops resided in the smaller arcades set back from the dirt and noise of the main thoroughfare. The Royal Arcade that connected Bourke with Collins Street, the elite street of Melbourne, was a highlight. Modelled on the arcades of Paris and London, the bow-fronted shop windows and high glass roof, decorated with wrought iron and coloured fanlights, conveyed pure elegance.

Another popular place to visit was the iconic Coles Book Arcade housed between Collins and Bourke Streets. Said to be the biggest bookstore in the world, it boasted a dazzling two million books as well as selling a huge variety of stationery, fancy goods and ornamental toys. The main building was three storeys high, with a glass roof and balconies that circled a long, internal court. To step into Coles Book Arcade was to enter a magical fun park with palm trees, live monkeys, funny mirrors, confectionary stalls, the 'goose that laid the golden egg', and a band that played every afternoon.

Alice also took clients to matinée and evening shows of light opera and vaudeville playing at Melbourne theatres such as Her Majesty's, Theatre Royal and – the most regal with its marble staircase and foyer – the Princess Theatre on Spring Street. Alice loved the theatre, particularly the fast, witty operas of Gilbert and Sullivan. To accompany clients to shows and be paid for the privilege was a marvellous perk.

Most popular with young women out for a day on the town were the strip shops of Chapel Street just south of the Yarra River. Alice took her female clients to visit Miss M. Lindsay's Ladies' Hairdressing and Toilet Parlor for the 'latest mode hairdressing', which in 1917 translated as a short clip at the nape of the neck with soft curls fringing the face. Holdsworth Brothers sold 'modern jewels' and D'Estelle's ladies' underclothing. If one was after coats and skirts, Miss Brownings had every style available.

While there were always exclusive designs and expensive fabrics for those who could afford them, the war did restrict fashions. Long, flowing skirts used too much fabric and corsets used steel required for tanks and weapons. Alice's clients discovered new, softer elastic corsets known as girdles and skirts with higher hemlines. The latest dress style of 1917 was the coat-dress, also known as the one-piece or chemise dress that stopped just above the ankles. The style was simple, with a narrow belt, pockets and a big collar.

Alice delighted in seeing her young female clients excited by the fashions on offer, though personally she had never been one for frocks. She was most comfortable in shirts and trousers, which Alice was seen wearing on most occasions other than weddings or funerals. Such attire worn by a woman was novel and daring. Even women's motoring fashions still focused on the feminine: 'smart motoring millinery' such as 'soft hand-made straw hats with veil attached in all the latest colourings', 'beautiful coats and wraps in tweed cloth with fur collars and cuffs' and soft leather gloves for motoring wear.[4] Some concessions were being made for the more physically active 'practical' woman, especially motorists, but only when the situation demanded. *Australian Motorist*'s first edition for 1917 reported:

> The woman is not born who does not desire to be stylishly clad and shod, but owing to the increasing demand for practical garments for women motorists, expert designers have given much time and thought to the requirements of 'Milady at the Wheel,' and brought before her many garments which ought to charm and satisfy even the most pernickety of the fair sex.[5]

Such fashions were highly influenced by activities on the Front, with an openly mannish, albeit feminine, twist: a symbolic deference to men at war rather than an attempt to mimic men themselves. A newly imported French coat of 1917 sported 'loose mannish lines and big pockets and buckled adjustable belt, similar to an officer's trench coat'. Designed to be worn with the coat was 'the new peaked cap, which is ideal for motoring, travelling, and all sports wear' but had 'a much slighter peak than a man's, otherwise it would not have the subtle distinction and air of true elegance that is its great characteristic . . . breeches and leggings have been adopted when the occasion demands, and have been invested with womanly charm'.[6]

Alice too wore breeches, laced boots and gaiters, a collared shirt, short tie, three-quarter-length belted overcoat, leather driving gloves and peaked cap, though she made no attempt to invest her attire with any more 'womanly charm' than her magnetic personality, and with curly hair cut short as a boy's at the back and falling forward into a wavy fringe, she was mistaken for a young male chauffeur more often than not. The clothing Alice chose to wear behind the wheel was not only practical: her outfits reflected several highly symbolic styles, the importance of which she was no doubt aware, such as the sporty woman's horseriding outfit, the uniform of a chauffeur and soldiers on the battlefield. Such attire aligned Alice and her business with a powerful trademark impression of adventure, of female daring, commitment and patriotic do-or-die. Still, the press not only 'feminised' Alice, some described her as practically prepubescent, incredulous at her motoring abilities as if she was a rare aberration. One magazine wrote at the time, 'Miss Anderson was the first girl (for she is only a girl) to enter the hiring business in Victoria and conduct her own car', then went on to say, 'Not only is she a splendid little driver, but she has obtained other experience also in mechanics and handling of the car', and 'Miss Anderson is a fearless little driver, unafraid to take on any dangerous run. She was the first girl to go through the Ten Mile up to the Goulburn – ten miles beyond Jamieson . . . To see her out of the car one immediately feels one would not credit her with so much ability, for she is "just a little girl".[7] In fact, Alice was twenty years old.

Despite such descriptions of Alice, when she drove her young female charges to dances held in the ballrooms and town halls across Melbourne, onlookers were shocked to discover that she, too, was a woman. Alice pulled up outside entrances in her beautiful, majestic motorcar and escorted her enthusiastic ladies inside, dressed as she was in full chauffeur attire. She enjoyed the frisson among the crowd as she passed for absent male dance partners while ensuring her girls kept away from mischief. She took to the floor as bands played wartime tunes, bush dances and American numbers by artists such as Irving Berlin and Al Jolson. She was never the only woman dancing with another – the war kept many young men away – but she was more than likely the only woman who looked like a boy.

Alice was pushing Australian motoring frontiers at a time when much of society was still uncomfortable with the idea of women being free and independent in the public domain, even as the war effort asked more of them. Alice positioned herself at the daring end of two opposing stories being played out in the press, most particularly in the pages of *Australian Motorist*. Alongside the idea that women were far less capable than men at handling anything to do with automobiles was the idea that women were capable enough drivers to transport soldiers, goods and ammunition when the war required it of them.

In 1916, the year Alice became the first woman to drive singlehandedly over the notoriously dangerous Black Spur, the *Australian Motorist* quoted Automobile Club Victoria's solicitor Mr Fay's personal view that:

women drivers lack the nerve and judgement of the stronger sex. They are not so alert as men, and become confused in a crisis. They are all right on an empty country road, but when quick action is necessary women have not the decision or strength to manoeuvre the car properly.[8]

This sort of attitude was everything Alice was determined to defy. And it was this statement that led a Mrs Betty Taylor of Frankston to challenge the gentleman to a driving competition so that he may 'eat his words'.[9]

Even motorcars and maintenance marketed to women drivers – invariably by men – implied female drivers were feebler and less capable than males. A 1917 ad in *Australian Motorist* for CAV Car Lighting and Starting showed a well-dressed woman at the wheel, with the promotion, 'A girl can start the heaviest engine – when C.A.V. equipped . . . so simple that the veriest novice can control it'.[10] Another ad for Bridgestone Light Car Wheel Sets also showed a young woman in a feminine dress coat, felt hat and impractical heels levering her small car's tyre as a young girl looked on. 'Simple, easy, no special tools required, and all done in five minutes! Consider how important this equipment is *now*, when so many women or inexperienced drivers are on duty at the wheel!'[11]

The counter story was mostly found within *Australian Motorist*'s 'Women Awheel' pages, where women's motoring abilities and achievements, including Alice's, were celebrated. While Alice was working at the Blacks' Spur Motor Service driving a char-à-banc in all weather and terrains, the reality for other women drivers hoping for a career in motoring was bleak. Men did not want women muscling in on a profession they saw as their own, as women writing for *Australian Motorist* were eager to point out. The December 1916 edition of 'Women Awheel' complained that women wanting to be chauffeuses were being held back: 'There are a number of certified wheelwomen in Australia who are anxious to take up this class of work but are finding it very difficult to overcome the prejudice of those horrible men.' Who exactly 'those horrible men' were was not elaborated upon; however, England, the journalist wrote, had many 'competent wheelwomen earning good salaries'.[12] Britain required women to drive lorries and ambulances to and from the Front. By 1917 the need for drivers in England was such that a recruitment advertisement was published in *Australian Motorist* encouraging Australian women drivers to join the Motor Transport division of the Australian Imperial Force. Suddenly women's driving capabilities were up to the sort of difficult and dangerous tasks the likes of the Automobile Club Victoria's Mr Fay would have had trouble contemplating.

Given Alice's patriotic stance and expert driving skills, she would most certainly have considered volunteering with the AIF had she not been responsible for earning her keep. Instead, she began making enquiries about obtaining a mechanic's licence. Her plan was to go beyond driving and eventually take charge of a fully functioning motor garage. As far as dreams of success on a large scale, Alice was certainly her father's daughter. However, a woman forging such territory with few resources other than her own ambition made the road to success far steeper and more treacherous. If Alice were to fail in business, it would not be due simply to poor decision-making or unforeseen circumstances: she was setting herself up as a spanner in the works of a self-proclaimed male domain. And she knew this only too well.

A woman working as a mechanic, let alone running a commercial motor garage, was unheard of in Australia in 1917. The expected role of women, even during World War I, was still managing the home and raising children. If a woman did have to work, it was mostly in the caring professions such as nursing and in industries such as clothing, food and printing. If women drivers in Australia drove for pleasure, the AIF recruitment advertisement was speaking to women wealthy enough to have the time to take up such a calling. Similarly, if women in Australia were to use their driving skills publicly at all they were encouraged to escort returned soldiers as Red Cross volunteers rather than taking up men's work.

There were two study options for trainee mechanics. One could attend the Melbourne Working Men's College in La Trobe Street or be apprenticed directly to a motor mechanic. Despite its name, the Working Men's College did take women students, though it was in courses such as bookkeeping and dressmaking. Mechanics were deemed strictly for men, of which there was no shortage throughout 1917–18 when the college accepted over 1500 servicemen for vocational training.

And female mechanic apprentices in garages at the time? When it came to driving tuition, some garages advertised 'ladies taught' or 'ladies a specialty', but no garage was offering women mechanical tuition and it is possible no other woman other than Alice was asking the question. In 1917 there were five motor garages close to Miss Cattach's cottage, all in the adjacent suburb of Hawthorn, and all managed and staffed by men. None could or would take Alice on.

Alice did have the possible option of learning mechanics from her engineering father, though he may not have been in a position to provide her with a mechanic's licence. In any case, she chose not to learn any more from JT or via any of his connections. She was doing this on her own.

Alice was knocked back time and time again. *Who was this little upstart who strutted around in boys clothes thinking she could take on the men? How many times did she need to be laughed off the premises before she got the idea men didn't want women poking around a garage where they swore and said things they would never contemplate saying in the company of the fairer sex?* Another woman may have given up but Alice persevered until she finally found a mechanic who would take her on. 'I just went into Dennys, Lascelles' garage one day, and asked for a job, and the manager laughed at me,' Alice said. 'You'd hear too much swearing!' he cried. 'But I probably would not understand it,' Alice demurred.[13] The manager laughed again and shook his head before asking a few pointed questions. Impressed by her already well-rounded mechanical knowledge, Dennys, Lascelles Ltd of 618–624 Elizabeth Street, Melbourne, accepted Alice as an apprentice employee for the next six months. She worked after hours, arriving first thing in the morning and returning at night. The manager could not have been more pleased with her dedication and abilities. Alice was his best student and obtained her mechanic's licence quicker than anybody he'd ever taught. 'Oh, she was a wonderful person, so gay and so happy and so intelligent,' he said.[14]

By mid 1918 Alice, now a fully licensed mechanic, was successful enough in her driving business to purchase another motorcar. How much debt she might have been in at this stage is unknown, but she had a clear vision and was taking one ambitious step at a time. The car was an American-built five-seater Dodge tourer. Not quite as large and luxurious as the Hup, but it was the first model to boast a modern, full-steel body.

Now that she had two cars, Alice asked artistically talented Frankie to design her a business card. Together the sisters concocted an audacious promotion that implied Miss Cattach's address was the fully functioning 'Kew Garage' with a fleet of cars for trips and tours, a testing and repair service, as well as driving and 'mechanism' tuition.

As soon as Alice promoted her enterprise in this way she was putting herself in direct competition with male counterparts employing more than one staff member, and with a great deal of infrastructure, who were also offering these services. She advertised her full course of driving and mechanism tuition at a rather expensive £10 and 10 shillings. She justified the cost by providing an excellent and thorough course in every aspect of car handling and maintenance. More importantly, Alice had built up an excellent reputation as a reliable operator and, being the only woman offering such services, naturally attracted female clients who may otherwise have felt intimidated or less supported by male tutors. Almost immediately Alice had seven female pupils lined up for driving instruction. This early success meant that purchasing the Dodge had probably been a good move, though the extra motorcar committed her to expanding the business and hiring another driver. If she were to continue, Alice would need to find a way to move beyond the limitations of Miss Cattach's backyard. The pressure was on.

In the meantime, Alice juggled her business duties and took advantage of the landlady's secretarial skills. Around this time she also acquired the use of a typewriter, which one cheeky person used to type a letter on behalf of her motorcars. Other members of the Anderson family were still using 67 Cotham Road as their Melbourne base, so it might well have been the work of a sibling. Could this letter, clearly sending up Miss Cattach's Scottish brogue, be the work of Katrine? It certainly bore the hallmarks of her particular sense of humour (spelling as typed):

> Yes'M, I ken weel ye want some bit noos, but what's a puir body tae do whin there's nane tae be had?
> 'Twas like this the day:-
> It rained all the day, an' the washerwoman came an' washed, but couldna iron save a wee few o' the clothes. Wee Alice had a sma' bit wi' frind Mathers — 12/6 I doot. She ran the Dodge Car, she toold me that that was the third rin she has had it forr. She has also bin fairly busy with herr accounts I doot, an' that is why she has commessioned me tae write ye a bit letter, tho' where I'll find yin stamp for eet I dinna ken at a'at a'.
> I'm main glad tae hear ye've been prunin' the orchard. It needed it bad I doot. I envy that lucky lassie Miss Susan Jardine, ferr I onderstand that she is payin' ye a wee bit visit come the King's (God bless him) birthday.
> So it has bin raining a wee up your side the worrl'? I doot it a'ways rains there.
> Och but its nae use tryin' tae fill this bit page, A can only pit doon any nonsense that comes in tae me haid.
> Sae, Farewell Wuman, and ye nicht let ken whin ye intend returnin' to the bosum of yeer beelovid da'ter
> DODGE THE HUP[15]

No matter the pressures, Alice was always up for a good laugh.

11

A WOMEN'S CLUB

'Only by goodwill and friendly cooperation can
we achieve the safety and convenience necessary
to really appreciate the pleasure of motoring'

(1920s *Shell Motorists' Index*)

By 1918 Alice had begun advertising for staff to join Miss Anderson's Motor Service. Her intention was to create an all-women garage – the most radical, groundbreaking business decision she could have made. There was no one else in Australia encouraging female employment in the motorcar industry, let alone establishing all-women motoring enterprises. Certainly women drivers were more or less socially accepted, but working in a garage, which invariably meant tinkering under the bonnet and the chassis, represented another step altogether. Again, Alice was breaking the mould and the public would decide whether her enterprise was a delightful novelty or something to be ridiculed, or both.

Alice announced her intentions in the August 1918 edition of *Australian Motorist*. The bold, matter-of-fact article was placed beside a large photograph of a boyish Alice in the driver's seat of her Dodge, dressed in a voluminous coat, peaked chauffeur's cap and driving gloves, with her hands planted confidently on the wheel:

> Miss A. E. F. Anderson has opened a public garage at 67 Cotham-road, Kew, Victoria. She is the proprietress, manageress and forewoman; capable of doing the jobs any male member of the automobile industry would undertake. Miss Anderson runs hire cars as a side line, and makes long-distance trips to wherever her clients demand . . . [She] has motored over long distances in Victoria, and finds 200 miles a day, over country roads, a mere incident in the week's work . . . Miss Anderson plans to make her business an 'all woman' organisation, and will shortly be increasing her staff; no man will have a chance on her pay-roll, but clients of both sexes will be taken care of, and expert attention will be bestowed on their cars.[1]

No formal records of Alice's employees have survived but the earliest known staff member was a Miss Sweetman, confirmed by a small notice that appeared in the following month's edition of *Australian Motorist*:

> Miss A.E.F. Anderson, Of Cotham-street, finds business booming, and has found it necessary to employ another hand at the garage. Miss Sweetman has taken her post at the steering wheel of one of the cars for hire, and finds the work most interesting and congenial.[2]

A few weeks after Miss Sweetman's appointment Alice put an advertisement in *The Argus* for another 'experienced woman motor driver, with or without car' for 'town and country work and running repairs'.[3] Business indeed was booming. Or perhaps Miss Sweetman, whose name never resurfaced beyond the short note in *Australian Motorist*, realised that after a few weeks' employment she no longer found the work 'most interesting and congenial'.

While one magazine hailed Alice's decision as expressing 'true loyalty to her sex', Alice did not speak of her business as a feminist enterprise.[4] It would be easy to conclude that she saw herself as a feminist championing women's rights but what did this actually mean in 1918 and the years immediately following the war?

The war saw active feminists rallying against conscription, opposing capitalism and generally pushing for better conditions and protections for women and children in the form of a 'maternalist welfare state'.[5] Given Alice's strong patriotic stance and her attempt to create a successful enterprise, she might not have identified with this particular brand of feminism. However, Alice did fit into a public feminist ideal prevalent at the time that came from women who 'were concerned with individual achievement in areas not traditionally female'.[6] This ideal continued to gain strength postwar when women of a certain education and standing had more freedom to choose 'unconventional callings', as a women's magazine wrote in 1926 in an article featuring Alice's garage, a female steel works manager and a woman analyst.[7]

Claire insisted Alice 'wasn't part of a movement or anything else, she just got on with the job and showed her capacity by doing it'.[8] Claire's comments somewhat resonated with a more courageous view that Alice 'acted as if sexual equality had already happened'.[9] Feminist motoring historian Georgine Clarsen has written that Alice was part of a generation of 'radical individualism' whereby one's individual accomplishments were emphasised over the idea of gender difference. Clarsen sees any idea of the garage being a feminist enterprise as 'an implied, non-collective kind of feminism that did not seek claim to that name'.[10]

———

Alice was well aware of and inspired by women in Britain who had motor businesses prior to the establishment of her own garage and throughout World War I. The man shortage had British women from all classes taking up a variety of jobs in military and civilian transportation. The first to be advertised was Miss Alice Hilda Neville's Women's Driving School and Garage at Worthing, established in 1913. Two years later Gabrielle Borthwick opened two ladies' automobile workshops in Piccadilly. Her slogan was 'Women Trained by Women', which most likely inspired Alice to later adopt the similar 'By Women for Women' motto. There was also a workshop in Mayfair providing mechanical repairs and courses in 'elementary and advanced motor mechanism', run by a Miss C. Griff.[11] In the upmarket suburb of Kensington the early war years saw at least three women's garages established: one by Miss Amelia Preston, one-time chauffeur to Mrs Pankhurst; another by Miss Nora Bulkley at the Warwick School of Motoring; and a garage in Cromwell Mews managed by Mrs Charlesworth of the Women's Volunteer Reserve, who trained women to pass mechanical and driving tests on ambulances and commercial vehicles.

The distinct difference between these garages and Alice's was the effect the proximity of war had on necessity over opportunity. Women in Britain drove motorcars, buses, ambulances and munitions trucks; Alice took returned soldiers and their families on picnics and scenic tours.

One of the keys to Alice's success was good public relations and making work fun. She took initiatives such as proposing a Melbourne-based Victorian women's automobile club. What better way to develop a strong female motoring community? Her first step was to make contact with the Royal Automobile Club of Victoria (RACV). The club had women motorists as members but the men tended to dominate the rooms and there was no area where women could congregate away from their male counterparts. Alice jumped on her typewriter and wrote a letter to the RACV's all-male General Committee. Could the club provide a writing room and lounge for lady members? If so, Alice would guarantee an additional number of women members to warrant the expense of additional accommodation. It was May 1918 and her timing was perfect. The club had outgrown its rooms at 243 Collins Street and was seeking larger premises. Consequently, the RACV was prepared to consider allowing space for a women's club, though the General Committee replied somewhat cautiously to Alice's request: 'We are endeavouring by every means possible to obtain new premises where we provide ample accommodation for ladies but in our present ones our accommodation is so limited that there is absolutely no space which we could set apart for this purpose.'[12]

Alice lost no time in approaching *Australian Motorist* to put out the call for women interested in forming a motoring club. The journal's July 1918 edition wrote:

Miss A.E.F. Anderson, 67 Cotham-road, Kew, is taking steps to form a Women's Automobile Club, and will be glad if women motorists who are interested in such a movement would communicate with her. Shortly a number will be invited to attend a preliminary meeting to form a provisional committee to carry the project further.[13]

Everything fell into place when the RACV announced it was moving to the Equitable Building on the corner of Collins and Elizabeth Streets and would indeed include a separate ladies lounge. However, to Alice's frustration, the arrangement was short-lived. A dramatic increase in membership meant the premises became more crowded than expected and the ladies lounge was the first space to be sacrificed. Without their lounge, women members 'were reluctant to join the male melee of the reading room', and tended to stay away.[14]

Disappointingly, the RACV was not as supportive of a women's club as Alice had hoped. Even when the club moved to its expansive premises at 94 Queen Street in 1925 a women's lounge was not a priority. Despite the newly established club journal announcing in its September 1925 edition that an 'at home' was given by the wife of the RACV president, Mrs Cox, 'to celebrate the formal opening of the rooms set apart for lady members', just seven months later the RACV made a backflip without reasonable explanation.[15] The April 1926 edition of the journal recorded Mrs Cox saying that while the 'exquisite furnishings and luxurious appointments' had attracted more women members, she was 'against making a separate women's section'. She went on to emphasise that her first consideration was to 'the Club itself, apart from interests of any section, whether of men or women'. While this, on the surface, may have sounded egalitarian, Mrs Cox's following statement carried more than a hint of chauvinism: she said it was 'a privilege of a woman member to give an afternoon party at the Club to her friends, it being understood that the majority of the guests will be members'.[16]

How much Mrs Cox was expressing her own views on the matter and how much she represented the all-male board's view of women members was open for question. The club certainly acknowledged and gave consideration to its female members; there was the *RACV* journal's regular 'Women's Interests' column to prove it. However, the journal also revealed a sexist side when it indulged in derogatory jokes about women drivers, particularly in the 'In a Merry Mood' column set aside for more humorous aspects of motoring:

> Wallace M. Bayliss, in the 'Saturday Evening Post,' notes different methods of imparting car wisdom.

> **1. <u>The Flapper Learns from Algernon</u>**
> To learn to drive the auto dear,
> First put your lever into gear,
> Then push your left foot in like this–
> That's fine. Now teacher gets a kiss.
> Now step upon the starter, so;
> That makes the precious engine go.
> Now bring your foot back just like
>   this–
> Good! Teacher gets another kiss.
> Now change to second; now to high–
> You do that just as well as I,
> Now stop the car right here, and then
> We'll do the lesson once again.

2. <u>Wife as Pupil</u>

First, see your car is out of gear.

How? By this gear-shift here.

How can you tell? Why, feel it. See?

The thing is simple as can be.

Now step on that to make it start.

Great Scott! You'll tear it all apart

If you don't take your foot off quick

The second that it gives a kick.

Now throw your clutch. For goodness sake!

Your clutch, your clutch! No, not

    your brake!

Why? 'Cause I tell you to, that's why!

There now, you needn't start to cry.

Now pull this lever into low;

Step on the gas and start off slow.

Look out! You almost hit that fence.

Here, let me drive! You've got no

    sense!

Undaunted by the RACV's response, Alice again took advantage of *Australian Motorist* to promote the idea of a separate women's motor club and to outline the type of premises required. Afternoon tea parties were not high on the agenda and the ability to further contribute to 'patriotic efforts' countered any suggestion that a women-only motor club encouraged any form of frivolity or, indeed, socially unacceptable behaviour, though calling for women with 'sportive instinct' might have raised a few conservative eyebrows:

The general requirements are a large reading and writing rooms, with refreshments procurable, and somewhere where one can have a warm bath after motoring into town on a dusty or muddy day; a place to rest before making a return journey; and a place to meet other women motorists . . .

A Club would do much to further the interest of women in the motoring world, as well as bringing motorists in touch with one another, when the novice may gain many 'tips' from an old hand at the wheel. It may be considered by some that this is not a time to start out on a new venture. But, on the other hand, this is a time when women are showing themselves to be independent, and anxious to advance with the times, to increase their status in the motor world.

The Club, when formed, could assist in many patriotic efforts, and prove its value in a hundred different ways. In time it will form itself into a good, strong body of women with sportive instinct, who have common sense in their composition, and who will eventually reap the benefit of their efforts in this direction.

It rests with the ones who come forward at the start to make a 'go' of it, and if the right women come forward there is little doubt that eventually they will have a membership to be proud of.[17]

The first meeting to discuss the formation of the club took place at the Patriotic Tea Rooms in the Centreway, Melbourne, on 20 August 1918. It included 'a small but influential member-ship of experienced, capable and patriotic women drivers'. Alice did not chair the meeting but she did propose that the club, based in Australia's capital city, become a national organisation called the Women's Automobile Club of Australia. The motion was seconded and Alice named as one of three vice presidents.

Fees were fixed at 1 guinea for entrance and 2 guineas for an annual subscription. The members also agreed to help the motoring women of the Red Cross Volunteer Motor Corps, who had been volunteering throughout the war as chauffeuses conveying wounded soldiers from the ships and taking soldiers and their families on outings.

Imagine scores of motorcars lined up at Princes Pier, Port Melbourne: individual drivers, members of the Red Cross Volunteer Motor Corps, and RACV members, all responding to the call that a ship carrying wounded servicemen was about to port. Many would have earlier farewelled these soldiers from the same location with great fanfare. But now there are ambulances at the ready and the mood is sombre. A quiet number of relatives stand in silence as the ship docks against the grey boardwalk. The gangway opens and 'men with empty sleeves, men on crutches and men hobbling with sticks' make their way down the plank followed by the stretchers that carry the ones unable to move themselves.[18] Alice's patriotic contribution had her driving one of her cars to Princes Pier many times to take soldiers to wherever they needed to go, whether it be home to family or to convalescent homes. Her experience moved her to write this poem on her typewriter:

I know when I come to my own immortal
I will find there
In a myriad instant all that the wandering
Soul found fair
Empires that never crumbled, and the wounds
All Glorious yet
And hearts E'er they were broken and eyes

E'er they were wet
(From recollections
Alice Elizabeth Foley.)[19]

Alice's dream of a world without battle scars was envisaged beyond death, as if this were the only dimension where such a world could exist.

Unlike Alice, most women volunteer drivers were wealthy wives and daughters who had the financial means to offer such a service. One of the first women to 'dedicate herself and her automobile to the services of the Red Cross' was a Miss Alice McCulloch, daughter of Mr and Mrs Colin McCulloch of North Woodlands, Stawell. She moved to Melbourne, resolved to 'do her bit' and at 'anytime of the day' was 'to be seen flashing back and forth between various military hospitals and rest homes, her soft tailored sports hat pulled well down over her bright young face'.[20] Presenting female youth, vitality and sacrifice as welcome salve to the confronting reality of weakened and damaged soldiers buoyed the public as well as the soldiers themselves. By August 1918 the predominantly female Red Cross Volunteer Motor Corps had completed an incredible five hundred outings, utilising an estimated ten thousand cars for a total of fifty thousand soldiers.

The Women's Automobile Club found suitable rooms at the Phair's Buildings in Collins Street. The badge they chose to represent the club was a motor wheel crowned by an outline of Australia with wings and, in the centre of the wheel, a helmeted profile of Minerva, the multifaceted Roman goddess of handicrafts, the professions, the arts and war. No design could have better signified a sense of movement and purpose, patriotism and female power.

In November 1918 the club reported that 'steps were being taken to organise a series of lectures to be given by experts, on various parts of the chassis'. Club members were also reported to be 'meeting incoming boats bringing the Australian soldiers' wives' and that there had been 'several propositions . . . before the committee with a view to start a garage, run by or in connection with the club, none of which have met with approval, although they have several schemes at present under consideration'.[21] There are no surviving records to confirm Alice's involvement around such a discussion, but one can assume The Kew Garage was considered and dismissed. Whether any tensions arose as a result is not known, but the fact that Alice's name was not mentioned beyond the club's first meeting is telling. Perhaps her business interests were ultimately at odds with the altruistic spirit of the club. Alice had no choice but to charge for her services and the time she could devote to volunteering was limited, though it was noted that Miss Anderson participated in collecting money for the Red Cross on Wattle Day in September 1918.[22] It is possible Alice gave some of the successful 'lecturettes' offered to members on technical aspects of the car, but with such luminaries as Mr Chas Perrin, chief engineer of the Vacuum Oil Company, giving his time to present the 'Fundamental and Elementary Parts of the Motor' perhaps she was passed over. Her absence from the list of elected patrons, office-bearers and committee members announced after the club's first Annual General Meeting in October 1919 suggested that, for whatever reason, Alice subsequently stepped back from the club she had initiated. Alice did, however, remain an RACV member all her life. (By 1920 the membership of the Women's Automobile Club of Australia had expanded enough to require larger premises secured at the

Centreway, Collins Street. The club then continued until 1928, when it was finally amalgamated with the RACV.)

By the end of 1918 Alice had become a member of an even more influential women's association in Melbourne: the Lyceum Club. Established in 1912, the club was modelled on London's Lyceum Club formed a few years earlier. It provided for women who, as experts in their fields, read carefully prepared papers from which questions and discussions followed. Eligible for membership were women with university qualifications; women distinguished in art, music, literature, philanthropy or women who had taken a prominent part in education; and women who rendered important public service.[23] Many founding members were graduates of the University of Melbourne, including Anderson family friend Jessie Webb, who had a penchant for lively discussion and debate among fellow intelligent and educated women. It was while Jessie was staying with the Andersons in Narbethong in 1912 that she invited Alice's mother to join just as the club was being formed. Ellen Mary was flattered and horrified in equal proportions. 'Oh, but I couldn't belong to a club like that,' she cried. 'I'm not a graduate!' 'But we want a good proportion of just cultured women who are interested in the Arts and reading and education and you are all of that,' Jessie assured her.[24] According to the club's guidelines, Alice's mother did not quite qualify but she did have the intellectual nous and musical ability to actively contribute, and was overjoyed when her application was accepted. It gave her the first opportunity she had had since moving to Narbethong to reconnect with Melbourne society on her own merits. In being accepted into the Lyceum Club, Ellen Mary had more reason to visit Melbourne – access to clubrooms meant she could both invite friends along, reviving and broadening her social circle, and rest comfortably between outings. This was especially important for a woman whose walking was impaired. Claire recalled that, 'Mother loved it because it was a nice place you could ask people to come and have afternoon tea with.'[25]

The first home for the club had been a humble room secreted behind Alston's corner tobacconist in Brunton's Chambers at the corner of Collins and Elizabeth Streets. Access was up a narrow staircase. At the top was a single room with a curtain that hid a gas ring on which members could make a cup of tea. It wasn't until 1919 that the club moved to the larger Auditorium Building in Collins Street and then in 1925 to the elegant Stock Exchange Building on the corner of Collins and Queen Streets. (Another move in 1934 saw the club at Bank House in Collins Street before the current premises in Ridgeway Place were specially constructed after World War II.)

Alice's sister, Frankie, was proposed at the beginning of 1917 and became a member of the Lyceum Club shortly after. Due to family circumstances Frankie never had the opportunity to graduate, but she was accepted on the basis of having, by this time, become a fully qualified art teacher. Alice's membership application was based on the fact that she was the first woman in Australia to run a motor garage. She wanted to become a member to promote her business with women who could afford their own cars and, as with Ellen Mary, have a central place where she could meet friends, enjoy a meal and freshen up for the evening. Miss Cattach's cottage was hardly a place where Alice could entertain women of influence.

On 4 December 1918, Alice was nominated by Margery Herring and seconded by Florence Young. Both women were connected to the University of Melbourne, giving credence to

Alice's entrée to the club. The affiliation with the University of Melbourne crowd of women through the Lyceum Club gave Alice direct access to educated women of independent means who had greater freedom to travel and maintained their own motorcars. Both Florence Young and Margery Herring owned cars: Florence, admitted to the Lyceum Club on the strength of her educational and philanthropic work, was a member of the Women's Automobile Club of Australia and had an Enfield car; Margery, who became principal of Janet Clarke Hall, Trinity College, in 1919, was later 'renowned for her Baby Austin'.[26]

University women were relatively rare in the scheme of things: women were still given little encouragement to pursue academic careers, and when they did it was expected that they choose between marriage and vocation. The career prospects of graduates were limited by a ban on married women in the public service, which forced many who wanted to teach into the private school system. The University Appointments Board, which assisted graduates to find employment, took little interest in those who had husbands to support them. It was not surprising, then, that most women in this set were single. Other members with whom Alice was to associate both personally and through her business included Frankie's close friend Ruth Derham (artist, sister to Frankie's husband, Alfred); Enid Derham (Melbourne University English lecturer and poet, sister of Ruth and Alfred); Ethel Bage (accountant) and her sister Freda Bage (biologist); Georgina Sweet (zoologist, academic, philanthropist and the university's first female associate professor in 1920); Elizabeth Lothian (classics teacher); Dr Constance Ellis (medical doctor); and Frances Taylor (journalist and magazine editor).

Alice had been accepted into the cream of Melbourne's intellectual society of women without finishing high school or even needing to wear a frock. When she attended her first Lyceum Club meeting in 1918 she could have been mistaken for a paperboy, dressed as she was in breeches, leggings and a tweed cap pulled down over her brow. At first, members did not know what to make of her, intrigued as to who she was and how she could possibly belong to their club. When asked her qualifications, all heads turned towards this girl looking like a boy, who replied with a disarming smile, 'Oh, I got through as the pioneer of women in the motoring industry!'[27]

The connections Alice made in 1918 extended her influence throughout Melbourne, especially in the wealthy inner eastern suburbs of Kew, Hawthorn and Camberwell. Her business continued to expand faster than Mrs Cattach's backyard shed would allow. The war that was expected in 1914 to see 'our boys home for Christmas' had finally ended and, despite the return of men broken in more ways than could be imagined, there was hope. Every time Alice pulled in and out of the laneway she cast her eye over the empty block diagonally across the road on the corner of Cotham Road and Charles Street and, like her father, dreamed of the best of all possible worlds. *If only she could find a way to purchase the land and build a garage to her own specifications. It would be unlike any other purpose-built motor garage in Melbourne: a huge, three-storey space catering for motor repairs, a large workshop and sleeping quarters for all the garage girls she would employ.*

In reality, how Alice could afford such an extravagance as a young, single woman would pose the greatest challenge of her career.

12

POSTWAR PRESSURES

'The motorist must rely entirely upon the
constitution of the fuel to safeguard his engine'

(1920s *Shell Motorists' Index*)

Alice had made influential connections and the public's response
to her enterprise to date had been generally positive. Her achievements thus far represented all that was possible for Australian
women in motoring. She remained the only woman in the
country with an all-women garage business and *Australian Motorist,*
with its regular 'Women Awheel' column, continued to promote
her as such. However, it would take more than just motoring
skills and clever public relations to establish the fully functioning
garage that Alice's business card implied. The stark reality was
that Alice was up against a financial system that did not cater
for women, let alone women in business.

In 1918, when Alice attempted to secure a loan to purchase the
block of land at 88 Cotham Road to build her garage, banking
and finance were still male domains, as they would be for many

decades to come. It hadn't been until the late nineteenth century that women in Australia even had a right to have their own bank account. Moreover, marriage, banking and property rights were inextricably linked. Victoria's *Married Women's Property Act 1884* enabled married women to hold property of their own, sue and be sued, enter into contracts and be subject to bankruptcy laws etc., but what of a single woman who was a sole earner? She could own property in her own right but could not obtain a loan without the signature of a male guarantor.

Although Ellen Mary did not approve of the direction Alice was headed, JT was happy to support her venture. Yet when she needed the money, Alice discovered his guarantee was no use at all. Given JT's financial history, this was not surprising. Alice loved and admired her father's intelligence but she was increasingly disillusioned by his ongoing, seemingly self-imposed financial woes. Katrine, who was working as a secretary, offered Alice what little she could but Alice politely refused. In fact, after JT's guarantee fell through, Alice decided it was best to keep her financial affairs altogether separate from family. She sought backing elsewhere and refused to disclose to her sisters and parents the name or names of those who agreed to support her.

Alice's family was left to speculate. Katrine thought she might have had assistance via 'the MacBeth woman' or the accountant Ethel Bage or possibly even Jessie Webb. However, any female friend would have had to either loan Alice money directly or have a man guarantee a loan on their behalf – a very generous and risky act. Claire imagined Geoff Gair, a solicitor friend who thought very highly of Alice, might have helped her. No matter how Alice managed to garner support, the fact was that she had secured the trust and goodwill of those with means. It was an incredibly brave leap for a single woman of twenty-one whose family had few assets.

Once in place, Alice's loan catapulted her into serious debt. The pressure to properly handle financial matters on a large scale had suddenly become crucial. It wasn't enough to know how to bookkeep, or how to foster good public relations or even to drive and maintain cars. Just because the training from her parents in such matters read like a manual of what one should never do didn't mean that Alice magically held the keys to successful business management. Alfred sent a warning signal to Frankie when he wrote in early 1919 that Ellen Mary 'had had a distressing interview with a Mr Jardine', who was 'annoyed because Alice could not give him a statement of a/c.' Alfred continued:

> *It appears she is <u>losing</u> not <u>gaining</u> money at present! And things are, as usual, all wrong. Alice seems to have the parental temperament too well developed to be able to squeeze profit out of anything. I believe half the secret lies in their inability or refusal to look after the pennies and even the pounds for that matter!*[1]

Alfred clearly felt Alice was headed for disaster. Though, seen in the context of Alfred and Frankie's relationship with JT and Ellen Mary, his comments revealed a broader family tension.

While there may have been some truth to Alfred's concerns, his hyperbole was as much about his opinion of Alice and Frankie's parents, and his relationship with Frankie, as it was about Alice. Ever since adolescence, Frankie's relationship with her mother had been strained. The pressure, compounded by JT's lengthy absences and fiscal irresponsibility, meant relations were often pushed to breaking point: the weight of expectation Frankie felt from an early age; the judgements and misunderstandings between mother and daughter; and being party to Ellen Mary's isolation and depression. There was also the unspoken jealousy Frankie had of Alice in particular, which might have unwittingly influenced Alfred's own impressions of his sister-in-law. The wound ran so deep as to be barely acknowledged, but to Frankie Alice was effortlessly more popular, more confident, more daring and, unlike Frankie, she cared little for what others thought. When they were children it was Alice who seemingly got away with everything while Frankie stayed close to Ellen Mary and took on what her mother physically could not. She sewed the family's clothes, cooked and cleaned, and mothered her younger sisters, all without a cross word. Alice did what she liked and was bossy to boot. It would be perfectly understandable for Frankie to have mixed feelings for a sister who took such risks as to open a motor garage supported by a huge loan she had to pay back on her own. It would not have taken much imagination for Frankie to see Alice's business as a reckless high-wire act that might collapse at any moment, just as each of JT's enterprises had, and Alice's inability to provide a client with an account as a sign of monetary incompetence.

Alice might have taken on more than she could handle on her own but she had a number of women friends and associates who were willing to lend a hand. Her accountant friend Ethel Bage more or less offered herself as a patron of Alice's business by providing accountancy skills free of charge as required. Thirteen years older than Alice, Ethel was typical of the women Alice surrounded herself with. She was from a wealthy Melbourne family and part of the University of Melbourne crowd. Ethel had

obtained a Masters of Arts at the university and her sister Freda
Bage held a Masters of Science. Both sisters were keen motorists,
particularly Freda who, in Queensland, was labelled a 'motoring
adventurer' and most 'unladylike' in her pursuits.[2]

Alice's financial situation was made even more complicated
by obligations to family. She was not only supporting herself, she
was taking on responsibilities and making financial decisions –
by an arrangement of sorts with her mother – that should have
otherwise fallen to her father. In June 1919, shortly after her
twenty-second birthday, Alice wrote:

My Dear Mother,
. . . Now, I have to break this news gently. I am in such a
position financially, that I cannot possibly keep Joan at school
for this term. I went to Miss Jones today and told her so, and
Joan will be up to you on Saturday, and the fees will go on to
the next term she spends at school – I arranged that, because
I cant afford to pay that £24 and she not benefit by it, but
cannot afford it yet.

I hope to be able to let her return for the last term of this
year, so that she could have a go for the Scholarship. In the
meantime I do not think that a term's rest will do her any harm
at all. She is not brilliant by any means, but she is not stupid,
and if she reads a bit – just anything, Miss Jones and I agree
that she will certainly not disimprove.

You may wonder why I took this in to my own hands so
drastically. Because if I did not do something right away,
I would have had to pay the whole fees and I can not, and you
have practically constituted me her guardian by letting me pay
for her.

> *By the way, I will be paying Miss Cattach any future rent,*
> *and will not worry you any more, you paid her to 26th May so*
> *I will take it from then . . .*[3]

Did Ellen Mary owe rent to Miss Cattach directly or had she been assisting Alice with her rent? From Alice's letter it would appear the former might have been the case. Alice was a dutiful daughter but she could be forgiven for losing faith in both parents in this regard. Whatever the situation, Alice was signalling a severance of any financial support either to or from family from this point on.

Despite Alice's precarious financial situation she still dreamt big, imagining an unconventional garage of enormous proportions. The June 1919 edition of *Australian Motorist* outlined her ambitious plans:

An All-Woman Garage Success

Miss Anderson, who has taken up motoring as a profession, has made an unqualified success of her venture. Her garage work in Kew, Victoria, has grown so rapidly that a three-storied brick garage is to be built to her special requirements.

The first floor is to house the motors in for repairs; the second will be a workshop, where girls will be employed; the third will be used as sleeping and eating quarters for the staff . . .[4]

Alice envisaged an ideal amalgam of female industry and collegiate harmony: a house of young apprentices and employees all sleeping, eating, working and playing together in the tradition of a religious order or boarding college. It was a wonderful dream but a terribly costly one. If Alice stuck to this plan she would risk going the way of JT and falling into a hole too big to crawl out of.

Apart from being cost prohibitive, there was a shortage of materials postwar. Alice put aside her dream reluctantly and set about designing a more realistic single-storey building. Even with the modified plan, however, the builder told Alice, 'I can't go ahead. I can't get bricks.' Alice, though, had already thought this possibility through. 'Oh, that's all right,' she replied, 'I've got the bricks already.'[5] (Perhaps JT's benevolent intentions had finally materialised via one David Mitchell – father to Nellie Melba – who owned a large brick and pipe works, and with whom JT had previous business dealings.)

———

Meanwhile, waves of returning soldiers arrived home with a weapon as innocent as a running nose and as deadly as a spray of bullets. When armistice was declared on 11 November 1918 Sir John Monash, recently knighted by King George V for his outstanding work as Commander of the Australian Army Corps, was charged with coordinating the return of two thousand men. It took over twelve months before the task was completed. In that time a mysterious illness developed among the soldiers. The Australian Government took quarantine measures to contain the disease but they were ill equipped to prevent its spread. The Spanish flu, as it became known, ended up taking more lives than all those killed in the Great War. No one was immune. For Alice, this could have meant disaster for her burgeoning business; certainly, it was not the best time to be working in a field that involved ferrying people around in cars.

The geographic origin of the disease is unknown but it was dubbed the Spanish flu because neutral Spain was free to report the outbreak before other countries that had censored initial reports to keep up wartime morale. Some experts suggested the virus started in China or France, but there is a general consensus that it most likely originated in the United States of America, in Fort Riley, Kansas. There, in March 1918, soldiers burnt tons of manure and, according to one report, 'a gale kicked up. A choking dust storm swept over the land . . . a stinging, stinking yellow haze.' Two days later the first soldiers reported feeling sick. Forty-eight soldiers died at Fort Riley and the virus was carried to Europe with the arrival of American troops in France, where more soldiers were infected. The sickness grew more deadly as it progressed. In a reversal of the normal mortality pattern, it attacked young and healthy adults rather than the very young, or old and infirm. Initial symptoms of the disease were no different to the common cold but could quickly develop into a viscous pneumonia that could kill within hours. One physician recalled that the patient 'dies struggling to clear their airways of a blood-tinged froth that sometimes gushed from their nose and mouth'.[6] It tended to affect an area for up to twelve weeks and then would suddenly disappear almost as quickly as it had arrived, only to return several months later.

Alfred Derham found himself at the forefront of the insidious virus when he was assigned to Point Nepean Quarantine Station as a medical officer in January 1919. Along with a nurse and medical officer in charge, Alfred's task was to assess and vaccinate all returning military personnel and further contain anyone showing symptoms. Throughout the pandemic, all incoming vessels passed through either this Victorian quarantine station or the one based at Sydney's North Head in New South Wales. Point Nepean was the ideal port to assess and control any outbreak, being situated on the tip of the Mornington Peninsula, a thin strip of land between Port Phillip Bay and Bass Strait.

Alfred was proud to take on the quarantine role, but in doing so he left behind an anxious wife and a baby son. Hilda Pickford, one of Alice's chauffeurs at the time, drove Alfred to Queenscliff, after which he took a motor launch across the narrow strait to Point Nepean. On arrival he wrote to Frankie:

> Quarantine Station
> Point Nepean, via Queenscliff
> 3-1-19
>
> Dearest Beloved,
> . . . work will only be strenuous in patches so long as no
> epidemic occurs and then I shall try and stick to the sea
> going job if I can . . . It is of course quite a beautiful spot
> <u>here</u>. Quarters very good — stone's throw from water (Bay) —
> fare food but tinned milk . . . My pay here is £3.30 per day
> plus expenses (plus military sick pay) = £4.5.6 . . . Don't
> talk about it or there will be questions asked in parliament —
> Anyway it is worth that to be away from you and Tommy
> for a month. I would not <u>dream</u> of bringing you down
> here . . . Quarantine have promised to release me in a month
> if possible and five weeks for certain . . . I did not pay Miss
> Pickford for the car as time was short and I had no idea when I
> would get any more cash. I should like you to settle with Alice
> as soon as convenient or could send a postal note . . .
> Sweetest possible kiss,
> xx Alfred[7]

The outbreak of the flu was first recognised in Victoria in January 1919 and on 21 January the government declared the state infected. The announcement sent a ripple of anxiety throughout the population. People were encouraged to wear masks in shops, hotels, churches and public transport. The government set up stringent protocols. They prohibited public meetings of twenty or more people and restricted travel in long-distance trains. Anyone in contact with someone with influenza had to report their name and address to their local council, and houses with any infected family members were immediately isolated under strict quarantine rules. Fear and suspicion became as contagious as the dreaded flu itself. *Was it safe to visit the next-door neighbour? Did little Mary's cough signal the Angel of Death? Were they putting themselves at risk taking a hire car?*

A letter Alfred wrote to Frankie on 23 January 1919 reflected the community fear building around the flu, and the anxiety Frankie felt being separated from her husband as well as her feeling that Tommy, being a baby, might be especially vulnerable. At the time, Alfred appeared to be unaware that the flu outbreak had already been publicly announced two days earlier. Ironically, his own isolation in quarantine may have kept him from receiving the latest public news. Alfred's advice to Frankie revealed the limited precautions available for infection prevention, as well as the lack of certainty around what medical doctors believed they were actually dealing with:

> *My dearest girl,*
> *You sounded a little forlorn over the phone. I _wish_ I was with you but little girl if Pneumonic Influenza does break out and I _were_ in Melbourne I could not come home to you and Tommy*

and I would in one way [be] further away than I am here — I
don't believe <u>any</u> of my family will get it if they are careful. All
the staff wear masks here <u>always</u> when they are near suspects or
away from the station and <u>none</u> of them get influenza.

It would be sheer moral cowardice for you to be ashamed to
adopt the simple precautions at once which will be enforced on
the public as soon as they get <u>frightened</u> enough. Re inoculation
— get Ruth to do you if she can[8] — otherwise wait and if the
risk seems to be increasing get . . . any local doctor to do
it . . . but once you make up your mind don't delay . . .

I enclose . . . a sample influenza mask — don't use anything
smaller. A few drops of carbolic acid (1 in 20) sprinkled on the
outside and rubbed in is what we have here. Keep a distance
from everyone and attend scrupulously to cleanliness of hands
etc. etc. <u>Personally</u> I think that a certain measure of isolation
for Tommy would be possible and for you too, but I leave that
to you — but darling girl don't worry.

I am still doubtful whether this is really Pneumonic Influenza
as I know it though it may be "Epidemic Pneumonia" which is
quite a well known thing . . .

Cheer up beloved — there may be a tragic time just ahead
but we can be as we have been — trust in God but keep our
masks wet with carbolic acid. (carbolic acid wants very careful
<u>mixing</u> with water and is liable to <u>burn</u> even 1 in 20) . . .

Good night my dearest dearest wife Oh! Frankie I shall
want to be <u>paid</u> in blood drop for drop for leaving you next
time . . .

<u>Yours forever</u>
<u>Alfred</u>[9]

As the flu spread, more people stayed home and theatres, schools and other public buildings, such as the Exhibition Building, were either closed or set up as fever hospitals and morgues. Those who did venture out wore masks, as Alfred had predicted. The Exhibition Building had hundreds of beds in close rows, with women and men in separate sections in the main hall. Their nurses slept on the verandah alongside State Parliament in the western annex. Hundreds of people died there and were sent to a temporary morgue in the basement. No one, especially those living in the city, felt safe. People had 'inoculation parties' at home or queued at the Town Hall for an injection. But the injections did nothing to save people from being infected. Churches held services outside for safety. Ellen Mary was ensconced at Springbank when Alice wrote her a letter on 26 January 1919 warning of the dangers:

> Spanish flu is rife. Don't let the kids come near town or back to school unless it is all away. Smithy [Jean Smith, Alice's employee] took a case in yesterday. Nice old liars they were too. They said it was not flu and when she got to Melbourne she looked at the slip they handed to her and it was the Flu. So she had . . . the trouble of disinfecting and then we don't feel safe.
>
> It starts with an ordinary cold.
>
> I took F [Frankie] to Portsea last night where she will be indefinitely as Alfred will be there. Strange as it may seem it is the safest place in Australia.
>
> Yr. ld [loving daughter]
>
> A.A.[10]

Thankfully, Smithy did not contract the flu and neither Alice nor any of her other staff appeared to suffer. However, Frankie's baby, Tommy, ended up contracting the virus, which must have been a terrifying time for the family. To everyone's great relief, he survived.

By the end of 1919 around ten thousand Australians, mostly young adults, had died of influenza. Given the statistics, it seems almost miraculous that the Anderson and Derham families survived the pandemic relatively unscathed.

Meanwhile, Alice continued working out of number 67 as she watched her garage being built brick by brick across the road. Despite the flu epidemic putting her business at risk, the fact that she would soon have the premises she had dreamed of for so long kept her as focused and forward thinking as ever.

Studio photograph of the Anderson and Monash families, 1897, posted to loved ones back home. Ellen Mary is seated to the left holding three-month-old Alice, JT stands behind Stewart and Frankie with brother Jack, and Victoria and John Monash, to the right. The Monashs' daughter Bertha is seated beside Frankie. (AUTHOR'S COLLECTION)

Frankie and Alice wearing their Sunday best outside their cottage at 'Springbank', Narbethong, c. 1910.
(AUTHOR'S COLLECTION)

Alice at nineteen in her first car – the Hupmobile – c. 1916.

A favourite family photo-
graph of Alice that captures
her cheeky, outgoing nature,
c. 1919.

Alice (right) pretending to be a client's boyfriend, c. 1919.
(UNIVERSITY OF MELBOURNE ARCHIVES)

Alice and two garage girls with the Hup, wearing full chauffeur uniforms including boots, coats, gloves, peaked caps and driving goggles, early 1920s.
(COURTESY MARK DERHAM)

Alice's garage girls at work on an engine in a photograph for *The Home*, 1 December 1920. Note that the car's bonnet has been lifted off and the hood is pulled back, leaving the windscreen free standing. (AUTHOR'S COLLECTION)

Alice at the garage lathe, c. 1922.

Jessie Millar (left) and other garage girls posing for a publicity shot at the rear of the garage, c. 1925. (COURTESY MILTON GREEN)

A private moment: garage girls in a romantic embrace, c. 1924.
(AUTHOR'S COLLECTION)

Outside The Kew Garage, 1925. (COURTESY MARIE MARTIN)

Five of Alice's garage girls pose outside, 1925. From left: unknown, Ruth Snell, Heather Buchanan, Marie Edie, Peggy Bunt. (COURTESY MARIE MARTIN)

Studio photograph of Alice
in chauffeur uniform, 1925.
(UNIVERSITY OF MELBOURNE ARCHIVES)

One of Alice's Chandler tourers being lifted onto the ship to Tasmania for
her popular Tasmania tour of 1925. (AUTHOR'S COLLECTION)

Alice posing with the Austin 7, prior to the Lyceum Club farewell, for *The Herald*'s article 'Ready to Set Out for Alice Springs', 7 August 1926. Jessie Webb is in the passenger seat and the doors have been left off to make way for extra luggage. (AUTHOR'S COLLECTION)

En route to Alice Springs, Jessie Webb crouches beside the Austin 7 checking a possible flat tyre, 1926. According to Alice, a single flat tyre was the only problem the little car encountered throughout the whole trip. (AUTHOR'S COLLECTION)

13

THE KEW GARAGE

'Less oil used and a greater mileage covered . . .'

(1920s *Shell Motorists' Index*)

By late January 1919 the building at number 88 had progressed to four walls and a roof. There was a long way to go before Alice could move in and set up shop, but this didn't stop her promoting all the services and equipment of a fully functioning garage. Her first large format advertisement in the *Sands & McDougall's Directory of Victoria for 1919* read:

MISS ANDERSON'S MOTOR SERVICE

(KEW GARAGE) Tel, HAWTHORN 2328.

67 COTHAM ROAD, KEW.

Seven-seater HUPMOBILE and Five-seater DODGE

Touring cars for hire.

Driving and mechanism taught.

PETROL, TYRES, and all Motor Accessories Stocked.

REPAIRS to all classes of cars.[1]

How Alice was able to provide all this from Miss Cattach's cottage is mind-boggling. As soon as the roof was completed at number 88, however, Alice and her staff began moving cars and equipment out of the backyard shed, off the street and into the garage. The building was nothing more than a cavernous shell but it was good for storage. The day Victoria declared the flu had broken quarantine lines, Alice sat at her typewriter and wrote to Ellen Mary:

21st Jan. 1919

Dear M,

Too tired to write. It has been a day and a half as you may imagine – for we have moved out of the Old into the New.

Of course, the New is not nearly finished yet, but it is burglar proof. It has yet to have the other two doors put on hinges and the floors asphalted and the office and petrol store floored and the windows put in the ground leveled up and the gate put on and the fence painted.

The Conversatsione, I suspect will be on or about the 1st of March next, and you are invited to attend.

What made the day busier was the fact of the two floors being done, which naturally turned the place upside down.

What made the day busierer was the fact of Miss Smith and I sitting at a/ac all day until 4pm.

What made the day busiest was the fact of my having to give 2 clamorous pupils lessons.

And busierest – the fact of their being a 7 p.m. run – Smith Hupp. That's all the runs and biz today and please say thank you for getting any epistle at all.

Yrs.

A.[2]

Often the letters Alice wrote to her mother around this time were full of exasperated comments about her lack of time to do anything other than garage business. Alice thought Ellen Mary was being overly demanding expecting her daughter to write regularly but Ellen Mary didn't see it that way. *If JT, who was always away chasing business opportunities, had time to write to her daily, then surely Alice did too!* It didn't help that Ellen Mary continued to feel cut off from the wider world and the latest news. As other family members made their way in the world she generally remained at Springbank with twelve-year-old Joan – who was still attending the local state primary school – as her only day-to-day companion. Ellen Mary wanted to know what was happening in everyone's lives and wanted to be able to respond with advice, opinions and concerns.

Five days after Alice had written to let her mother know of the move from 'the Old into the New', she wrote again. This time Alice's lack of frequent correspondence was justified by her listing a section of her engagement book as proof of how little time she had to dedicate herself to anything but work, work, work. Alice listed the client's name, the car to be used or the driving lesson to be conducted, the staff member responsible, the times involved and, if it was a long-distance chauffeured trip, the destination:

67. 26ᵗʰ Jan. 19

Dear M.
I don't see how you can expect letters from me

1. Wednesday.
   Arnold Best. Dodge, Pickford, 9 to 4
   Prell Elgin A. A. 2 to 3.30

Cooper, Dodge, Pickford, 4

5.30. Dr. Cowen Pickford Dodge

8.30 Gillespie A.A. Elgin

11.15. Dr. Cowen Pickford Dodge

2. Thursday.

6. Pearson Rowe, Elgin, A.A. Heathcote

3. Friday.

8.0 Jones lesson

9.30 Dr. Cowen. Hupp. Smithy

9.30. Mrs Bean Dodge Pickford

10. Mrs Dredge lesson A.A.

11. Miss McBeth 11 to 6p.m. Pickford

3 Dr. Cowen

6.30 Sherbrooke A.A. overnight

4. Saturday

9. Wills lesson

9.30 Run Town Smithy

11. Smithy Macedon Elgin

Pickford Sherbrooke as driver weekend.

7 a.m. Dodge Spencer St.

2.30. Swanson Dodge A.A.

3.0. Dodge Dr. Cowen Jones

6. Swanson Hupp. Lander

6. Derham Portsea Dodge

And I did not get home till 1.45 this morning had to be home
— I had kept Smithy all night. She is off today with Dr Cowen
to Mornington Elgin. No other trips. Father has just been and
gone. I am just up having had a good laze.

Everything has gone on greased wheels with the Boss so much to the fore to keep things smooth. And Miss Cattach has been an angel and answered the phone and is really excellent on it. Never loses anything. Arent you jealous?

A new driver is in evidence — on trial only. She is out from England. Drove for two years in London. And is EXCELLENT. Knocks spots off all here. Ella Jones . . .

Jones has passed the Royal Auto Club of England's exam for Chauffeurs and mechanism —

True Blue— . . .[3]

As her letters show, Alice was certainly busy with little time for herself. How grateful she must have been for Miss Cattach, who fielded all telephone enquiries as building works continued across the road. Alice still had to base herself at the cottage but she madly worked to expand her enterprise ahead of the garage's completion. Any profit made was ploughed back into the business. As her letter to Ellen Mary attests, Alice had two regular staff, Hilda Pickford and Jean Smith, with a promising third, Ella Jones, 'on trial'. By this time Alice had also acquired her third motor vehicle, the Elgin. As with the Hup and the Dodge, the Elgin was an American model that promised comfort and reliability. Manufactured by the famous Elgin Watch Company in Illinois, which also built clocks for cars, the vehicle was promoted as 'The Car of the Hour' and 'Built Like a Watch'. What better emblem for an efficient, all-women garage service whose time had come!

Outside the front of number 88 Alice installed two petrol pumps, one close to the roadside so drivers could be served at the kerb, and the other in her driveway. Inside, Alice had compensated for the lack of storeys by designing and building an unusually large floor plan and an unusually high ceiling with windows. Compared to other garages that were often dark and somewhat cramped, Alice's design was a breath of fresh air, literally. It was a practical, breezy space that housed a front office, sleeping quarters for Alice, a kitchen, bathroom with shower and general work-shop. The large entrance and generous interior allowed exhaust fumes to dissipate quickly and noise to be reduced. In fact the garage was so ample there was reportedly enough room to store up to twenty-two vehicles, the size one would expect of a car showroom. Not only could Alice park her Hupmobile, Dodge and Elgin undercover, her mechanics could repair and maintain several vehicles at once. She also had room to house motor-cars for her most wealthy clients who entrusted Miss Anderson's Motor Service to keep their vehicles in tiptop shape and be at the ready with chauffeur on hand to drive the owner wherever and whenever he or she desired.

Once the flooring was complete Alice installed a lathe against the rear left-hand wall. The lathe would be used to fashion metal car parts for replacement or repair, as car manufacturers were yet to provide commercially made spare parts. Towards the back wall she set a large table on which was placed an industrial sewing machine for making and repairing the cloth hoods that motorcars relied on for protection against the elements. Her well-equipped mechanical workshop also included cut-away engines for driving and mechanical instruction.

Alice's garage design skills were such that she was praised by a journalist who wrote of women in architecture in the *Adelaide Chronicle*:

> There is, in a neighbouring State, a woman architect who designs
> and supervises the erection of houses. Her opinion is that women
> are no better architects than men, but they have a keener insight
> into the details of a house as they affect the work to be done by
> the women of the household. Some women, even without training,
> seem to have a gift in this direction. One of the best balanced and
> most attractive looking dwellings with which I am acquainted
> was built to the design of the lady who was to live in it. Miss
> Alice Anderson, the only woman I know to run a motor-for-hire
> business, designed her own garage. For utility of purpose com-
> bined with a smart appearance, it would take some beating.[4]

Although Alice had no formal architectural training she would
have acquired some engineering and design nous from JT, and
possibly from those with whom he had an association. When
the Commonwealth appointed JT between 1916 and 1917 to
investigate and estimate the costs of the proposed federal capital
parliamentary works in Canberra, for instance, he became friends
with the winning designer, Walter Burley Griffin, and his wife,
Marion Mahony Griffin. The American–born architects and landscape designers had settled in Australia in 1914 as a result of
Walter's prize win, and, although Marion's name did not appear
on the Canberra plans, she was a significant contributor. In fact,
as well as being an artist, Marion was one of the first female
licensed architects in the world – a fact that would no doubt
have especially impressed Alice, if not all the Anderson women.
When the Griffins were invited to stay at Springbank, it was
interesting that Claire perceived Marion as having more brains
than her husband, as well as being 'the better architect'. However,
she also thought Marion looked like a wayward gypsy, with

her 'dark clothes, very unfashionable, and beads and things on her' – a bohemian style that possibly put Marion ahead of her time.[5] One can only imagine the interesting conversations the Andersons had with the Griffins in their humble, tumbledown cottage in the bush.

———

Alice finally took possession of her completed garage on Christmas Day 1919. The first mechanised war in history had been won and, despite the flu throwing a pall over the world, Alice was jubilant. Here she was, still in her twenty-second year, with keys to the great padlock that opened the large wooden double doors to the garage she had designed, built and fitted out to her own specifications. After three years of hard work and planning, Alice had made manifest the garage she had previously owned in name only. Its handsome stucco Art Deco-inspired façade fronted Cotham Road, displaying the moniker 'The Kew Garage' in large relief between two decorative pillars.

Now Alice had not only her own business premises but a new home replete with kitchen, bathroom and a tiny, window-less bedroom adjoining her office. Moving in freed Alice from paying board and gave the garage greater after-hours security. More importantly, Alice's constant presence permitted the smooth running of a 24-hour chauffeur service – even if it meant she got little sleep, which was often the case. As soon as the garage was up and running, Alice employed a woman called Maisie Rooney as office manager. It was one of the best decisions she could have made. Rooney was pleasant, neat, efficient and, as the only woman on the premises to wear smart feminine attire – no breeches for her! – she added a little class to The Kew Garage.

Seven months after Alice moved into number 88 she sent out invitations for an 'at home' at the garage. The guest list would have included the families of staff, garage clients and their friends, the university crowd, members of the Lyceum Club, Alice's benefactors and certain dignitaries connected either personally or professionally to Alice: the Griffins, Robert and Patty Menzies, Sir John Monash and family, Dame Nellie Melba, garden designer Edna Walling and the Syme newspaper family, to name a few.

It was Wednesday, 28 July 1920 when, for a few hours, the garage girls downed their tools. They had spent the morning ensuring every car was gleaming, that the floor and all surfaces were free of dust, oil and grease, and every piece of equipment was in its place. The girls wore the smart brown uniforms Alice had chosen for them: cap, white shirt, tie, short coat, breeches and leggings. They looked professional, neat and proficient – the fresh public face of women in motoring. The garage girls, used to dealing with all the messiness of motorcars, made cups of tea for the guests and passed around sandwiches, cakes and biscuits on delicate trays. There was a short tour, some demonstrations of the garage girls' mechanical skills, a rousing speech or two, and then it was official: The Kew Garage, the first women's garage in Australia, was open. It stood to rival every male-run garage, with a well-equipped mechanical workshop, driving and mechanical instruction, petrol sales, a 24-hour chauffeur service and organised tours.

Alice announced to every women's magazine in the country that The Kew Garage was open for business. Each journalist who visited the garage was charmed into writing articles that would encourage even the most 'womanly' of women through Alice's doors.

A journalist from the women's magazine *The Home* gave the impression of something otherworldly, describing the space illuminated from above as if it was a theatre or a church and Alice a curious creature who, at the appropriate moment, appeared centre stage among her props in full costume right down to the grease (paint):

> One enters a roomy modern garage with sunlight streaming through lofty windows. Along the walls are various cars, and in the more immediate foreground is one jacked up in process of repair. From beneath this a voice hails one, and a shock head is perceived. The head extricates itself from among wheels and implements and a boyish-looking figure in dungarees generously ornamented with very real grease emerges. It is Miss Alice Anderson.[6]

No dingy, dark spaces or a male in sight. This was a garage designed to attract women to the joys of motoring in the most inspiring and congenial of atmospheres.

Alice's sister Claire, who worked with Alice for a time on weekends, did not need to wax so lyrically. She described the garage based purely on its practicalities:

> The big doors go right in, with a very, very high roof. Alice wanted it that way. It was good; good you didn't get the noise so bad. It was always fresh and you got rid of the exhaust fumes and so on. You went in the big front door and on your

right there was the little office, with one little bookshelf, one desk, one little basket chair and one ordinary chair. That was the office – and about two pictures and a few books on the bookshelf but not many. She didn't have time for that. And next to that there was a tiny bedroom, totally dark, no window, no lighting at all. Not much bigger than the average loo. It had enough room for her bed. I think there was a little table beside it and there must have been some sort of cupboard for the few clothes that she had. All the cars and the machinery then were in the big part of the garage. Over on your right was a side door with concrete where the cars were washed. It was a nice place, it got all the sun. In between that door and the end of the garage there was the kitchen and the shower. Tiny kitchen, very little in it. A tiny little gas stove – think it had one ring on one side of it. A tiny little black cast iron thing, very primitive. The bathroom consisted of one cold shower. You took in a kettle of boiling water to wash in. Couldn't afford any luxuries like hot water.[7]

Then there was the journalist who interviewed Alice onsite for *Woman's World* magazine. This article created the impression of a bustling enterprise with a charming hostess whose bedroom was not a dark, windowless space the size of a toilet but a repository of femininity hidden from the public eye:

> If you wait your turn among the motorists who are garaging cars, arranging for repairs, or booking tours, Miss Alice Anderson will tell you how she did it; but you will come away knowing that the secret of her success is her own bright, dauntless personality.

> Seated in a cosy armchair in her own den, a dainty room fitted
> with every comfort dear to the heart of a woman, and camou-
> flaged on the outside by the severe lines of office architecture,
> she reminisces of the days when she took the plunge into motor
> mechanics and new breeches . . .[8]

Again, this was a women's magazine article specifically designed
to attract female clientele to a world in which women did all the
jobs a man would do and more. The workspace and its female
staff might have been necessarily masculine in their service of
machinery but the hidden heart, central to the proprietor, was a
room that was soft, comforting and feminine. Alice and Claire
would have had a little laugh about that one.

A journalist from the *Brisbane Courier*'s 'Home Circle' section
went so far as to describe the garage as one would a home, as
indeed it was for Alice, and she the lady proprietor:

> Small feminine touches – flowers, books, a piece of knitting, and
> a big tabby cat purring on the window ledge indicated that for all
> its ledgers and records the office was the domain of a woman . . .
> Before leaving the garage, I was allowed to peep into the gauze-
> screened kitchen, which is also the dining-room, and into the
> proprietor's bedroom, for, having to be on call early and late,
> Sundays included, it is necessary for her to sleep on the premises.
> A garden runs the whole length of the garage and, with pride,
> Miss Anderson and her lieutenant drew my attention to the array
> of flowers and the promising show of vegetables which rewarded
> their efforts.[9]

With the war over and the flu receding, the new decade was
free to redesign itself. A fresh optimism hung in the air and the

motorcar was set to become the plaything of the next generation. The era would see Alice and her garage girls becoming more than just a novelty: they were set to become the embodiment of the 1920s 'modern girl'.

14

A THOROUGHLY MODERN GIRL

'The modern spirit for the modern engine'

(1920s *Shell Motorists' Index*)

It was the 1920s and young women across the industrialised world were dressing for action. Time to shake off the horror and drudgery of war and have a bit of fun! The siren call issued from phonographs, women's magazines and the wireless; it flashed across movie screens and landed in dance halls with the Charleston, the Tango and the Shimmy. Hollywood showered us in glamour and jazz gave us a new rhythm. In Melbourne, the 'modern girl' practised dance steps waiting for the tram. And the motorcar was the sexiest symbol in town.

There were fancy cars of velvet and brass, and cars built for speed. For the first time motor spirit began to outsell kerosene. Wages rose and cars became cheaper to buy. A Chevrolet that cost £545 in Australia in 1920 cost just £210 in 1926. More and more motorcars crowded city thoroughfares and took to roads out of town. In 1920 there was one car for every fifty-five people; by 1929 it was one for every eleven. Still, the continued high costs of maintenance ensured most cars belonged to the middle and upper classes – the core of Alice's clientele amongst which there was no shortage of young women seeking driving lessons and car maintenance. Freedom, independence, mobility and vigour: the motorcar and the modern girl went hand-in-motor-glove.

The quintessential modern girl was the 'flapper' – the poster girl for a new idea of youth, that fun, flirtatious time between leaving school and getting married. To be a flapper was to have a good time and darn tomorrow. Her ideal physical attributes were, as one Australian women's magazine wrote, 'young, slender, tanned, fit but not muscular, attractive but not sensual'.[1] She flattened her chest, cropped her hair, wore flexible girdles, low-waisted frocks and shorter hemlines. The look was sublimely sexual, separate from any hint of the maternal.

Androgyny and the 'boyish' look was also part of the costume game. Suddenly women were seen wearing trousers, shirts, ties and jackets. Still, their look retained a cute, playful edge. To mimic men entirely would have been considered unnatural. Whether the modern girl wore baggy dresses with dropped waists or pants-suits and ties, they all gave the impression of a child on the loose, wearing her parents' dress-ups and, like a child, having little concern beyond the present.

Alice and her garage girls easily embodied the spirit of the times, and Alice's life, in particular, reinforced the underlying per- ception that Australian women were more practical, independent, familiar with the bush, and more at ease with a masculine world of action than their European counterparts. The old world ima- gined Australian women through the lens of a certain physical and spiritual resilience: a blend of pioneering and convict grit forged in a harsh continent far from the motherland. Alice had learnt to do the sorts of things one would expect a man to do and she did them as well as, if not better than, any man could. 'I always loved the outdoor life and before I left home I was handyman about the place. I suppose mechanics have always fascinated me,' declared our modern girl of motoring in 1922.[2]

Despite Alice's chauffeur uniform shocking a lot of people in what was still a very conservative Melbourne, the boyish look was generally accepted as a sign of 'youthful capability'.[3] In 1920 *The Home* magazine tempered that capability with a touch of femininity to ease the minds of its more traditional readers. Alice was a 'very feminine business person' the journal wrote, and 'the cropped hair she tosses out of her eyes suggests a sturdy reliant spirit'.[4] What was meant by 'a very feminine business person' could only be guessed at, though it implied Alice was socially acceptable and therefore acceptable to do business with. It was a stamp of approval to and from the establishment. What no one wanted to suggest was that Alice and the women she employed might have been sexual inverts. The press promoted the garage's dress codes as both necessary to requirements as well as displaying an innocent, jolly-hockey-sticks kind of camaraderie. Importantly, garage staff were described as attractive in the most innocuous sense, and always as girls rather than women:

All her [Alice's] assistants are girls and they manage the entire business themselves, from racing to some urgent call to roadside repairs and the varying phases of the garage work. Clad in business-like khaki coats and breeches, they make attractive and reliable chauffeuses.[5]

One newspaper described Alice's face as, rather than ruddy from outdoor work, 'rosy with the caresses of the sun and wind'.[6] The same article also described the picnic hampers Alice put together for her touring parties as 'a truly feminine touch . . . she always carries a hamper of chicken, ham, fruit, cream, and, in fact, everything a picnicker's heart could desire, and this is slung in a big canvas bag to the footboard'.[7]

Despite these attempts by the press to reinforce the femininity of Alice and her garage girls as much as possible, they more accurately depicted the boyish end of 1920s fashion, as seen in photographs taken of Alice and her staff at the time: Alice catching some sun outside her garage entrance, papers in hand; Alice dressed in white shirt and breeches working at her lathe; the ever-reliable Heather Buchanan – who 'enjoyed a social life'[8] and 'always drove with a flourish'[9] – wearing peaked cap, shirt, tie and breeches as she helped Alice pack the Chandler for touring. Ann McBean, another garage girl, was photographed for a newspaper posing in full chauffeur uniform with feet together, arms behind her back, looking out beneath her peaked cap as if she'd proudly dressed in her new uniform for her first day of school. She told the reporter that the garage was 'a great adventure and, though it entails long hours of work, they [the garage girls] recommend the life to those of their sex who seek independence'. The newspaper was also keen to note that this particular garage girl came from good stock: '[she] is a daughter of the former well-known head of the firm of Joseph McBean and Son'.[10]

Other employees in some of the many photographs taken at the garage reveal a generally happy group of women free to dress and behave in ways that suited the times and their profession:

smart-looking garage girls sipping a cuppa on a tea break; working at the sewing table; washing a client's car – all wearing shirts and breeches or overalls, and sporting cropped hair. Of course, many of these young women donned the flapper look after hours. But their other fashionable option was to maintain the boyish look beyond the garage doors, which Alice did as a matter of form.

Garage girl Peggy Bunt looked very boyish in her overalls at the garage but a photograph of the after-hours Peggy shows a different, more stylish woman. Sitting with her friends at the beach round a gramophone on a picnic rug, she rests back on one elbow, a gasper held loosely between her fingers.[11] Her short, straight hair is parted down one side and combed smartly behind one ear. She wears shirt, tie and blazer with matching skirt, which sits just below the knee, and cream stockings – a smart combination of both masculine- and feminine-style attire. Other women sitting round the gramophone are dressed in loose, drop-waisted frocks and matching cloche hats. Two of them wear shirts and men's felt hats placed somewhat playfully on their heads. All sport cropped hair. Who could have imagined a group of young women looking so bold even fifteen, twenty years earlier?

For five hundred years women's tresses had been long and flowing, the crowning glory of womanhood; skirts barely revealed a well-turned ankle, and waists were slimmed with laced, whale-boned corsets. The changes the modern girl ideal brought to women's fashion and lifestyle were nothing less than revolutionary.

———

Margaret Louise 'Peggy' Bunt had just turned seventeen when she arrived in Melbourne from London with her 25-year-old sister Constance, or 'Consie', in 1920. It was a new start for both of them. They had been orphaned at an early age, and the war had taken two of their four brothers. The remaining two brothers had settled in Australia a few years prior, and the boys were looking forward to reuniting with their sisters. Though Peggy was the younger, she felt protective of her sister, who carried an extra burden of the heart. Consie was still grieving terribly over her fiancé, who had also been killed in the war. For Consie, it was one loss too many: she vowed she would never, ever consider marriage again. In support of her sister, Peggy also vowed she would not marry. Together, the two would take on the world and shape it in their own fashion.

It was on their brothers' properties at Wandin East in the Yarra Valley that Peggy became an accomplished horsewoman. This, and the receipt of a small inheritance when she turned twenty-one, gave her the sense of independence she needed. Peggy obtained her drivers licence and took to the road – all the way to Alice Anderson's garage.

Peggy's apprenticeship at The Kew Garage began towards the end of 1923. At first Alice allocated her to the junior tasks of washing, cleaning and dusting cars. Peggy also had to pass an additional driving exam to meet her boss's high standards. She studied hard, reviewing all the current road rules. She practised difficult manoeuvres, smooth braking, and learnt to predict the behaviour of other drivers on the road. Next was the intense mechanics training under Alice's firm instruction. Alice's motor-cars came with a basic toolkit designed to cover every mechanical mishap and it was the driver's responsibility to get out and fix the problem, whatever it might be.

The mark of a successful garage girl was to provide every service with good humour, confidence and a calm demeanour, no matter the circumstance. Before Peggy became the regular driver for a wealthy Melbourne grazier, whose property was 224 miles (360 kilometres) away towards Casterton, in Victoria's Western District, she had to prove to Alice that no mechanical failure was beyond her capability. It was a proud day when Peggy chauffeured the gentleman in his impressive Bentley motorcar with the car's long-handled brake outside the driver's side of the vehicle and the bonnet secured with leather straps. Peggy eventually drove clients to Sydney, approximately 545 miles (878 kilometres) from Melbourne. This was at a time when the roads were so undeveloped that the route still offered serious motoring enthusiasts dangerous speed trials between the two major cities.

Another garage girl, Jessie Millar, grew up on a sheep and wheat farm in Prairie, a flat, remote part of Victoria's north, halfway between Kerang and Pyramid Hill. The family's square mile of land was small as far as sheep and wheat farms go, and the soil was poor. The contrast with farmers living on the rich volcanic plains of the Western District, boasting sprawling estates and expansive homesteads, was stark. As soon as Jessie was able, she worked on the farm alongside her father. There was always something to do: mending fences, checking paddocks for feed and dams for water, sowing and harvesting wheat – not to mention chopping and carting wood for the fireplace and stove. The list was almost endless. For Jessie it meant getting up before sunrise and putting in a couple of hours on the farm before school, then working after school, sometimes until dark. Weekends meant even more work. Jessie was also required to help her mother with domestic tasks.

Jessie had a brother who was four years younger. A strict, conservative man of his day, their father didn't believe girls should receive an education. Jessie was simply expected to work on the farm until she got married. It was the boy who required the best possible education and entry into society. While the farm always struggled to make ends meet, a small inheritance, possibly from Jessie's grandmother, was used to send her brother to board at prestigious Wesley College. Once he had completed his schooling he was rewarded with a round-the-world trip set up by the Young Australia League. Jessie's education was limited to four years at Castlemaine High School.

Despite the long hours, Jessie made time to read after all her chores for the day were done. There was no electricity in the house so she read by the poor light of a hurricane lamp. Reading was her escape from farm life and fed her very intelligent brain. She loved history and poetry, and could quote Shelley, Keats and Byron as easily as she could drive a tractor. Jessie was the clever one in the family. Her brother, on the other hand, was not so smart and had no interest at all in reading. 'He was a lovely guy but he was a bit of a dodo,' declared one relative.[12] It looked as though Father had chosen the wrong child on which to bestow an elite education.

Jessie was still working on the family farm in her late teens. She was an eligible young woman stuck in the back of beyond with no eligible young man within cooee of the place – the war and her geographical remoteness made sure of that. More importantly, she was desperate to escape the drudgery and her father's controlling ways. Eventually, Jessie built up the courage to approach her father with the proposition that she move to the city and find work. Perhaps she would have a better chance of finding husband material there, she argued. Thankfully her father relented, and she was on the train to Melbourne before he could change his mind. It was 1924 and Jessie was now a robust twenty-year-old more than ready for independence. Her first steps were finding a place to stay and a way to make her own living.

Jessie ended up boarding with a few other young women from the country in suburban Malvern, in a house close to where Alice Anderson was born. Alice's garage was only a couple of suburbs away in Kew and Jessie fronted up to see what work could be had. As an outdoors girl, she couldn't imagine working behind a desk or in a factory. Getting paid to drive about and tinker with cars was an attractive proposition. In her interview with Alice, Jessie handed over references that boasted well-oiled family connections. As Australia 'rode on the sheep's back', so did the Millar family's reputation, rubbing shoulders, as her father did, with others of the pastoral class. Jessie's most impressive reference came from no less than the recently retired Premier of Victoria, Harry Lawson, MLA. On parliamentary letterhead Mr Lawson wrote, 'I have known Miss Jessie Millar, of 15 Soudan St, Malvern, all her life. I have known her parents for many years. She is of excellent family and character, good habits & thoroughly reliable & trustworthy. I have confidence in commending her for a position of trust.'[13]

Jessie was 'over the moon' when Alice agreed to take her on as an apprentice.[14] The garage girls, particularly during their apprenticeship phase, did not earn a great deal but to Jessie her salary was as good as a fortune – on the farm she was expected to do hours of backbreaking work for no pay at all. She had never felt so free and happy. Jessie cut her hair fashionably short and donned the garage girl overalls, which were not so different to the boots and trousers she'd worn on the farm practically every day. As for driving, she had been manoeuvring tractors round paddocks and driving motorcars along dusty old roads since she was a kid.

It didn't take long for Alice to recognise that she had taken on a clever garage girl with an aptitude for hard work, and for Jessie to realise she was working for a very smart woman. Jessie admired Alice's love of reading that matched her own, and appreciated their shared ability to apply themselves to pretty much anything. It wasn't long before Jessie was donning the chauffeur uniform as well as teaching students to drive. Her favourite jobs were taking people on scenic trips or going to the races. Many of her clients resided at Cliveden Mansions, a large, English-style apartment block situated on the corner of Wellington Parade and Clarendon Street, East Melbourne. It was a guesthouse for the well-to-do, and many of the residents were graziers from the Western District. Jessie always drove one of Alice's large tourers that could take as many as seven passengers at a time and headed off for a day of betting on the horses at Caulfield or Flemington, or winding up and down the lush hills of the Dandenong Ranges. It was so much fun it didn't even feel like a job. As with other garage girls, Jessie would always be included in the gathering and be given lunch. *If this was work, what marvellous work it was!*

Alice's younger sister Claire, who by 1923 had turned nineteen, was also given work at the garage. She had followed directly in her father's footsteps and begun an engineering degree at the University of Melbourne.[15] Claire was the first woman to enter the engineering course at Melbourne and she held her own with the male students, many of whom dismissed her as a singular aberration. *What had the world come to when a woman was allowed to study engineering, of all things?* She lived on campus at Janet Clarke Hall and worked at the garage on weekends, where the 15 shillings she earned at least 'helped pay for books and things'.[16]

If not for her big sister, Claire would never have attended secondary school, let alone university. She had studied hard under Alice's tutorship and received a full scholarship to Merton Hall as a result. And her acceptance into the University of Melbourne's engineering degree was based on her excellent final year marks in physics, maths and chemistry. Claire was just as smart as her sister, though she did confess to living in her books and being a little vague when it came to the pragmatics of life. Perhaps she felt somewhat overshadowed by her big sister, who proved to be so popular and so capable. However, once Claire had found her feet she became the most modern of modern girls, throwing herself into everything, playing hockey, smoking Camels and whooping it up with fellow university students and garage girls alike.

The first job Alice gave Claire was to clean and grease two cars every Saturday in upper-class Toorak. From her Carlton campus it was a seven-mile journey on public transport. It meant rushing from a prac class, missing hockey, spending a tuppence on the cable tram to the city, another tuppence to Toorak, then down St Georges Road to the large house where a Cadillac (or something similar) and an 1910 Argyle sat in the drive. Claire recalled the Argyle being a fiend with 'brass everywhere'.

> It had three things that had to be lubricated – three systems – and some of them were practically inaccessible, underneath the car, awful! And all that brass to be made clean and shining. They didn't cover it up with colourless lacquer: it was straight brass and lamps and all that.[17]

However, Claire's greatest sense of achievement at the garage came about in one solo after-hours marathon:

> [It] was when some work came in unexpectedly, and she [Alice] had promised to have [a] Buick – reline its brakes. There was no chance of having it done. She said it had to be done by morning. That was the evening. Everything had cropped up the way things do. And I was there and she threw me *Dyke's Encyclopedia* and said, 'get on to that'.[18] She said, 'You'll find it a bit hard because Buick doesn't use studs and nuts and bolts, they use rivets' . . . I went through *Dyke's Encyclopedia* . . . it was three big volumes with absolutely everything. Everything. And I had that. And it was a very greasy, well-thumbed volume I might tell you. And I was under that car, working on that: taking the brakes to pieces and back, and everything. I don't remember but it took three hours. I'd just have to stop and look in the encyclopaedia et cetera on my own. But I got it done, I think, about two or three in the morning. Alice got home from wherever she had to be – I forget – and she said, 'Have you done it?' I said, 'Yes, it's finished and all put back together, grease where it needs grease' and so on . . . I remember feeling very pleased with myself and very happy about it . . .[19]

Alice was a tough boss even when it came to family members. She expected her employees to work as hard as she did, and without paid overtime. They were paid for approximately forty-six hours a week over six days, which was the average for full-time female workers at the time. Rates of pay were based on age and experience. Her apprenticed junior staff earned just over £2 per week, well below the average female wage of around £4, and there was no rise until they had reached the age of twenty-one (or, as one newspaper article in 1925 wrote, wages at The Kew Garage rose after four years, from 15 shillings to 35 shillings a week to the award rate £4 and 10 shillings a week).[20]

One garage girl, Marie Edie, whose family lived close by in Kew, applied for an apprenticeship as soon as she turned sixteen – the minimum employment age at the garage. Edie still looked so young that she could have passed for a twelve-year-old. She knew nothing much about cars, really, but she had seen the chauffeuses come and go all through her school years and decided that was what she would like to do.

Edie chose to work at Alice's garage because of her 'spirit of adventure', though her family was by all accounts so eccentric and unconventional that home was a daily adventure in itself.[21] According to a family friend, Edie actually went to work at the garage as an act of rebellion against her family.

Edie's father was an Irish actor and theatrical entrepreneur who thought, like Alice's father, that a fortune was to be made in speculative mining ventures. He was rarely home, and when he did turn up he was usually broke or in debt. He eventually made a precarious living giving elocution lessons to the children of middle-class parents who wanted to cure their offsprings' colonial accent. Edie's mother was strong-minded and extremely unconventional, with very definite ideas about almost everything. She did not believe in bureaucracy and behaved as if it didn't exist by refusing to register the births of her four children. She was a militant vegetarian, imbuing in her children the horror of animal slaughter to the point that Edie fainted when she first stepped into a butcher's shop as a young married woman.

Edie's mother was a pacifist and anarchist-cum-socialist. She constantly corresponded with notable people of influence who she understood to be of the same social and political persuasion: George Bernard Shaw, Bertrand Russell, Charlie Chaplin and even Stalin. Her religious beliefs were founded on basic concepts of Christianity and spiritualism. She was a tremendous fan of Annie Besant, the British socialist, theosophist and women's rights activist, and a rabid follower of Indian philosopher Jiddu Krishnamurti. She believed children should be schooled at home rather than taught by the state, and actively took up this idea by keeping her youngest child from attending school until her teens, though Edie and one of her brothers went to the local Catholic school. But her greatest passion of all was saved for the theatre. All four children were taken to practically every play, opera and ballet performance that came to town, even if it meant pawning jewellery or accepting gifts of food from a family friend who owned a bread shop. Home itself was even a stage of sorts, with visiting international artists invited as a matter of course, including Anna Pavlova, the Russian prima ballerina famous for her rendition of the Dying Swan. For many, such a life would have been seen as wildly exciting; for little Marie Edie, not knowing what any day would bring was unsettling. Despite stating that she joined the garage because of her 'spirit of adventure', what she really craved was stability and predictability – and a regular income.

As a junior apprentice, Edie was given the task of cleaning and dusting clients' cars stored in Alice's garage. Not all cars were the latest models but, as with the cars Claire maintained in Toorak, they reflected the wealth and prestige of many of Alice's clientele. The most extravagant by far was a Rolls-Royce parked inside the garage under a tent canopy. The owners had gone overseas for a couple of years and it was Edie's job to keep the 'most elegant' car dusted and its interior and windows clean. It was upholstered in silk velvet with two crystal vases held in silver brackets in the passenger compartment. Found in only the most sophistic-ated of automobiles, the vases were designed for long-stemmed, perfumed flowers – the earliest form of car deodoriser. At the back was an ivory speaking tube from which the chauffeur was given directions. It was Edie's favourite car and she took pride in keeping it looking as good as new.

Another car held in the garage was a British Stanley Steamer, which represented the epitome of steam cars in the early 1920s. It was promoted as preferable to petrol-run cars for performance and was simplicity itself: a car with a single lever over clutch and pedal, using common paraffin to make steam. There was no gearbox, no magneto, no plugs, no carburettor and only thirty-seven moving parts. Edie recalled the car as having strong bodywork and a 'beau-tiful line for those days'. However, it would take twenty minutes for the gentleman to start the motor each morning, 'then he would silently move out of the garage with just a gentle hiss coming from the motor'.[22] Though the steam car was a viable alternative to cars that ran on petrol in many ways, there were issues that were not perfected in time to compete with petrol's overwhelming efficiency. The steamer's popularity, therefore, was short-lived. Apart from taking too long to 'fire up', it had difficulty maintaining consistent pressure, the acrid smell of the kerosene used in many burners was off-putting, and the cost was three times that of the Model T Ford.

Edie worked up to driving motorcars and wearing the chauf-feur uniform she had admired since she was a kid. However, by this time she knew that garage work was not all fun and games, and was definitely more demanding than school:

[We] had one day a week off, mostly week days, sometimes on Sunday, Saturday was always the busiest day . . . The hours were also long with no over-time . . . We did not mind the long hours as our work was always interesting (apart from washing and greasing of the cars. No one liked that job). We mended punctures, did mechanical repairs, attended to phone calls and the petrol bowsers, went out on taxi calls, and the older ones taught driving. Customers could also hire drivers for their own cars . . . After working in greasy jobs it was not unusual to have several hot showers during one day . . .[23]

Almost every garage girl deemed the work to be hard and not so well paid – at least at first – but the majority stayed on because Alice's training was invaluable and she made the work count in a way male garages took for granted. To be a garage girl meant joining an elite team of capable young women led by a young woman with loads of personality and shrewd business sense. Alice reinforced the work as varied, purposeful, exacting and enjoyable. Garage girls tinkered with tools, got messy with oil and grease, and took to the road in a very public way. By 1925 Alice had reportedly trained twenty-nine chauffeurs, many of whom had been placed as live-in 'cook–chauffeurs, companion–chauffeurs, etc'.[24] And each was, indeed, a thoroughly modern girl.

15

A VERY CLEVER INVENTION

'Here is an experiment worth making . . .'

(1920s *Shell Motorists' Index*)

The year 1924 was one of great expansion at The Kew Garage. Alice took on more staff than ever and she invested in four more American cars: another Chandler tourer, a Chandler sedan, a small Willys-Knight sedan (used by the more petite garage employees due to its small size and easy handling) and a Willys-Knight Overland Tourer (used as the message car and driving instruction vehicle if a student did not come with their own). The tourers had hoods but the sedans were the new hardtop variety.

A 1924 advertising poster for the Willys-Knight Overland headed 'No Vibration' boasted, with more than a hint of exaggeration, that the drive was 'Smoothness beyond comparison. A new thrill of vibrationless motion. Velvety performance . . . the nearest approach to gliding through space yet attained in a motorcar.' The car's point of difference was balloon tyres: 'Realise what it means to float over the road on cushions of air.' Pneumatic tyres had been around almost since the beginning of motorcar production but balloon tyres were a 1920s development that changed and enlarged the shape, and lowered tyre pressure. Balloon tyres did indeed offer a smoother trip with fewer punctures and greater longevity. A Willys-Knight Overland poster advertisement showed a plane flying through clouds overhead – a clever nod to the optimism of the decade and the future of commercial flight that was, at the time, in its infancy.

The renewed consumption of the postwar years also saw magazine culture flourish and create, for women in particular, an endless array of products for the maintenance of beautiful, slim, youthful bodies. Australia's Helena Rubenstein and America's Elizabeth Arden took make-up from stage, screen and ladies-of-the-night, and made it a respectable and fashionable beauty enhancement for all women. Women's magazines in the 1920s were a hodgepodge of progressive and regressive ideas about a woman's place in relation to men. Women's bodies were being pushed into forms of unrealistic perfection and women were being sold the latest electrical appliance to create an even more perfect home.

Between such pages of advertisements, however, were stories of women who were not just breaking the rules but achieving remarkable things outside traditional female roles. Wherever possible, Alice made sure she was attached to such forward-thinking stories. A 1920 article in *Adam and Eve* headed 'Women in Unconventional Callings' showcased Alice's 'First Woman's Garage' alongside a woman 'Steelworks Manager', a 'Woman Analyst' and a 'Linotype Operator'. It was in articles such as this that Alice promoted the initiatives that stood The Kew Garage apart from the average male garage:

Women motorists sometimes find that mechanics have more than a lurking scorn for women's ignorance of machinery, and this scorn occasionally finds outlet in slurred work when the biggest mysteries of the car require overhauling. Miss Alice E. F. Anderson, whose garage at Kew, Melbourne, was the first of its kind in Australia, was quick to realise the possibilities of a garage run entirely by women, at which women motorists could leave their cars in perfect trust that the 'once over' would be thoroughly done.

Cleaning, oiling, greasing, repairing and adjusting are performed by her expert staff of girls trained by herself, or the woman owner can attend to her own car if she so desires under the guidance of one of the girls and thus learn how to be independent when an emergency arises.

The story of Miss Anderson's rise to consideration in the motoring world is stimulating. As an ex-school girl she indulged her passion for motoring by learning to drive around her home environment at Blacks' Spur near Healesville, one of the nerviest of training grounds for an aspiring motorist.

Ten years ago she came to the city, and during the week earned her living as a municipal clerk.[1] Over the weekends she enjoyed herself to the full by utilising her car for taking tourists around to the beauty spots, and with a woman's insight into what would be required to make the tour really comfortable, she planned all sorts of pleasant accessories to the trips. Making a name for herself, she built up a sufficiently large business to be able to devote the whole of her time to the work, especially to teaching women and girls how to drive.[2]

Such articles promoted the idea of women learning in a trusted, supportive environment, safe from male 'scorn'. This did not mean

Alice took a softly-softly approach with her driving students, however. Marjorie Horne, who went on to develop her own chauffeur business close to the University of Melbourne in the 1930s, told how she was taught to drive 'correctly' by Alice in 1925:

> You'd ask her a question. You might say, what happens if I push the clutch down going down a hill? And a big booted leg would come crash on top of yours on the clutch and you soon found out what happened. And she also taught you – you'd be going along Bridge Road – very busy with trams and cars and that sort of thing. And her idea was that you had to assess what was happening on both sides of the road so that you knew when a tram or car got to a certain point, where you were, what you were going to do. See, she taught you correctly.[3]

It is important to point out that Alice was in the habit of encouraging women of any age to drive, not just the young. This added to the garage's respectable reputation. Claire said:

> She used to persuade these women to drive. They'd say, 'I'm too old, I've never been anything but a housewife, I'm sixty!' So what? They didn't say so in those days, but she [Alice] said the equivalent of it, and she had these women who were always conscientious, good, middle-class mothers of families and wives of husbands and giving them a taste of freedom and being your own person and there's nothing like learning to drive a car – nothing like that.[4]

The 'once over' noted in the *Adam and Eve* article was a brilliant initiative of Alice's, whereby a client's car would be 'completely overhauled in eight hours for 30 shillings every 500 miles'.[5] It appeared that Alice was the first – at least in Australia – to offer what we now call a scheduled service. The idea and the practice was a streamlined process, as modern and efficient as a postwar production line. Note her advertisement placed repeatedly in the *RACV* journal throughout the mid 1920s:

THE

KEW GARAGE

KEW

–

A 'ONCE-OVER'

includes

All Greasers greased thoroughly, the Sump drained, Gear Box and Differential inspected and filled if necessary. Battery inspected and specific gravity read. Radiator drained, flushed and refilled. Loose nuts tightened. We also tell you if any repairs are necessary.

–

ALICE E. F. ANDERSON[6]

The 'once-over' service, as described by Claire, is familiar to us today. Though without the extensive electronics and testing devices of a twenty-first century garage, it was a far more labour-intensive affair:

you leave your car before nine in the morning and we will take it all to pieces. If the cylinders need realigning, the gaskets needed – anything – the whole engine. Everything was taken down and gone over. She [Alice] had her girls so that each did a different [task] – you know, carefully working out the work of it . . . there would be Alice and two or three mechanics working on that as a team . . . And you picked it up at 5 o'clock and paid for it and it was all put together absolutely reconditioned like new, with a report on anything that might need doing or whatever.[7]

The idea that women car owners could attend to the work themselves with the aid of the garage workers was also an original and clever idea of Alice's. She offered a number of options, from the basics in car maintenance to full courses on repairs. Customers could attend by-the-hour sessions to learn from Alice's apprentices, as noted in the *Australian Automobile Trade Journal*, which wrote: 'A rather novel idea has been introduced by The Kew Garage . . . whereby girl car owners can wash, grease their cars and receive mechanical knowledge with the assistance of an apprentice of the garage at 2/6 per hour.'[8] In addition, Alice held lectures every Tuesday evening on 'The Care of Your Car'.[9] Alternatively, Alice offered a more intensive three-month course in maintenance and repair that was called 'a minor apprenticeship or finishing school in the arts of technological modernity'.[10] In Australia's motoring world, Alice was the epitome of female motoring achievement and, through her promotional efforts, its spokeswoman.

Alice was determined to make garage work a legitimate and respectable career for women. Her trainees were either kept in her employ or were placed in private chauffeuring positions, both in Victoria and interstate. Every garage girl Alice had trained and employed represented Alice's enterprise no matter where they worked. Each promoted Alice's 'brand' and was responsible for upholding her reputation, not only as Australia's first and only garage proprietor but as one of the best in the business. She was on top of her game and she expected the same exacting stand-ards from her trainees. In 1922, when asked by a journalist what she looked for in an assistant Alice replied 'without hesitation':

> The bright intelligent girl from college. Education is essential. I can train a girl to be a good driver in a year; but if a girl is to qualify as a thoroughly competent garage assistant, she must be in a position to undertake any repairs and to make spare parts if necessary. This involves a working knowledge of mechanics and trig – an eight years' course.
>
> ... Of course, a girl who qualifies fully can earn £5 per week and over. Then she must be able to use the lathe and make spare parts, which is a department in itself.
>
> My ambition is to turn a trade into a profession for women, and it is well within the grasp of those who have initiative and grit. It is a lack of initiative ... that makes the average immig-rant girl such a poor success in this branch. The department has sent out to me a large number of girls who have driven cars abroad. One soon learns that there is but one make of car that they can drive – the only make they will drive – that they have no knowledge of repairs, and, further, that they seem to find it impossible to learn Melbourne.
>
> Quite recently I have placed five of my trainees in positions, one in Sydney. There is a growing demand for the girl driver, as in most cases she undertakes a dual position, acting as com-panion to the woman of the house in the hours in which she is not employed on the car. Splendid opportunities await the girl who can combine gardening with driving. [11]

When commenting on the 'immigrant girl', Alice may well have been referring to the likes of Gabrielle de Fleurelle, known in the garage as Fleury. Hailing originally from the French country-side, Fleury had also worked for the British Land Army during the war. She was a 'first rate mechanic' and a 'very good driver'[12] but was hopeless at directions and, according to Marie Edie, 'most temperamental'.[13] Alice always told her staff, 'never admit to your passengers you don't know where you are', but Fleury was too honest to hide her flawed internal compass.[14] One day she became so lost in a maze of streets that she not only told her passengers she had no idea where they were, but broke down and cried in front of them. 'I did cry, I did cry!' Fleury told Claire, who thought it hilarious.[15]

It was rather ambitious for Alice to say that a garage assistant required eight years, training before becoming fully qualified. She was influenced by her father's exacting engineering stand-ards and Claire's university studies. Alice had not received any formal tertiary qualifications herself, nor had several of her staff, including Marie Edie, Lucy Garlick and Ruth Snell, her capable all-rounder and second-in-charge. But in order to succeed, Alice knew she had to set the bar higher than the standards set for men who, after the war, had access to mechanical training through the Working Men's College.[16] Alice's garage, therefore, was prac-tically the only avenue for women to gain successful training and employment in the motoring world in Australia. However, according to a March 1925 newspaper article, it seemed that Alice had created a more realistic four-year apprenticeship, at the end of which an employee could earn the award rate of £4 and 10 shillings per week.[17] At the time, Alice had nine employees, had placed twenty-eight others in employment and had had fifty mothers try to place their daughters since Christmas. With those numbers, she could afford to be choosy about the apprentices she took on.

Alice was wily enough to project her garage girls as being invaluable to her educated and upper-middle-class clientele in more ways than one. Those who were placed in positions as chauffeur and 'companion' to the woman of the house somewhat filled the domestic help gap in Australia. Many women's magazines of the day bemoaned the fact that upper-middle-class Australian households were suffering a 'Mary Jane shortage'. Apparently this was due to the tendency towards 'shorter hours, towards social equality, towards Bolshevism (if you like).'[18] Postwar, young working women took up increased opportunities in factories and offices, where the pay was higher and the work more social. On the domestic front, it was a far more attractive prospect for a young woman to be out and about as the family driver and gardener than being tied exclusively to the more tedious indoor tasks of cooking and cleaning. One article wrote with great enthusiasm:

> There are infinite and undreamt of possibilities for women in
> this profession, for, instead of a girl having to go into a home as
> a cook, or a companion, she can have the added qualifications
> of chauffeur, with added financial security, and can get a post
> as cook-chauffeur or companion-chauffeur.[19]

As Alice placed her trainees all over the country and took her tours beyond the Victorian border, the rest of Australia was taking notice. A newspaper article written when Alice took a group of passengers on a tour to Sydney in 1925 noted her novel trade and youthful 'boyish' qualities as a uniformed chauffeur. At this point Alice's enterprise had been going for eight years, yet no other women's motor service had appeared elsewhere in Australia. She was still the only all-women garage business and therefore a rare sight beyond Victoria. Alice made a point of saying that her garage girls were a well-known feature in her hometown: 'Oh, yes, everyone in Melbourne knows us, and all are quite used to seeing us in our uniforms.'[20]

In the same year another reporter – who, under the nom de plume 'Verity', wrote the regular woman's column 'Between Ourselves' in the *Brisbane Courier* – visited Melbourne's Lyceum Club. There she highlighted a number of women, including Alice, who had forged independent careers. Aside from the proprietor–manager of a motor garage, she met the chief medical inspector of Victorian schools, a university coach, a bookseller and a domestic science 'expert'. In an attempt to legitimise such Lyceum Club women who, apart from Alice, would have been older and most likely unmarried, the reporter wrote:

> among the attributes which I noticed they had in common were the air of happiness and a quiet confidence which was free from any hint of aggressiveness, but sprang from the knowledge that they were thoroughly efficient in the work they had chosen to undertake ... one might see a little party of women in no way eccentric or dowdy – as popular fancy still imagines the 'brainy' woman to be – but in appearance and demeanour quite indistinguishable from those who find their lifework in the home.[21]

It is telling that Verity felt the need to point out that such women were no different from housewives. It was a reminder that career women, particularly older women, were far from the norm.

Despite the freedoms of the decade, there were constant subtle and not-so-subtle reminders that a woman's primary place was in the home. There seemed to be a concerted effort to remind any woman who participated in a public space usually dominated by men that the domestic realm was her true calling. The combination of electricity and mechanical inventiveness that opened up possibilities for work and pleasure promised to improve the efficiency of housework. The domestic science movement even gave household management a somewhat professional status, with scientific guidelines for health and hygiene improvements backed by public health reforms – all with the presumption that women were responsible for such tasks (naturally, said tasks did not involve payment). A company that advertised itself as 'The House of Efficient Electrical Goods' even sold a 'home motor' that promised to 'lighten her housework'. It was a powerful motor, shrunken and domesticised, to 'run her sewing machine, clean her knives, polish her silverware' and 'drive a mixer for all cooking operations'.[22]

Such tensions between new opportunities for women and the pressure to remain in the home rendered Alice's business fragile despite her successes. Her youth, charm, public relations skills, and the direct benefits of her business to women shone a positive light that kept flickering only as long as the public supported her enterprise. Verity did just that, commenting on the 'roomy brick garage' and 'its large block of land, and a valuable stock of accessories'. Out of all the Lyceum Club women Verity interviewed, it was with Alice she spent the most time, visiting the garage and commenting on the 'young and capable' women she found there. The other Lyceum Club women might have been more academically qualified, but Alice was the one who most personified the modern era.

The era also continued to be one of mechanical inventiveness. In Victoria, the RACV received so many requests for endorsement of motoring devices that in 1921 the club formed a technical subcommittee. The committee managed to conduct proper tests on, among other things, a windshield cleaner, unpuncturable tyres and tubes, a steering lock and light dimmers.

Alice came up with some interesting inventions of her own, though there is no evidence that she sought such endorsement from the RACV. With her own well-established business and positive public relations profile, she probably didn't need to. A 1922 article in *Woman's World* tells us of the 'Anderson Hood', a canvas hood that was 'a combination of bright ideas from her own inventive brain', though it was produced on 'a sewing machine of quaint design' situated in the back of the garage.[23] No details of this design have survived, but the 'popular' Anderson Hood would have been successful at least until the mid 1920s. Hoods, detachable windscreens and car bodies were accessories made locally, particularly in the couple of years after 1917 when the importation of cars was restricted to engines and chassis. However, with the lifting of import restrictions came the increasingly popular hardtop – a result of improved mass-production techniques together with developments in fully enclosed metal body technology. Prior to the war, body frames had been constructed of joined wood covered with a thin body of plywood, mahogany or sheet metal by local coachbuilders, but now cars were more robust and protected passengers from the elements.

One of Alice's more quirky inventions was the 'Radi-waiter', a clever device that would have been very handy on her day tours. *Australian Motorist* described the Radi-waiter as 'consisting of a special tank, standardised in shapes to fit to popular makes of cars, which is clamped on to the rear of the top of the radiator beneath the bonnet'. One could then fill it with hot soup, tea or coffee, and be assured the contents would remain simmering throughout the journey by way of heat from the radiator. A tap at the base of the device provided instant hot beverages.[24] Without a photo or diagram, one can only imagine what the Radi-waiter actually looked like, or how much liquid it could hold. Presumably there was enough capacity for the six or seven people seated in a tourer to each have a cup. It was certainly a novel idea, pulling over to the side of the road with picnic basket at the ready and raising the hood for a steaming refreshment. The article mentioned that the Radi-waiter had been patented but this was not the case and, if not for the article, the Radi-waiter would have been lost to history. What were the pitfalls, if any? Did the Radi-waiter overheat? Lose its contents over a few bumps? Lace the beverage with an oily, petrol aftertaste? Perhaps, in the end, it was simply too quirky and not cost-effective enough to manufacture.

Alice invented another device that really had the motoring world stand up and take notice – and had motorists and mechanics lying down. She called it, rather awkwardly, a 'Get-Out-and-Get-Under', most likely a reference to a popular early automobile song 'He'd Have to Get Under – Get Out and Get Under (To Fix Up His Automobile)' written in 1908, the title of which was used for a film in 1920. The device consisted of a 'light platform on castors fitted with a head-pad of leather' used to slide underneath a motorcar for repairs. It folded smartly into a compact space to travel in the car. Claire said the two halves were 'about fourteen inches each, quite comfortable, on little castors – four castors, and a headrest'.[25] This was a very handy piece of equipment for anyone needing to examine under his or her vehicle, whether at home or on the road. In the trade, Alice was well known for her Get-Out-and-Get-Under, which she put to good use on the road and in her garage. She applied for an Australian patent for her device in September 1918, describing the invention as 'improvements in body supports for use under motor cars and otherwise', but she let it lapse the following year.[26] According to Claire, Alice didn't have the money to develop it or to take out a world patent, 'it was just too expensive'.[27] Had Alice known what lay in store, she might have reconsidered her patent's worth. In a 1922 interview she divulged for the first time how her Get-Out-and-Get-Under escaped Australia's shores and became an international hit for which the garage world is still grateful:

> In speaking of this device, Miss Anderson ruefully tells the story of how by failing to register the patent in America, the idea was stolen. Soon after the device was patented here, she had a visit from an American to whom she showed it. The American returned to his country, and a few weeks afterwards American trade journals arriving in Australia were loud in the praises of the 'Creeper', which had been patented by a U.S.A. firm – a device exactly similar to Miss Anderson's. 'Now', she adds, 'you can see my "Get-Out" and "Get-Under" illustrated in any American newspaper.'[28]

As Claire said, 'If there had been some businessman who advanced the money and done what had to be done, she might have made a nice thing out of it . . . now every garage has got them.'[29] The only kudos for Alice was a private one, knowing she had been the first to come up with the concept. She continued to use her invention in the garage, with one journalist being impressed in 1925 when she saw the device: 'Almost immediately I saw it in use, when, a "differential" being in need of attention, Miss Anderson's chief mechanic, very workmanlike in her blue jeans wheeled herself under the car and commenced operating on the faulty mechanism.'[30]

There is irony in the 'Get Out and Get Under' song, a risqué number full of double entendres about a man on the road whose car keeps breaking down while he is trying to make love to his sweetheart. It is about a man's frustration but the implication is that a young woman in a car with a man at the wheel is at risk of going too far if he gets his motor running – all the more reason for a woman to take charge of the wheel herself! The chorus goes:

> He'd have to get under
> Get out and get under
> To fix his little machine
> He was just dying to cuddle his queen
> But every minute when he'd begin it
> He'd have to get under
> Get out and get under
> Then he'd get back at the wheel
> A dozen times they'd start to hug and kiss
> And then the darned old engine it would miss
> Then he'd have to get under

Get out and get under

And fix up his automobile.[31]

This early automobile song foreshadowed the conservative uproar around the freedom and mobility of motorcars in the era of the modern girl. Despite the positive press, Alice's enterprise was always under one threat or another. The scandals that continued to plague her – both professionally and personally – threatened to damage her successes more profoundly than a stolen invention.

Those supporting Alice's garage, including Alice herself, encouraged women to occupy the very public space hitherto dominated by men. But in the act of playing at the edge of gender roles and expectations, Alice and her garage girls walked a fine line between acceptable perceptions of postwar modernity and rumours of darkly sexual transgressions.

16

DANGEROUS FREEDOMS

'It is not possible to estimate pressure by appearance'

(1920s *Shell Motorists' Index*)

Leading into the mid 1920s, among positive articles about the modern girl, there seeped a creeping social backlash that signalled female emancipation had gone too far. In Australia, comments in the press equated shorter skirts and freer clothing with loosened morals. Young women publicly smoking, drinking liquor and wearing the latest diaphanous gowns – especially in male company – was, to many, shaking the very foundations of civil society. One of the more reactionary responses, which happened to blame American influences, read:

> Returning to Australia after a long residence in the East, a worthy citizen seems to find that Australians are degenerating. He disclaims all wowseristic tendencies, but is aghast at the hold these American stunts – physical charms and popularity competitions – have taken on our womenkind. He fears that in a few years' time

there will be no standards of womanly modesty and reticence left. Publicity, he says, may be necessary for professional women and the like – but if he were Prime Minister any girl entering a beauty or popularity competition would be deprived of citizen rights, of a vote, a position in the public service, entrances to scholarships, the old age pension, etc. etc.: and he adds that at present we are only one step away from the 'gum-spitting' competition, which is the latest in the U.S.A.[1]

A letter to another newspaper from a concerned male citizen opined that:

the whole fact of the matter is that the present-day woman has received too much rope in the way of immodest dressing – diaphanous blouses, short skirts and silk stockings, etc. Seeing as she appears in a next-to-nothing state she thinks she has the charms of the male at her feet . . . have we not a clause within the Police Offenders Act whereby steps could be taken to compel women from dressing indecently?[2]

However, it wasn't the social backlash against the flapper and accompanying ideas of female freedom and sexual identity that threatened The Kew Garage so much as the idea of women publicly looking, behaving and working as men. Alice was caught between the cultural norms of the all–pervasive all–male garages and striking a unique note of female competence that was acceptable to the public. The press supported the garage by coupling the boyishness of dress and behaviour of Alice and her staff with concepts of femininity and businesslike efficiency. But it was a tightrope Alice walked between the idea that they were all marvellous modern women and that her staff housed a bunch of inverts. Postwar androgyny might have extended to fashionable ideas of lesbian chic with movie stars such as Marlene Dietrich and Greta Garbo, but it did not translate into the real world, especially in conservative Melbourne. The 1920s might have seen more women daring to identify and acknowledge their sexual tastes, but this was not necessarily reflected public opinion. If one happened to be sexually attracted to other women it wasn't illegal, as it was for male homosexuals, but it was still the 'love that dare not speak its name'.

In the 1920 edition of *The Home* there was a feature article about Alice and her garage, complete with photographs: one, a formal portrait of Alice in full chauffeur regalia behind the wheel of one of her large tourers; the other with two staff in breeches attending to a car's engine, one straddled over the bonnet. The article, headed 'The Woman Who Does', appeared to cast a positive light on the young woman garage proprietor, but it also threw a shadow of scandal by playing on the title of a notorious novel, *The Woman Who Did*. One of the most popular of the so-called 'New Woman' novels published in 1895 – and made into a film in 1915 – *The Woman Who Did* by Grant Allen tells the story of feminist heroine Herminia, who chooses to believe in an independent life rather than follow the conventional plans set out for her by her parents. She falls in love with a man and lives with him out of wedlock. After Herminia gives birth to a daughter, her lover suddenly dies and she is barred from inheriting his money. Despite her dire circumstances, Herminia's clergyman father rejects his daughter because she refuses to repent, and Herminia is eventually driven to suicide. The novel was typical of its genre in which male writers 'pathologised feminist aspirations by linking them to sexual decadence, immorality, and emerging homosexual identities'.[3] The article in *The Home* danced delicately around these noble and dangerous ideas:

> An air of youthful capability and the cropped hair she tosses out of her eyes suggest a sturdy self-reliant spirit. This very feminine business person is justly proud of her garage and the progress she has made thus far in her business . . . In the early days she met with some opposition. Women had not at the time encroached on this field of activity and it took a while to wear down the prejudice of the opposite sex. Now, only the rivalry of good fellowship exists between other garages and her own.

And of Alice's staff:

> All her assistants are girls and they manage the entire business themselves, from racing to some urgent call to roadside repairs and the varying phases of the garage work. Clad in business-like khaki coats and breeches, they make attractive and reliable chauffeuses.[4]

Alice was plagued by rumours intended to undermine her business. Ironically, some of the most damaging gossip came from internal sources. Jean Smith (Smithy) and Hilda Pickford allegedly became jealous as more staff were hired. According to Alice's sister Claire, Alice was partly to blame, as she made the mistake of developing too personal a friendship with them and not keeping enough of a professional distance:

> she got this first girl and she treated her as a buddy, which she discovered was a mistake. Then she got a third car and another

girl, and she was teaching them to do everything. They were good drivers. They were businesslike, quite good BUT they had tongues and they were jealous – and women, and they started spreading awful things about her . . . those two girls – then she got appendicitis and she thought, 'I mustn't let anyone know, if they think I'm not in their command', so she sort of cracked hardy about it and it was a ruptured appendix. That was pretty bad. And those two bloody girls spread round that she'd had an abortion. If you knew Alice, you'd know how impossible, Alice was the religious one and really the most moral one of all of us.[5]

Abortions, of course, were illegal, so this was a very serious accusation. The other issue was the hospital where Alice had chosen to be treated. Lancewood was closest to the garage, being just round the corner in Glenferrie Road. However, it was Alice's friendship with the matron of the hospital that added to the gossip mill. The matron was Jessie MacBeth, one of the women who had come upon Alice saving her Hupmobile from plummeting down the steep, muddy bank at Keppel Falls. She and her lover, nurse Kate Griffiths, lived together in Warrandyte and worked together at Lancewood. The fact that the two were a lesbian couple was the worst-kept secret in town. Alice's association with Jessie MacBeth helped spread the rumours that Alice, too, was a lesbian.

Claire thought Alice dismissed Jean Smith and Hilda Pickford immediately after she discovered their betrayal, but Alice's sister Katrine recalled two troublemakers being around for much longer and causing further havoc. By Katrine's account, it is not definite whether these two were the same two women Claire mentioned, nor whether the abortion rumour occurred around the appendicitis incident or earlier, when Alice had had her tonsils out at Lancewood. Katrine said she remembered two of Alice's employees being 'antagonistic and really hurtful people – really spiteful nasty people. She should never have had them on, these girls.'[6] Katrine couldn't recall one of the employees' names but she remembered a Jean Wilson (whose maiden or married name might have been Smith). This is what Katrine had to say about the time she took matters into her own hands:

> There was a hospital called Lancewood run by a Sister MacBeth. It was the nearest hospital and Alice had to have her appendix out very suddenly. She had her tonsils out at this place – and that was a disaster too because she hadn't told the girls that she'd be doing this. She thought that she'd be back the next day, but she wasn't. So they started a rumour about her that she was having an illegal abortion. So she had that to get over. Well then this appendix thing. She got somebody to post a letter from Ballarat, to say that she was taking the week off and going to stay up there. Well I went to the garage – this must be about 1924 I think – I used to make her a meal, she was no cook, and do her accounts and we'd have a talk and then I'd go home. On this par-ticular night I went to the garage and she wasn't there. She had two girls who were very jealous of – Alice was very naughty, really, she had at the time about eight on the staff and she had favourites, there was no doubt that she did. And two girls felt slighted. They never were given the driving jobs to do at night or trusted to do the more pleasant jobs, I suppose. Well when I went there, they said 'Huh. She says

she's gone to Ballarat, but we know where she is, she's round at Lancewood having another abortion'. Well in those days abortion was illegal and really the hospital would be in great trouble. So I went round to Miss MacBeth and said, 'Is Alice here?' And she said, 'No she isn't.' And I said, 'I'm not leaving unless you show me every room in the place – every ward!' And we had the most terrible stand-up row. I said, 'You've done the most terrible stupid thing! The girls know she isn't in Ballarat, they know she's here. Why ever couldn't you say that – let them come to see her.'

MacBeth said, 'She doesn't want that. She wanted to let [Ruth] Snell run the place while she's away. If she knows where she is she'll be round every 5 minutes wanting to know what to do.' I said, 'You should have known better.' Alice was absolutely furious with me . . . but she was, she really did a number of pretty stupid things. In that sort of way. She didn't realise – of course they spread talk that she was a lesbian and that she was always around at Lancewood having a go with Sister MacBeth (laughter).[7]

It was to her friend MacBeth that Alice went, not only when she required medical treatment but also when she needed a quiet night or two away from the garage. It was her only respite from the 24-hour, seven-day-a-week work cycle. At these times Alice ensured another employee stayed overnight at the garage in her absence. When asked about Alice's relationship with MacBeth, Claire remarked:

Oh, she [MacBeth] must have been 50. It was more a mother-hood relation. To her, Alice was a child – her child. And there would be nothing physical to it. It was a kind of mother love. And she was so protective and so understanding of Alice's needs. To just escape for a little while from the garage and have a quiet sleep and be looked after for one night. That sort of thing. She kept that little room for Alice. Whenever she wanted she could go in there and just put herself to bed. And I think that was real love. Mother distrusted her extremely . . .[8]

It was understandable that Alice needed to escape from relentless garage work. She was running a business that included holidays for her customers but Alice was lucky to ever get a full night's sleep. It wasn't unusual for her to be up until three or four in the morning. It was obvious Alice didn't have time to properly consider her own needs. When she cooked on her little gas burner in her tiny garage kitchen she threw together what was quick and simple: porridge, bacon and eggs, maybe a steak or a chop.

MacBeth gave Alice a good hot meal and a quiet place to sleep whenever she needed it. This is what Ellen Mary would have loved to offer her daughter, and, as Claire suggested, she most likely resented Jessie usurping her 'mothering' role – especially knowing she was a lesbian with influence over her daughter. It was only when Alice's parents left Narbethong and settled back in Melbourne that Ellen Mary had the opportunity to keep a closer eye on Alice's welfare.

———

In 1922 JT and Ellen Mary moved to Mont Albert, a suburb only a couple of miles east of Kew. JT had secured what appeared to be a relatively prestigious position as Consulting Engineer to the

Shire of Richmond, though it was only part time at two days a week, with the weekly salary of £4 and 4 shillings on par with Alice's garage girls. How the family managed to rent a house on such an income can only be guessed at.

The youngest Anderson, sixteen-year-old Joan, lived with her parents while she continued her two-year course at Burnley Horticultural College in Richmond. It is not surprising that Joan decided on Burnley. As Alice had written to their mother in 1919, when Joan was studying at Melbourne Girls' Grammar, her baby sister was not academically inclined. And again, the family could not afford for Joan to continue her secondary schooling unless she could acquire a scholarship, as Claire had done. Ellen Mary might have swayed Joan in this direction, having herself been one of Burnley's first female students when she studied rose pruning at the college in the 1890s, though she might not have approved of the idea of Joan becoming a professional 'lady gardener', which was almost as rare and unladylike as Alice working with cars. The fact that her youngest daughter ended up being employed by Edna Walling, the definitive female gardener increasingly lauded as one of the best garden designers in Australia, would not have stilled Ellen Mary's heart, however. Edna worked with men as their equal, and she designed and built houses as well as gardens, including her own dwellings in country Mooroolbark, where she only ever lived with female companions. Perhaps Ellen Mary's disapproval was somewhat assuaged when Edna appointed Joan as head gardener to maintain her design at Nellie Melba's Coombe Cottage Estate at Coldstream. Joan, along with two other women gardeners, lived in a cottage on the estate and it was Joan who was often invited to the 'big house' for a chat and a meal if Melba was feeling lonely.

Despite, or perhaps because of, Ellen Mary's geographical closeness, Alice kept her mother at arms-length by always reinforcing her busy schedule. There was no doubt Alice was incredibly busy but she was also acutely aware of her mother's disapproval of her chosen profession, of the way she dressed and the company she kept. Jessie MacBeth was not Alice's first female friend introduced to Ellen Mary who appeared to be lesbian. When she was younger, Alice had brought a few women home to Springbank whom Claire suspected were homosexual. Claire thought that even if Alice attracted lesbians, she was probably naïve and didn't know lesbianism existed until she was in her twenties:

> I think Alice, like me, never knew anything about lesbianism. I didn't until I was approached by another woman, when I was up at Mooroopna with the fruit canning thing when I was twenty-one . . . because these things were not publicised . . . I know Alice was having the experience. I know because twice when she only had the one car she brought a friend up. She said, 'Oh, this is Con' . . . That went on for not long – only about a week . . . [She] was a very nice woman, about her own age at the university, who rode a motorbike, who was a bit of a butch. And she and Alice had so much in common. Great fun and highly intelligent – did a science course, I think. Alice and she thought each other was fine. And then it got – suddenly it ended – bang. And I can think of why. The only reason why that was was Alice's first experience of homosexuality.
>
> And I know there were one or two much other more obvious cases of people who have sucked up to Alice. And Alice liked it for a while. Very feminine people. And brought

them up to show them Narbethong. Introduce them to the family and so on. I think Mother probably spotted it straight away but it doesn't take Alice long. And she was not. That just wasn't her at all. And Mother said to her, 'I'm worried because you want to get married and have children'. Alice said, 'Yes, I do but I can't saddle any man with the debts I've got. Until I'm clear of this, I can't think of it.'[9]

Claire's views on her sister's first experience of homosexuality may well be true but it is highly unlikely Alice was as naïve as Claire thought. Exactly what year Alice first met Jessie MacBeth and Kate Griffiths at Keppel Falls is not known but certainly it was early in her career. From that point on Alice would have been aware that lesbianism existed, if she hadn't realised before, and was taken into the bosom of experienced women 'in the know'. Moreover, Alice would not have begun her all-women business aged twenty without coming across lesbian women. The very nature of the work and the opportunity to dress in masculine attire naturally drew women who were sexually attracted to women. For butch lesbians in particular, Alice's garage was a safe place to blend in and be gainfully employed in the company of other women who were either like-minded or at least accepting of their sexuality. And of course Alice's business attracted lesbian clients. The 'university crowd', for example, was shorthand for a group of lesbians who worked and lectured at the University of Melbourne, many of whom had their vehicles maintained at the garage. As Claire mentioned, homosexuality was not publicised but once a young woman like Alice, who dressed like a boy and was an expert in mechanics, was 'in the know' there would have been every opportunity for her to act on any lesbian attraction she might have had. Who knows whom Alice might have shared the little bed with in her den next to the office. Once the garage was empty of staff Alice had full privacy.

Ellen Mary continued to be deeply concerned that there appeared to be no eligible man in Alice's sights. She was even more afraid Alice might have found men unattractive altogether or, at the very least, that she was putting her business in the way of any marriage proposition. Certainly postwar there was a shortage of eligible young men, but a letter Alice wrote to her mother the year her garage was being built suggested there were other reasons for Alice not stepping out with a man.

> 67 Cotham Road, Kew.
> 26 June 1919.

> My Dear Mother,
> . . . I will at once ease your sore heart by telling you that I have no understanding with any young man, and that you will be the first I will tell when I have.
>
> And if I choose to wear a ring because a bloke wished me to, need it worry you or anyone? No, certainly not.
>
> You are my Mother and ought you not have enough faith in your daughter Alice to trust her not to make a fool of herself? Because I have not the slightest intention of marrying until I get a man a durn sight better than me. Which is going to be jolly hard to find.
>
> I may as well tell you at once that I have already had one proposal of marriage this year, from a man who is now the other side of the world and whom you do not know, and are not likely to know. 'Twas the scream of the garage, and if you

had been here within the last month of course you would have
shared the scream . . . because the poor man was very much in
earnest and in love! Will tell you when I have time some day.

Now I have made you sit up and take notice, haven't I?

Ha. Ha. However, I adhere to my promise made above.
Conceited little cove your daughter is aint she? Well, who made
her so, I'd like to know? All your doing. I am keeping the letter
you wrote me last buffday, in which you say that you ought to
receive the congratulations not me. I agree. And am glad such
is your opinion.

. . . This letter will give you a variety of feelings but I cant
help it. I am always your faithful daughter and will stick to you —
ld. Alice[10]

Alice deftly dodged her mother's (and anyone else's) concerns
and, in doing so, raised more questions than answers. Is her reference to wearing a ring purely hypothetical, or did she in fact
wear one? If so, could it be that Alice chose to wear a ring to
discourage men from asking her out, or could it have been from
a woman? Why, indeed, did the garage girls think the idea of a
man serious about Alice such a 'scream'? Was it because he was
just not Alice's type or was it because women in the garage knew
Alice was not sexually attracted to men? No wonder Alice stated
it would give her mother 'a variety of feelings'.

When Ellen Mary visited, hoping for some time with her
daughter, she was often disappointed. A short repartee might
have been sufficient for work purposes but not for family. Even
a phone call to the office did not allow for a decent conversation between mother and daughter. Alice eventually wrote to
Ellen Mary:

It hurts me when you come to see me, and I cannot show you
outward sympathy as of old. It is all there but hidden. But
you know that. You could not help but feel it. It pains to have
to rush on with every day work, with you sitting pathetically
waiting for a single glance from your child.

That is why I hate one I love coming to see me at work.
Because I cannot think of the two at once. And work suffers.
And there are consequences.

And I hate the telephone for an ordinary conversation.
I can not talk easily over it ever, always am I wondering who is
waiting to speak next, and perhaps been switched on listening,
while we talk. Also, there is nearly always someone by when I
speak on the line . . .[11]

The conversations Ellen Mary seemed to want to have with
Alice continued to revolve around marriage and children. No
wonder Alice was concerned about people overhearing such
private conversations, be it those within earshot of the phone
or those listening in – inadvertently or otherwise – via the telephone exchange.

Aside from her mother, Alice was feeling pressure from other
sources. She was increasingly up against male proprietors of local
garages who didn't like her 'muscling in on their business', even
though Alice had established the first garage in the local area,
which meant that they, in fact, were muscling in on her.[12] The war
might have given women a greater sense of their own capabilities,
but the public arena was still dominated by men – especially in the
field of motors and mechanics, which was technically and physically demanding. By 1920 there were two other motor garages
in Kew: Oliver's in High Street and Owen's, also in Cotham

Road. The adjacent suburb of Hawthorn, which had started out as a hub of coach and carriage builders and dealers, had consolidated its motor garage services to eight establishments by 1920. There was also chauffeur competition close by with an exclusive taxi service, the Glenferrie Taxi Cab Company, which opened in Burwood Road, Hawthorn, in 1920.

Ilsley-Holliss, which moved from Wellington Street, Kew, to diagonally opposite Alice's garage at 71 Cotham Road in 1923, was particularly nasty. Staff there tried to steal customers and, as Claire said, 'did the dirty' on Alice by 'spreading stories, lies, the usual sort of things . . . all the things that business people do'. No doubt some of the stories included sexual transgressions. Of all the local garages, it was only the men at the Williams Garage round the corner in High Street who, according to Claire, were 'honest people who didn't do the dirty'.[13]

Alice was professional enough not to complain publicly of any problems she had with other local garages. They might have used underhand tactics to steal customers but no one, it seemed, could fault Alice's skills as a chauffeur, and her mechanical abilities rivalled those of any man. One newspaper reported that Alice 'pioneered the way to motor garages for women, and made a greater success of it than most men could', and that 'many men have watched her repair a car or even change a wheel where they had failed and marvelled at her resource and initiative in driving'.[14] Alice also trained her staff to a greater standard than most. It was more than likely the male-run garages were disparaging of The Kew Garage because Alice's talents could put many a mediocre garage man to shame. Other garages would have perceived the high standards of Alice's garage girls as proof that they were 'unnatural'. It must have riled many men in the motor business that Alice was so capable and savvy. Her garage girls were well trained, polite and impeccably dressed. No one more than Alice knew she had to be better than a man to thrive in a man's world, and she instinctively understood the importance of developing and promoting a brand that would be attractive to the public.

———

Despite both internal and external pressures, Alice was undeterred in appointing women who were not only boyish but could easily pass as men. In fact, there was an element of enjoyment in shocking and confusing the public at a time when youthful female masculinity was being celebrated. One day a male passenger who hurriedly jumped into the front seat abruptly turned his head towards Alice and, looking confused, asked, 'Are you a man or a woman?' 'I'm a woman and you'd best watch your step!' Alice replied with a grin.[15]

A similar thing happened to Ella Jones, who drove for two years in London before working at Alice's garage and was described by her colleague Lucy Garlick as 'tall, thin and not feminine-looking'. Garlick tells of Jones having fun one day with a man who had rushed into the garage while she was working on a car. The man, desperate to relieve himself, called out, 'Anywhere here where a bloke can have a leak?' Apparently Jones looked up and simply pointed ahead to the one toilet at back of the garage. The man had naturally expected to see another male but once he recognised Jones as a woman, his face suddenly became 'covered in confusion'. Meanwhile, Jones 'did not bat an eyelid'.[16]

Two other garage girls, Ruth Snell and Fleury, were also masculine in appearance. Snell was Alice's most loyal and dependable all-rounder, who Alice had left in charge when she had her tonsils out. Photographs of Snell dressed in overalls and shirt require a keen eye to determine that the image is actually of a woman. Snell is naturally stocky, with a handsome face and square jaw. Her hair, rather than fashionably bobbed, is cut short back and sides with a slight fringe and parted like a man's. Her physical stance, too, whether pouring oil from a can, squatting or standing legs akimbo, is tellingly masculine. Photographed in a dress coat, stockings and ladies shoes, she looks awkward and uncomfortable.

Fleury was by all accounts a rough sort with a sharp sense of humour. She was 'country French, not Parisian . . . a very masculine type: thickset, sturdy, strong, definite, practical, emotional. Terrific person, great talent,' recalled Claire, who had befriended Fleury when they worked together in the garage.[17] Prior to working for Alice, Fleury had been in the British Women's Land Army and had been badly burnt when a farm tractor caught fire. Marjorie Horne, another boyish garage girl who lived with three other unmarried women, recalled that Fleury's temperament was just as explosive: 'Oh, she was a character. All round the garage were French phrases. And if she lost her block – Oh!' She had a temper, did she? 'Oh, did she what!!' laughed Horne.[18]

The garage girls had their collective independence from men and freedom of movement on public display. The daughter of one of the garage girls, on reflection, even stated that wearing breeches and laced gaiters had the added benefit of protecting the garage girls from sexual assault, especially when they were out on the road. For those 'in the know', their acts of gender bending opened up within the garage a communal (though still private) sense of a new sexual identity. They dared to dream of another way of life different from that of their mothers. Alice's garage was also as safe a public haven and workplace a woman attracted to women could hope to find.

Then there were the women customers who supported the garage, a number of whom were in lesbian relationships. Apart from nurses MacBeth and Griffiths, there were the University of Melbourne women, such as Margery Herring with her Baby Austin, whose sister-in-law, Nancy Houston, worked at the garage as driver and mechanic. Margery was a lecturer at the university and principal of its residential college, Janet Clarke Hall, from 1925–27. She was in a relationship with a woman called Dorothy McIntyre, a mothercraft nurse, who owned a large property in Vermont where they both resided.

A photo taken in the garage shows two garage girls in breeches, gaiters, shirts and ties, sitting on the running board of a car in a romantic embrace. Their arms are around each other and they are smiling, staring into each other's eyes. It is a private moment in a public space that tells us something of the relationships at play between women in the garage. Whether the women were reflecting a reality or acting out of fun does not change the fact that they felt free enough to be photographed in this manner. Another such photo exists of a young Alice in full chauffeur uniform, complete with driving cap covering her short hair. She is sitting on a bank with a client, an attractive young woman, whose long hair is woven into plaits. They are holding hands. Alice's head is turned towards the young woman and her arm is around the woman's waist. Alice's sisters commented on this particular photo, stating that the woman with Alice was a 'family friend' and that Alice was just pretending to be her 'boyfriend' as a bit of fun. Again, whatever the context of the photo, it reflects a freedom to play with gender stereotypes and sexual identity.

Frankie and Claire denied Alice was a lesbian, often suggesting certain men she might have had an interest in or men who were taken with her, though neither provided names of any man she definitely courted at any time. Katrine, on the other hand, suggested Alice's probable proclivities by saying that Alice 'walked with the girls', though she never qualified anything beyond this slightly oblique yet suggestive phrase.[19]

It was garage girl Nancy Houston's only child, Mary, who, in her late eighties and suffering from Alzheimers, said without any prompting: 'She [Alice] was a lesbian. How do I know? I don't know, maybe my mother told me. But everybody knew. Everyone just knew.'[20]

Mary fondly recalled going to work with her mother around 1923, when she was just four years old. She remembered Alice being very amenable to the barrage of questions she threw at her as Alice slid in and out from under cars on her Get-Out-and-Get-Under. 'She [Alice] didn't treat children as nuisances,' said Mary, though Nancy kept telling her daughter, 'Miss Anderson [is] taking lots of parts out and needs to concentrate on putting them all back in the right place' and, 'Please wait for Miss Anderson to come out from under the car to get some fresh air before you ask questions!'[21] Mary, however, took her cues from Alice, and Alice didn't seem to mind at all. To Mary's great delight, Alice would often pop her in the back seat when she drove passengers round town. Some of Mary's most exciting childhood moments were spent in the back seat of one of Alice's cars, seeing the world whizzing past as Alice took passengers to their destination.

She also recalled her mother saying that Alice was physically very strong. 'They were simple engines. You opened up the two sides [of the bonnet] and the engine was just sitting. I was brought up to just not touch it. Mother said she [Alice] would lift a whole engine out of the bonnet on her own – something that it often took two men to do.'[22]

Mary also remembered Miss Snell, although her little ears heard 'Smell' when she was first introduced. Alice called her staff by surname only and it became the cultural norm at the garage, just as it was with every other garage in town. Clients would have known them as 'Miss' or 'Mrs So-and-So' but among garage staff it was, 'Pickford!' 'Fleury!' 'Jones!' First names were only used for Alice's motorcars, all of which were female: the Chandler was known as Natalie, and there was a Noel and a Phyllis. As one newspaper remarked, 'in a woman's garage there can be no cars with men's names'.[23]

There is no doubt Alice and her staff enjoyed subverting the masculine/feminine dichotomy by calling each other the name their fathers or husbands had passed to them by way of surnames. This put them on par with their male counterparts but outwardly put their femaleness, or at least their femininity, into question. Giving Alice's cars female names, on the other hand, was not so much about public perception as an in-house joke. They were flirting with the idea of sexualising and controlling vehicles just as men were wont to do. And they were also continuing the long tradition of all vehicles – be they motorcars or ships – being denoted 'female'.

It wasn't surprising that Alice decided to adopt Joan of Arc, the masculine, sexually ambiguous cross-dresser, as an emblem for her enterprise. Canonised in 1920 by Pope Benedict XV, Joan of Arc was a popular figure in the 1920s and a symbol for feminist movements of the time. Joan of Arc captured the essence of noble difference and magnificent quest and the same could be said of Alice, albeit on a more pedestrian scale. Joan of Arc's military success in pushing the English out of France in the early 1400s also resonated with the Great War just ended; a war that Alice, full of nationalistic fervour, would have dearly loved to be part of. In 1917 *Australian Motorist* even reported on 'A Jeanne d'Arc in Khaki' – the name given to Lady Dorothie Fielding by a wounded French soldier, when she worked as a British ambulance driver and received many honours and decorations from several Allied countries 'for giving to all, almost daily, the finest example of contempt for danger and devotion to duty'. [24] Alice created her own armour in the form of a tiepin inspired by Joan of Arc and inscribed with the phrase 'Qui n'a risque rien, n'a rien' (nothing ventured, nothing gained).

———

Alice's armour, though, was never going to protect her from JT. She had learnt from him, looked up to him, worked alongside him, helped to make his Blacks' Spur Motor Service a success, but the disappointments kept coming with all the failed businesses and all the financial pain that followed. Alice felt her father's pain as well as her own, and each time it drained a little more of her respect for the man she adored. The worst disappointment her father gave her finally pushed Alice over the edge. Not only did she ban JT from ever stepping foot in the garage, she refused to ever speak to him again.

It was Katrine who was first burdened with the discovery of what their father was up to:

In 1920 I was working down at John Sharp's in South Melbourne
– I was 19 I suppose – and Father came down one day and asked

me to come into town to meet his mistress. I knew nothing at all about his mistress – nothing at all. I said yes. I was always very close to my father, although Alice was his favourite. She went on trips with him and looked after the horses and they were very close. We went to a restaurant . . . Here was a beady-eyed woman . . . I was very embarrassed. Apparently I was supposed to persuade her not to have an abortion – she was pregnant by him. He was nearly frantic with fury at the idea of her doing this and he thought I'd persuade her. It just didn't do any good at all. I was so horrified . . . We thought that all the time he was up at Traralgon it was on his engineering business. Meantime he was keeping this woman down at Traralgon as another Mrs Anderson . . . anyway Alice was always the person that I'd talk to. I rushed out and told her. If I had ever realised the effect it would have on her I would never have told her. It was only – we used to share everything.

And she said I will never speak to him again . . . She said I don't care how many women he has, it's the deception. I trusted him all these years and when he said he didn't want me to come to Traralgon with him . . . He lied.

She said I can't forgive that. And she never did. And he was absolutely . . . he was broken up enough by Stewart, but he was more broken up in a way by Alice. I felt really guilty about telling her. Not knowing that she would react like that.[25]

On one level his affair was surprising, since despite all the family's ups and downs Ellen Mary and JT, it seemed, remained very much in love. No matter how often JT admonished Ellen Mary she rarely had a bad word to say about him, even though there were times she was sorely tested. Years back, before Stewart was born, Miss Annie O'Neil, previous governess to the Andersons, discovered a letter from JT's sister-in-law to JT telling him he needed to sire a son to inherit the old family property back in Ireland. Miss O'Neil hid the letter but Ellen Mary soon found it and Katrine recalled there being an awful ruckus when Father came home.[26] By the time Stewart had died, 49-year-old Ellen Mary knew she was never going to be able to bear another child. How it must have plagued her, knowing her husband's grief at losing their only son and the pressure he was under to have a living male heir who could inherit his family's property. She must have dreaded the moment JT might introduce another boy to their family by way of another woman.

Unfortunately for JT, his mistress chose to have an abortion despite his begging. There was no child, no boy. And there was no need for his wife to know anything of the affair. Except that he'd made the grave mistake of bringing Katrine into the picture. Perhaps it was the guilt he felt over this mistake, and the fact that his favourite daughter was not speaking to him, that drove him to confess everything to Ellen Mary. Of course this did nothing but rub salt into every wound his 'Dear Life' had ever suffered. Her lameness, being forced out of Melbourne society when the family had no roof over their head except for the summer cottage, losing Stewart in the most terrible of circumstances. Katrine thought her father's misdemeanour was the result of 'the male menopause' but the truth was, aside from JT's urgency for another son, men of his stature were practically expected to have a mistress as a matter of course.[27] It was the done thing and wives, if they ever knew or suspected, simply turned a blind eye. For Alice, however, turning a blind eye was never something she could do. The two were so close she could not imagine Father ever deceiving her, but he had. She had believed him when he said she couldn't come to Traralgon with him because of 'business', even though she worked beside him through every other town, he the surveyor and she the chainman and general sidekick dutifully following orders. Alice was too principled to accept any excuse. In her eyes their special bond as father and de facto son could be no longer.

17

BEYOND THE GARAGE

**'Should the owner wish to proceed further than five
miles from the border, he must obtain a permit'**

(1920s *Shell Motorists' Index*)

In The Kew Garage's first few years Alice was central to all that
happened onsite: motorcars pulled into the driveway for petrol or
a top-up of oil; women arrived for driving and car maintenance
lessons; the office phone rang with requests for chauffeuses, roadside repairs and tour enquiries; drivers came and went, signing
themselves in and out of the large appointment book on the office
desk. Alice thrived on the busyness, working the lathe, checking
an engine, sliding beneath a car, jumping into the driver's seat.
No matter her task, she was always up with a ready grin and
a bit of friendly banter. Frankie, who'd never possessed Alice's
natural ease with people, once asked her sister, 'Why are you so
popular?' Alice laughed and said, 'Well, nobody sees me for any
more than ten minutes!'[1]

It was true. Alice *was* the garage; she made herself indispensable and there was little time to gather breath. When justifying her workload to Ellen Mary, Alice wrote, 'When you think, you must see that you it is that have taught me how to work and work and work, thinking work a play. So how then one must stop?'[2]

Claire also understood her sister's position. 'She was caught up in it. She had to go on. If you didn't go on, you might as well give the whole thing away.'[3]

Alice's only respite, it seemed, was Jessie MacBeth's spare bed at Lancewood Private Hospital, where Alice continued to go despite the vicious gossip her visits generated. Lancewood had become Alice's bolthole, and Jessie her chief friend and confidante. MacBeth and her companion, Griffiths, were no strangers to the rumour mill themselves. They ignored the sniggering regarding their sexual proclivities, got on with the business of running a hospital and chose their friends carefully.

On one rare occasion when Alice did take time off to spend with a friend, the results proved disastrous. Alice was determined to go horse riding. She sorely missed her Narbethong days when riding was an everyday joy. No motorcar could replace the feeling of moving as one with an animal born to gallop. Without the time to take off to the bush, Alice enquired locally and found a riding school willing to hire out horses a few streets from the garage in Princess Street, Kew. She chose a bay mare for her friend and a cob for herself. Alice would have preferred more lively horses than these short and sturdy beasts, but since her friend was a horseriding novice, they were a sound choice.

It was a November day in 1920 when the two trotted along the back streets of Kew. Some roads were still without asphalt and the hooves made a gentle clopping on the compacted earth. The fragrance of late spring drifted from gardens fronting Victorian and Federation homes of varying splendour, the larger ones with expanses of front lawn and pebbled, semicircular driveways. There was also the occasional paddock. They passed one or two motor-cars parked in the street and a few moving vehicles of the motor and horse-drawn variety. As they headed east along Wellington Street, beyond the recreation hall and bowling club, the sound of a cable tram and several passing cars signalled Glenferrie Road ahead. Lined with shops, people and traffic, it was a busy thoroughfare. Affected by the noise and the timidity of its rider, Alice's friend's mare quickened its pace and was suddenly out of control in a runaway gallop. Alice forged ahead, attempting to get herself between her friend and the upcoming intersection but she could do nothing except watch in horror as the terrified mare ran into the intersection and collided with an oncoming car. The blow to the horse was fatal. Miraculously, Alice's friend survived without any major physical injury, though emotionally she was a quivering wreck. Alice was mortified. If she had possessed a gun, the mare would have been put out of its misery in an instant.

Unfortunately, such accidents were not uncommon. More and more motor vehicles were taking to the roads but horses, and particularly horse-drawn vehicles, were far from disappearing. While there had been road accidents since roads had existed, the unprecedented strength, weight and speed of motor vehicles compounded the dangers. The combination of animals, people, trams, motorcycles, bicycles and motorcars all sharing the same thoroughfares was becoming increasingly precarious. In Victoria alone, horrific accidents involving all sorts of gory combinations of wheels, hooves and humans were reported regularly in the newspapers: 'HORSE BOLTS WITH LORRY. COLLISION WITH TRAM. DRIVER'S SKULL FRACTURED'[4]; 'SENSATIONAL COLLISION. TRAM AND LORRY. MOTORMAN INJURED.'[5]; 'FATAL COLLISION: BOLTING HORSE DASHES INTO MOTORCAR'[6]; 'FATAL ROAD COLLISION: MOTORCAR STRIKES HORSE'[7]; 'MOTOR-CYCLIST KILLED. ACCIDENT AT BRIGHTON. STRUCK BY MOTOR CAR'.[8]

Traffic volume in the 1920s was far less than it is today but traffic control and accident prevention measures were poor. Motorcars had no electric indicators and relied on hand signalling. There were no traffic lights and little signage, and speed limits varied depending on the council district. In Victoria, it was a matter for a policeman or witnesses to confirm that a motorist had been driving 'recklessly, negligently or at speed' – all of which were open to interpretation.[9] Motorcars had been fitted with speedometers since the early 1900s but the ability to randomly clock a driver's speed was difficult, if not impossible. It took until 1926 for speedometers on Victorian police motorcycles to attempt to measure excessive speed by motorists, but many of the readings proved inaccurate. The Royal Automobile Club of Victoria inaugurated its Vigilance Corps in 1920 in an effort to control reckless and inconsiderate driving, and by the mid 1920s the RACV was delivering public campaigns warning all forms of traffic to take greater care. Those riding bicycles and horses were advised to keep to the far left of the road, and faster-moving motor vehicles were to pass on the right. Motorists were warned to look out for tram passengers carelessly jumping off in front of cars; pedestrians were warned to look out for traffic before stepping onto the road and not to loiter in the middle; cyclists were told not to hitch lifts on other vehicles.

Even Alice, a consummate driver, had not been exempt from a collision when at the wheel. *The Argus* reported that she knocked down a fifteen-year-old cyclist in Bridge Road, Richmond, on a Tuesday morning in May 1924. How the accident happened and who was at fault wasn't mentioned but the boy suffered a severely lacerated scalp and had to be admitted to the Melbourne Hospital.

As the road toll in Victoria in the 1920s increased from well below one hundred to over three hundred per annum, many outraged citizens sent letters to the editor demanding changes. Alice was no exception. Her letter to *The Argus* of 6 April 1925 made suggestions for accident prevention in the high-traffic areas of Melbourne's popular beachside suburbs.

MOTOR ACCIDENTS
TO THE EDITOR OF *THE ARGUS*

Sir – The accidents occurring in ever increasing numbers at each week-end horrify everyone, yet no laws are framed to help prevent this increase. Would it not be possible to make the St. Kilda Esplanade to Elwood, and the Brighton to Mordialloc roads only open to one-way traffic on Saturday afternoons and Sundays? This has been done in every other great city the world over where necessary and has been found most effective.[10]

Improvements came gradually over the next decade with traffic lights, increased signage, parking restrictions, pedestrian crossings and better-quality roads. The number of horses used for transport purposes gradually decreased as the number of motorcars continued to rise. By the mid 1930s Australians ranked fourth in the world as motor vehicles users. Cars were here to stay and, along with them, the ongoing conundrum of traffic control and accident prevention.

As a result of the accident involving Alice's friend and the death of the bay mare, the horse's owner sued Alice for damages of £37 and 2 shillings – an unusually large sum and much more than the deceased horse was worth. Alice chose young lawyer and Kew Garage client Robert Menzies to defend her in court. She had come to know Mr Menzies through Frankie, who had rented rooms from his parents when he was at university. *The Age* reported that the plaintiff claimed 'the mare, a quiet animal, was hired to [the] defendant for her use, and that no authority was given to her to permit anyone else to ride the mare'. This seemed a ridiculous argument seeing that Alice had hired two horses in the one transaction. Mr Menzies then contended that 'the hirer of the mare had a right to allow the animal to be ridden by a friend . . . and that the accident occurred through the mare proving so hard-mouthed that is was impossible to check its career'. Unfortunately for Alice, the judge concluded that, while Alice's conduct in attempting to save the mare was 'meritorious' and 'while there had been no breach of contract', he 'considered the defendant's friend had not taken reasonable care while galloping the horse' and so ordered Alice to pay £21 to the plaintiff.[11] Claire was of the opinion that Australia's future prime minister did not fight the case hard enough, nor was he interested in doing so:

> she [Alice] hired Bob Menzies, who'd just got through and was a very young barrister and very full of himself and all his possibilities. And he went to court and lost the case. And he didn't even ask how old the horse was or get any evidence as to its condition. That's the brilliant Bob! He wasn't

especially interested, petty sessions and all that . . . of course
Bob, after all, what did he know about horses?"[12]

By the mid–1920s Alice had relaxed her hold on the garage
enough to take on activities off the floor. She led interstate tours
that went for weeks at a time and began to write articles for
women on motoring. Alice would not have taken on these sorts
of commitments if she hadn't felt confident there were garage girls
able to run the business in her absence. It was late 1925 when
she told a women's magazine that of all the young women who
had signed on with her for the four-year apprenticeship, not one
had turned back. The magazine suggested that:

> this may be due in part to the condition on which she takes a girl
> into the garage. She [Alice] insists on a three-month's trial. If at
> the end of that time she sees the making of a good chaffeuse in
> the applicant she apprentices her. As a rule if the girl is unsuit-
> able she tires of the work herself before the probation period
> ends. If, on the other hand, she 'sticks' the first three months of
> grease and instruction she is almost certain to turn out to be a
> good chaffeuse.[13]

It appeared Alice had taken great caution after the two trouble-
some garage girls who had caused so much havoc, by setting up an
apprenticeship system that weeded out problems before they could
negatively affect her reputation or the smooth running of her
business. Alice was never wanting when it came to eager applicants: there were plenty in the city and Alice also had country
garages on the lookout for her. However, suitable girls were 'not
so easy to find as one might think', she remarked. 'Only a few

of those who apply are the right stamp of the work.' In regards to those who were successful 'motor girls', Alice said they had such characteristics as 'patience, good temper, reliability, a certain amount of daring, but good judgement to know when taking a risk is justifiable and when it is not'.[14] In other words, a garage girl was required to be not unlike the boss herself.

The tours Alice took beyond the Victorian border weren't exactly holidays, in charge as Alice was for the whole operation. But they were an enjoyable way of varying the work, creating income and reinforcing her presence nationally. By 1925 Alice had conducted tours of Tasmania, South Australia and New South Wales to the Queensland border. Prices of £2 and 2 shillings a day per person included 'every expense', namely a daily hamper and quality overnight accommodation. For the most picturesque scenery Alice would travel 'as slowly as forty miles a day so that it can be really seen and appreciated'.[15]

It was the summer of 1925 when Alice's enormous Chandler touring cars were winched over the top rails of a steamer headed for Tasmania, the island state known for its pristine wilderness and magnificent coastline. Among the passengers on board were Alice, at least one other chauffeuse and their touring party. The steamer took them through the quiet waters of Port Phillip Bay and beyond the heads to Bass Strait – a choppy 310-mile (550-kilometre) strip of ocean with a reputation for making many a traveller seasick. The trip included driving and walking tours through rainforests, waterfalls, lakes, beaches and the ruins of Port Arthur's convict penal settlement. They stopped and picnicked along the way, collecting twigs to fire up the billy tea. All around was bush that was home to a host of native birds and animals including cockatoos, galahs, parrots, wallabies, wombats, iconic Tasmanian devils and the soon-to-be-extinct Tasmanian tiger.

Then, in early autumn of 1925, Alice drove a party the 540 miles (870 kilometres) to Sydney in one of her Chandler tourers. The 'straggling collection of roads and tracks' they took were still used for unofficial Melbourne-to-Sydney speed trials.[16] (Three years later the stretch would be known as the Hume Highway.) The tourers passed through historical Victorian towns such as Euroa, where the infamous bushranger Ned Kelly robbed the local bank in 1878 and Glenrowan (where the Kelly gang had their final shootout with police two years later). They crossed over the mighty Murray River to New South Wales and continued inland through numerous towns, villages and dots on the map, gradually heading northeast towards the coast. Once the party had arrived in bustling Sydney, Alice met with a journalist who, as with other reporters, perceived Alice as novel, youthful, capable and boyish.

> During the last few days Sydney has witnessed the unusual – a girl chauffeur, complete in uniform, cap, knickers, coat and leggings driving a large new Chandler, christened by its boyish owner, 'Natalie' (says the Sydney Daily Telegraph).
>
> You ask this slip of a 'boy-girl' (who looks about 17, and confesses still to being on the happy side of 30), for her credentials, and out of voluminous pockets in her chauffeur's jacket comes a heterogeneous heap of letters and tickets; in fact everything to which a man's coat pockets imagines it holds exclusive rights, except a tobacco pouch and pipe . . .
>
> . . . Miss Anderson had just returned from a trip to Tasmania when some passengers wanted her to bring them to Sydney. And

here she is, driving about our streets, waiting to make the caves trip on Tuesday, and later to return to Melbourne. [17]

This tour was so successful that Alice advertised yet another leisurely three-week round trip to Sydney and the Blue Mountains in 1926. The cost was an extravagant £35 per passenger, confirming that Alice was continuing to cater for society's well-to-do.

In 1926 Alice also began writing motoring columns for one of Australia's most popular monthly women's magazines, *Woman's World*. At the time *Woman's World* had twelve thousand readers Australia wide and was also popular in Britain. Journalist and fellow Lyceum Club member Frances Taylor, who was three years Alice's senior, founded the magazine in 1921. Frances and Alice were sisters-in-common. Born in St Kilda, a seaside suburb of Melbourne, to British-born parents, Frances's childhood was also partly spent in New Zealand with her family. Her entrepreneurial streak and sense of adventure matched Alice's. In 1916 Frances rode a horse from Mildura to Melbourne in twelve days – a trip of 337 miles (542 kilometres). Five years later, *Woman's World* arrived at the beginning of a burgeoning market in postwar women's magazines, and became one of the most longstanding in its class. Not only was Frances the magazine's founder, she was also its editor and business manager, something unique in the British magazine world. In keeping with her profession, Frances wore smart tailored suits but she was equally at home mucking about at her country property in Kangaroo Ground wearing breeches, riding boots, shirt and slouched hat. Like Alice, Frances had a slim, boyish figure, and her vivid blue eyes were a match for Alice's cheeky browns. She was described as having a 'casual' manner and her speech as 'brusque', suggesting a no–nonsense woman with unswerving confidence.[18]

Alice's first article appeared in the May 1926 edition. Her writing was authoritative and direct. One can imagine Alice speaking these words face to face with her pupils, ticking off points as she went.

> You will hear many people say, 'Oh but it is nothing to be able to drive; it is the mechanical part of the car that takes time to learn.'
>
> One may say with equal truth, 'It is not hard to learn to dance – a few lessons will teach you all the modern dances.' True – but how well?
>
> The advertisements say: 'Six lessons licence guaranteed.' Also perfectly true, but what of the car the lessons are given on?
>
> . . . What one cannot possibly learn in a few lessons are things such as: 1 – What is happening inside the engine to make it go? 2 – How to know if it is making a sound that it should not make. 3 – What that creak means in the right back wheel as one turns a corner to the right? 4 – Why the engine is hot? 5 – Why the gears will not slide in smoothly?[19]

Alice also shared her own experience of learning to drive, though she always referred to herself in the third person. Hers was an example to readers to persevere despite the difficulties they may encounter as women.

> The writer was taught on the Blacks' Spur Road, ten years ago by men who considered that women should never be allowed to drive over the Spur. Every time the query was put, 'Do you think I will ever be able to drive over the Spur?' the answer

was 'Perhaps, some day, but it is no place for a woman to be driving.'

The consequence was that it was five months before she was taken up for her licence; but, during that time, she had been through the boggiest tracks on the mountain, and learnt how to get out of them without damaging the car . . .'[20]

Other articles written by Alice for *Woman's World* were equally pragmatic. Her advice for a basic on-board toolkit was to have 'a Jack, a Pump, a Lever or two, Some Patch-quick, a Hammer and Pliers, A Spanner, Screw-driver, and Chains if it's wet. And several assortments of wires.'[21] She listed all the technical reasons why a starter may fail to start the engine; how to check and test tyres; how to look well ahead and develop 'the use of brakes into a fine art'. Similar motoring advice appeared regularly in several journals and newspapers, though articles providing practical motoring advice written by women for women were so scarce as to be practically nonexistent. By the 1920s even *Australian Motorist*, which had championed women's motoring almost from its inception in 1908, had done away with its 'Women Awheel' section, although the occasional article on women and driving still appeared within its pages. In Australia, Alice was by far the most authoritative voice on women and motoring.

———

The year 1927 was to be a milestone for Alice: she would be turning thirty and would have been in the motoring business for a decade. Celebrations were in order. Alice began by planning her most ambitious group tour yet: an eight-month world trip limited to six clients only, commencing in February 1927. The trip would depart by boat from Melbourne to America where, on arrival, Alice would purchase a motorcar to 'tour Uncle Sam's country at leisure'. Since American motorists drove on the right-hand side of the road and their cars were accordingly left-hand drive, Alice thought it best to purchase a motorcar in the United States rather than take one of hers. From America, Alice planned to cross over to England and then go on to the Continent. Unsurprisingly, the booking was full, save for two seats, as early as January 1926.

By 1928 Alice hoped to revisit Great Britain without paying clients. This would be a holiday she would cherish, giving her time to catch up with relatives she had not seen since childhood. It would also give her the opportunity to finally meet some of the women garage owners who had inspired her own enterprise. She would especially want to meet the women proprietors of the X Garage in Kensington, for which Alice's Kew Garage was the Australian agency.

Established in 1920, the X Garage – so named as an inside joke to indicate its unknown quantity – was set up by a group of women friends who had been ambulance drivers during the war. Its main financier was the notorious lesbian oil heiress Marion 'Joe' Carstairs who had inherited her grandfather's fortune as one of the founders of Standard Oil. Three years Alice's junior, Joe's roots were American but she was born in London and spent her childhood being shuffled back and forth across the Atlantic. When World War I broke out Joe, like Alice, wanted to support the war effort, though Joe was driven more by a thirst for adventure than nationalistic fervour. She was just sixteen when she joined the American Red Cross in 1916 and was sent to drive ambulances in France, the same year Alice was learning to drive over the Black Spur.

As Alice was building her garage, Joe continued her life of action in Dublin, driving British officers who were fighting Sinn Féin. She then headed to northern France and, with other women, relieved male drivers clearing battlefields, supervising prisoners of war and reconstructing towns. While Alice and volunteers of the Australian Red Cross took returned soldiers on picnic outings, Joe and her cohorts chauffeured officers responsible for clearing ammunition dumps and for the reburial of the dead in Imperial War Graves cemeteries. The conditions under which Joe perfected her driving skills were more severe than Alice had ever dealt with: roads sunk with craters, buried artillery, barbed wire, blasted trees and trenches. When tyres were punctured or springs broke, as they frequently did, the women carried out their own repairs. With such experience under Joe's belt it was a natural progression to return to England after the war and set up a chauffeuring service with two of her friends, sisters Barbara and Molly Coleclough. In similar fashion to Alice, Joe cut her hair short and wore masculine clothes for work and pleasure, though her crew cut and tattooed arms made her more mannish than boyish.

The X Garage chauffeuring business was situated in a converted stable in a cobbled cul-de-sac off Cornwall Gardens in Kensington. The three women lived in a flat above the stable. Just as Alice had done, they purchased large touring cars, though the Daimler landaulettes were more luxurious than Alice could ever have afforded. In 1920 the plush six-seater Daimler, a British brand favoured by the Royal Family, was priced in English pounds at £1000 to £1300 for the chassis alone. The X Garage had a list of illustrious clients to match, including James Barrie, author of *Peter Pan*, and the Sultan of Perak. As with Alice's chauffeurs, the X Garage staff wore jackets, caps and ties. On their advertising brochure a quote from Sir Ernest Birch, KCMG, described the X Garage women in terms similar to those that appeared in the Australian press when describing Alice and her staff: 'I have always admired in all of you your pluck, your enterprise, your hard work, your excellent driving & your cheeriness.'[22]

Joe took advantage of her wealth to fashion a lifestyle as glamorous, adventurous and outrageous as anyone living through the roaring twenties could envisage. She was intelligent, stylish, sporty and theatrical. Her numerous affairs with beautiful women were legendary: Dolly Wilde (who was as mannishly lesbian as her uncle Oscar had been effeminately gay) wooed her; she seduced the stage and film actress Tallulah Bankhead, and had an intense affair with Marlene Dietrich. How Alice and Joe would get along meeting face to face for the first time would be fascinating: their similarities were as numerous as their differences.

Before Alice ventured overseas, however, she planned to travel through Central Australia with her friend and fellow Lyceum Club member, Jessie Webb. 'I think everybody should know something about her own country first,' Alice remarked when discussing her intention to travel to Britain for her next holiday. The heart of Australia, known as the 'never-never', represented what was arguably the real Australia: it was vast, relatively unspoilt and largely unknown to Europeans, the majority of whom clung to cities and towns on the eastern seaboard. This six-week round trip, commencing on 6 August 1926, would be the first real holiday Alice would have taken in nine years. However, she was not going to let up on an opportunity to pursue publicity: she purchased a new Austin 7 – the smallest car on the market – to prove that such a vehicle was capable of completing the 3558 mile (5774 kilometre) return journey. More specifically, Alice purchased the Austin 7 chassis and fitted up the rest of the car, including a partial body, in her own garage. Of course it was common at the time to import car chassis and purchase locally built bodies, giving Alice not only an economic advantage but the ability to allow for extra luggage by doing away with car doors altogether.

The challenge of driving a Baby Austin over record distances leveraged a sponsorship deal with a South Australia–based Austin distributor, Butler Nicholson, as well as Universal Oils. Butler Nicholson agreed to publish updates of the trip in South Australian newspapers in return for telegrams detailing Alice's progress. Universal Oils would arrange for the necessary fuel and oil supplies to be delivered along portions of the route from Adelaide to Alice Springs in the Northern Territory. Alice would also have a notable send-off involving a celebratory farewell and evening departure from Melbourne's illustrious Lyceum Club.

18

TO THE NEVER-NEVER

'Go where you will'

(1920s *Shell Motorists' Index*)

The heavily laden Baby Austin had just come off the most comfortable surface it could hope to feel against its tyres. Roads in the cities and major towns had only recently been refurbished with macadam and bitumen that was relatively smooth, and too new for potholes. However, the deep V-shaped gutters needed to be negotiated with great care. All other roads beyond were simply packed earth that was dusty when dry and muddy when wet. The motorcar was equipped with pneumatic tyres but the wheels still did not afford much comfort on the rougher roads. The Austin 7 model compensated for this somewhat with two hidden weapons: the front seats had 'float-on-air' cushions with air-filled rubber bladders beneath the leather, and the chassis was an unusual triangular shape that flexed over uneven surfaces so that the car seemed to glide over bumps and dips. Alice and Jessie were as equipped as they could be for the harsh terrain to come, though conversation would be almost impossible over the incessant engine noise from which the open-aired Austin had no insulation.

The most direct route to Adelaide from Melbourne is north-west through central Victoria via the large gold rush mining town of Ballarat. But this was not the road they travelled. Alice and Jessie decided to take the longer, coastal scenic route, passing through Geelong and on to Torquay, Lorne, Apollo Bay and Port Campbell. Here, the Great Ocean Road carved into the rugged cliff face was yet to be completed. The survey work had begun in 1918 when thousands of returned soldiers worked to build the road, but it was a painfully slow process with only picks, shovels and horse-drawn carts at their disposal. This was not just a matter of giving returned soldiers work: the road was viewed as a lasting monument to those who had died in battle. Soldiers who had survived the trenches physically intact sweated for their mates who lay buried on foreign soil. A memorial arch at Eastern View was the tollgate where Alice paid 2 shillings and sixpence as the driver, and Jessie 1 shilling and sixpence as the passenger.

Any newness the little motorcar possessed was soon washed away along this strip. It was cold and rained heavily, making the narrow road muddy, slippery and full of grooves. To their right were steep cliffs; to the left, a sheer drop to the ocean. The two women clung on, battered by the salty winds and driving rain against which the motorcar's canvas hood gave little protection. Once at Peterborough, the Great Ocean Road met with the Prince's Highway, recently named as such following the Prince of Wales' visit in 1920. Alice and Jessie continued along the highway, driving a little inland and then back along the coast, through Warrnambool and towards Portland, the bay of which was the site of the first European settlement in Victoria.

Why did Alice and Jessie choose this treacherous stretch when they could have taken a safer inland route? George Broadbent, manager of the touring department at the RACV, provided a possible answer when he wrote, 'the coastal road to Port Campbell is the approach to some of the most remarkable and wonderful coastal scenery in Australia'.[1] In 1925 Broadbent bemoaned that the road had shown little improvement and still carried 'a good deal of sand and rough tracks', though he had also written in one of his many popular *Broadbent's Motor Routes* that certain routes 'render the passage arduous enough to make him feel – well, that he has accomplished something, and imbuing him with that pleasurable sense of self-satisfaction through conquest'.[2] The combination of magnificent scenery combined with the arduous challenge was more than enough to attract the likes of Alice. And she also had her sponsors to consider: they wanted her to test the Austin to its limits. The more exciting Alice's progress reports, the more readers would travel vicariously alongside her. An *Adelaide Mail* promotion depicted Alice and Jessie as two 'intrepid lady motorists' attempting a great feat in a tiny car that, with patriotic echoes of the recent war, would 'win through and through' because it was 'British'.[3] Such confidence was boosted by the telegram Alice sent to her sponsors once they had survived this coastal stretch, published in *The Advertiser*: 'even without chains the Austin 7 came through easily'. The newspaper championed the 'two plucky women' and their success thus far.[4]

From here the women most likely pulled away from the coast at Portland to continue northwest along the Prince's Highway. They crossed the Victorian–South Australian border and continued west to Mount Gambier, an extinct volcano surrounded by picturesque lakes and mountain scenery. It is generally hotter and drier in South Australia than Victoria, but being early spring the weather was still mild. It was reported that Alice and Jessie intended to stop and explore the 'interesting caves said to be inhabited by huge wombats' at Naracoorte on the South Australian border.[5] The caves are famous for preserved fossils of mega fauna, including giant kangaroos and wombat-like creatures that became extinct approximately sixty thousand years ago. If they did take time to see the caves, however, it had to have been a short visit, because Alice and Jessie arrived in Adelaide on the afternoon of 10 August, only four days and approximately 879 miles (1414 kilometres) after their departure from Melbourne. Assuming the little car averaged a realistic speed of 30 miles per hour (48 kilometres per hour), Alice and Jessie would have needed to drive around seven hours each day to make it to Adelaide in four days; if they averaged 20 miles per hour (32 kilometres per hour), they would have driven eleven hours a day!

Just outside Adelaide, the Austin's sponsors from Butler Nicholson and the Universal Oil Company met Alice and Jessie on Mount Barker Road. After a few handshakes and congratulations all round, the gentlemen escorted the women to the Butler Nicholson Garage in town. Once there, a newspaper photographer set up a publicity shot with the four sponsors standing side by side behind the motorcar. The Austin's hood was drawn back and Alice remained in the driver's seat, wearing her full leathers and driving cap. Her left hand rested on the wheel while her right arm leaned casually on the car's outer body. The photographer caught her wry, nonchalant smile as she turned to face the camera. Jessie, seated beside her in hat and overcoat, looked pleased, if a little weary.

The two women spent the night resting in Adelaide. Although it had less than a third the population of Melbourne, Adelaide was booming, mostly due to Holden's Motor Body Builders Ltd, which by 1926 produced more than half the national output of motor bodies.

The following afternoon Alice and Jessie, replenished with food, water, petrol and oil supplies, were on the road again. This time it took them only one day to drive the 208 miles (335 kilometres) north to Quorn, South Australia. They travelled through the flat plains of Banggarla and Kuyani country, now populated by wheat crops and sheep and cattle, towards stretches of desert and scrub where tiny outposts replaced towns. As they approached the southern base of the Flinders Ranges the soil turned from pale yellows and greys to the deep rusty red of the outback. Quorn was a centre for the railways. Sheep and cattle sales kept the place busy and there were four hotels to choose from. Jessie rested while Alice sent a telegram to her sponsors advising all was well. The only misfortune, Alice reported, was the loss of a wallet containing £1 between Wilmington, a mere spot on the map, and their current stopover. Echoing her father's engineering nous, Alice also remarked in her telegram that 'it seems to me a tremendous mistake to set the railway up before they have got the water. Sometimes the people have to dig 1500 ft. for water, and then after all their trouble it may turn out to be brackish.'[6] Fresh water, even in the towns, was a precious, sometimes rare, commodity.

Newly laden with supplies, the Austin departed Quorn on 13 August and forged further northwest, bypassing the Flinders

Ranges to the east towards Oodnadatta. This was Australia's vast never-never stretching far beyond the horizon. Here, the world's most ancient continent lay unmasked, ruggedly beautiful and unforgiving. Man-made roads gave way to sandy riverbeds, scrub and gibber plains scattered with crimson pebbles. Kangaroos and wallabies bounded in the distance and emus strode on their ungainly legs faster than a horse could gallop. Alice navigated the Austin carefully, avoiding dangerous stretches of sandy soil and damaging rocks. To be stranded here could spell disaster. Some motorists went so far as to carry carpet runners to roll out to drive over the sandiest patches. However successful, it was a slow and ponderous business, getting out and laying a few feet of two tyre-width lengths of carpet, driving over them, then repeating the process as needed. The Austin, though, was far too small to carry such bulky items and the two simply relied on their driving skills and a few doses of good luck to get through.

Few motorcars travelled through the outback. The exceptions were local lorries and cars with truck flatbeds – a precursor to the classic Australian 'ute' – on which drivers carried children, dogs and provisions. In general, motorcars were neither affordable nor practical for desert travellers. Roads were patchy at best and motor engines radiated heat into the cabin, which made travel in desert daylight hours potentially scorching, and there was the risk of breaking down miles from any garage or access to spare parts. Aside from rail, people traversed by camel.

For anyone less prepared, it would have been extremely risky. Alice pulled the hood across for shade, rolled up her sleeves and did away with her driving cap. She was happy to have the breeze through her hair and her face and arms tanned while Jessie kept her mosquito-netted pith helmet on and wore long sleeves to protect her delicate skin from burning.

As planned, they travelled off the beaten track but always kept the great Overland Telegraph in their sights. Operational since 1872, the miraculous strand of electric wire stretching from Adelaide to Darwin not only provided communication between towns but was often the only lifeline for the stranded traveller. The trick was to damage the line and wait in hope for a camel-riding linesman to appear on the horizon. Linesmen spent their waking hours traversing the 1988 miles (3199 kilometres) of overland telegraph ensuring essential communications were maintained. It was a desperate soul who risked fines or even imprisonment by deliberately sabotaging the line, and it could take several days for a linesman to appear, but the alternative was to risk perishing alone.

Each day before sunset Alice and Jessie stopped and stretched. After hours of noise, engine vibration and rough terrain their bodies took time to adjust to the stillness. The air smelled of dried earth and eucalyptus. Sparse scatterings of ironwood and coolabah trees made long shadows across the pebbled desert sand dotted with mulga and spinifex. Galahs, magpies and red-tailed black cockatoos called overhead. After examining the best spot to set up camp, they stomped on the ground to deter venomous snakes and cleared their sleeping space with a shovel. Rocks were not only uncomfortable to lie on but the scorpions that hid beneath them were nocturnal hunters with powerful stingers that could cause long-lasting pain and swelling. The two also made sure to collect firewood before the sun became a dusky crimson disc on the horizon. In the desert, darkness fell as quickly as a lid is shut and, with it, the heat of the day disappeared. The fire warmed them against the chill air and, above, the great dome of stars twinkled across inky blackness. Small nocturnal creatures scuttled about and the howls of dingoes in the distance reminded them they were not alone.

The two women were still making their way through the desert when they came to the end of their food rations and three-day water supply. The open air only increased their hunger and, left with only bacon, bread and jam, Alice took the on-board rifle and shot them something to eat. The only way to quench their thirst was to make billy tea from the warm, brackish water that bubbled up from the mound springs and rusted pipes of man-made bores. The tea, even with a few spoons of sugar, tasted like Epsom Salts. Their lips swelled and cracked when they washed their mouths with the water.

The Austin continued northwards. To the east they spotted Lake Eyre, the largest salt lake in Australia and the lowest point of the Great Artesian Basin that covers almost one-sixth of the continent. Its dry bed was an alien landscape glistening on the horizon and playing on the eye so that its distance from any point was unclear. Far beyond its outer edges, stretches of white pebbles and patches of yellow, pink and lavender stone glared under the sun, but there was not a plant in sight. To the parched traveller, it was a cruel mirage promising a quenched thirst but offering only salt. To the Arabana people, it was the sacred Kati Thanda. The little Austin made its way above the enormous underground water system as it tackled desert plains that had suffered the worst drought in forty years. Alice and Jessie witnessed a landscape ominously strewn with animal carcasses and bones, and stone piles marking the graves of people who had succumbed to the elements.

While the women struggled for food and fresh water, rain finally hit the dust further north. As they drove on, desert flowers burst from seeds lain dormant for years, throwing up a carpet of dazzling colour. In some parts the ground was covered in royal purple. There were patches of marshmallow flowers with mauve or pink petals on tall stalks that reminded Alice of hollyhocks. Scarlet peas in the distance looked like bright parrots squatting on the roadside. Among the spinifex were large yellow daisies and white everlastings with yellow centres. The two women danced about in delight, picking samples as they went. In a few days the flowers would disappear as if they had never existed.

Further to their west lay Coober Pedy, an anglicised version of 'Kupa Piti', where opals had been found in 1915. To protect themselves from the desert heat, opal miners had built their living quarters in underground dugouts. Decades later Coober Pedy would become the opal capital of the world and the original one-room dugouts would be expanded to accommodate a unique underground city.

On 20 August, exactly fourteen days after they had left Melbourne, Alice and Jessie arrived in Oodnadatta, the tiny township just south of the Northern Territory border with a population of approximately two hundred and fifty. The only doctor for many miles resided here, but thankfully the women were healthy enough not to require his services. Oodnadatta was the terminus for the Great Northern Railway, also known as The Ghan, which originated in Adelaide. Oodnadatta would have to wait three more years before the rail extension to Alice Springs would finally come into operation. Meanwhile, camel drivers provided the most efficient transport for goods and people, especially from Oodnadatta to coastal Darwin in the Northern

Territory. Camels had arrived in the mid 1880s, along with their cameleers, from Afghanistan and India to assist with expeditions to the outback. They quickly became essential to communications and transport throughout remote Australia, but their days were numbered: it would be only another ten years before these ships of the desert would be superseded by planes, trains and automobiles.

Aboriginal people had a strong presence in Oodnadatta, where a home had been established by the United Aborigines Mission, a religious organisation for assimilating children. The missionaries, like most settlers, had little if any understanding of the local Arabana culture. They labelled the Aboriginal people 'nomadic blacks', and regarded them as wandering, unsettled and 'steeped in superstition'.[7] One missionary wrote: 'They came to Oodnadatta in the course of their wanderings, made a camp outside the town, of any odds and ends of rubbish that they could pick up, settled there for perhaps a few months, and then disappeared into the bush from whence they came.'[8]

In reality, they were highly skilled nomadic hunters and gatherers. And around Oodnadatta they found ways to survive as best they could – there were Aboriginal camel boys employed by Afghan teamsters, while others attempted to continue their traditional lives on the fringes of the settlement. A 1923 article in *Woman's World* titled 'Woman in Central Australia' interviewed a Mrs Aiston who lived on Mungerannie Station, east of Oodnadatta. She reported that a local Aboriginal group came to trade hand-carved wooden clubs, 'wirrahs' (boomerangs) and 'pirrhas' (bowls) at her homestead each week. 'Recently I told them that all provisions, tea, sugar, flour etc., were now very dear,' Mrs Aiston said, 'and one old maker of weapons replied, "Yes, boomerang be very dear too now!"'[9]

The trauma of colonisation and their brutal casting as a race of savages without status or state would have been starkly confronting in places like Oodnadatta. It was likely the first time Alice had come into direct contact with any of it. Aboriginal people were not so present in the cities and even in the Victorian bush, where Alice grew up, groups had been killed or taken to mission stations years before her family had settled there. In fact, Aboriginal people were practically invisible to the majority of white settlers except when they appeared in what we recognise today as racist and derogatory advertising. One of the recurring ads at the time featured 'Lubra Kate', a smiling Aboriginal woman who was the face of McCarty's oil and grease lubricants. Aside from its obviously lewd inferences, the word 'lubra' is itself an offensive name for an Aboriginal woman.

Alice and Jessie finally made their way across the South Australian border into the Northern Territory. Their first stop was Charlotte Waters, the site of one of the most desolate homesteads. It was also one of a few key strategic points where the Austin's sponsors had prearranged delivery of essential oil and fuel supplies. Such homesteads were tiny domestic oases many hundreds of miles apart. It was a feat to even find them and the lady of the house was often alone, waiting weeks at a time for her husband to return from working on the station, as was the case with a woman Alice noted simply as 'Mrs A'. The Austin's noisy little engine and the dust plumes stirring from its tyres brought Mrs A out on her verandah when Alice and Jessie were still a mile away from the house. She greeted her bedraggled guests with great enthusiasm, inviting them to sit around her large kitchen table while she poured the best cup of tea the two travellers had tasted in a long time. The three women chatted, sharing stories and experiences. Alice was particularly taken with Mrs A's fashionable appearance and her cheerful outlook. *She even wears her hair short and shingled as young women do in the cities*, Alice observed. Mrs A brought out her collection of up-to-date fashion books and catalogues. 'I make all my own clothes you see, and I like to keep up with the new styles.' Alice and Jessie were surprised to learn that many of the settler women in the outback were similarly fashionable, and positive in their outlook. Jessie wondered if Mrs A felt lonely being so far away from everything. No, she didn't really. It was her friend 'Mrs B', who lived in an even more isolated place further north, who Mrs A felt sorry for. Alice and Jessie were to hear this story time and again from women in similar circumstances, but 'none ever complained of being lonely', Alice quipped.[10]

The three women sat down to a simple meal of beef and vegetables. To Alice and Jessie it felt like a royal banquet. The meat came directly from a bull slaughtered on the station. How did meat in such quantities stay fresh in the heat, Alice wondered. Mrs A showed them her meat house, the most important room at the station. It was a shaded wooden structure built high off the ground with reeds from a nearby creek and protected with a dado of wire netting at the bottom. Alice was impressed at how 'beautifully cool' it was. Mrs A also explained that the slaughtering was usually done in the cool of the evening and the meat salted while it was still on the gallows. With each kill the meat was shared with others. 'When my husband kills one of our bulls he divides the carcass with our nearest neighbour. Then our neighbour returns the compliment. No money is exchanged here, you see. Everything is paid by cheque.' Despite the coolness of the meat house, the Charlotte Waters homestead was surrounded by nothing but gibber plains. The only trees Alice saw were in the dried creek beds. 'Do the creeks ever have any water in them?' Alice asked. 'Well, they ran last Sunday, but that was the first time in five years!' the lady of the house replied.[11]

Alice gave the Austin its usual once-over. Despite it looking worse for wear, the little car was holding up extremely well. The two women bid fond farewells, Alice promising to post Mrs A pins and needles on her return to Melbourne, which she did. Such basic items were hard to come by in the outback and Mrs A was keen to keep her treadle sewing machine in working order.

Off they drove to Horseshoe Bend that curved in the shape of a horseshoe round the Finke River, one of the largest rivers in Central Australia. Alice and Jessie were relieved to see fresh water, even though it was mostly shallow. The surrounding area was very sandy and a challenge for any motorcar. Here they met a woman who had been on the road for three months. Her husband was bringing down cattle and she was driving ahead in a motor truck to prepare their camp. The woman looked exhausted, and when she told Alice and Jessie she had just 'ploughed through sixty miles of thick sand with only an aborigine to help her', they were not surprised. She could not believe it when Alice and Jessie said they were on a driving holiday. 'Anyone who took a trip through central Australia for pleasure must be a lunatic!' she cried. Both Alice and Jessie laughed, though Jessie was beginning to think the woman was right even as Alice rattled on about how getting accustomed to the primitive conditions was 'half the spice of adventure', confessing to finding fun in 'trying to get a morning wash out of half a cup of water'.[12] Further on, the two met a woman who was happy being as far away from city life as possible. The only thing she regretted, she said, was missing out on meeting Pavlova, the famous Russian ballet dancer who had toured the country earlier that year.

Motoring ahead, the little Austin passed through Heavitree Gap, a huge crevice from which the MacDonnell Ranges soared. Beyond this 'gateway to the north' a flourish of galahs and sulphur-crested cockatoos burst from clusters of date palms planted by Afghan cameleers to remind them of home. Then, three weeks from starting out, Alice and Jessie finally arrived at their destination, Alice Springs. Success! Not only had the Baby Austin proved it was more than up to the task of traversing the harshest of conditions, it had achieved what it had set out to do: be the smallest car to travel from Melbourne to Alice Springs – an estimated distance of 1620 miles (2607 kilometres). Covered in red dust, the Austin tooted its arrival and the few townsfolk on the street waved enthusiastically. No one in Alice Springs had ever before set eyes on such a tiny motorcar.

The town of approximately forty settlers was completely unre-markable, famous only for the fact that it was situated in Australia's centre and was the nearest town to iconic Ayers Rock some 292 miles (470 kilometres) away. The name Alice Springs was a mis-nomer, as were so many other outback town names promising generous bursts of fresh water when all that was available was the now-familiar brackish artesian water that had made Alice and Jessie's mouths so sore. The place was dry and dusty, but to two exhausted women it was paradise. Alice sent telegrams to her sponsors, telling them the car had travelled from Oodnadatta to Alice Springs in three days without a hitch. In that distance, she told them, the car had used three tins of Tydol Oil and twelve gallons of petrol. Alice pronounced the Baby Austin a 'perfect car' and was full of praise for her sponsors, stating the arrangements had been 'excellent'.[13]

It was tempting to rest and enjoy the local hospitality but there was no time to dillydally: Jessie was expected back at the university and Alice had a business to run. The next day they turned the Austin around and tracked south back to Oodnadatta. However, between Alice Springs and Oodnadatta, the plans for their return went awry: Jessie decided she would leave Alice and find her way home by train from Oodnadatta. The plan had always been for the two to set aside six weeks for a round trip. But Jessie, at forty-six years old, had had enough of the never-ending driving and harsh conditions. For three weeks she had sat next to Alice with hardly any room to move. The Austin was so tightly packed, even getting in and out was an awkward clamber with little legroom and running boards stuffed with gear. There was the incessant engine noise, the heat, dust and flies, freezing desert nights, the lack of fresh food and water, and terrain one would only attempt today in a four-wheel drive with two spare tyres. For three weeks the two women shared everything from personal hygiene to their most intimate thoughts and feelings. Alice might have thrown a positive spin on the whole adventure but the conditions were ripe for testing even the best of friendships to the limit. As one newspaper reported:

> Miss Jessie Webb, who set out on the journey with Alice Anderson, found that life on this route was not all that she fondly imagined. Conditions were too primitive for her and she retreated in good order, leaving Kathleen Hall, of the Methodist Ladies College to step into her sleeping bag and share the campfire of Alice Anderson.[14]

Alice waited in Oodnadatta for her mate to come up by train. It was a long way for Kath to travel, especially at short notice, but it was still school holidays and she was happy to pick up the mantle and ride in the little motorcar that had made the news-papers. It was a welcome sight to see Alice standing on the station platform when Kath arrived on the evening of 27 August. She waved madly out the window and Alice ran alongside the slowing train to meet her carriage. After greeting and hugs, Kath picked up her luggage and looked around. 'Where's the motorcar?' she asked. 'Oh, I sold it to someone in town earlier this evening,' Alice said. Kath stood, mouth agape, certain her friend was joking. Alice shrugged and smiled. There was no car to take them home so they were going to 'train and walk', Alice said matter-of-factly.[15] What was Alice thinking? How many necessary items could the two of them carry on their backs? This was not what Kath had signed up for.

At least Alice agreed the two could stay a couple of nights in the transit town before setting off. Whether Alice had planned it or not, staying in Oodnadatta gave them the opportunity to cross paths with another adventurous traveller who was also being reported in the newspapers, and who was making an even greater journey halfway round the globe.

―――――

On 5 August 1926, the day before Alice and Jessie had set out on their mission to drive to Central Australia in the smallest car ever built, a young British pioneer aviator by the name of Alan Cobham was landing his de Havilland DH50J seaplane in Port Darwin. World War I had given aviation technology the impetus required to develop effective fighter planes and now the race was on to conquer the challenge of distance. Cobham was almost halfway towards his goal of breaking the world's long-distance flying record, which would be achieved once he successfully made the return flight to London. However, his single-engine, four-cabin, wood and canvas biplane was extremely flimsy and dangerous. This was also before the age of jet propulsion and by necessity the plane required many refuelling stops and regular overhauls. It was the main reason Cobham added floats, which converted the plane into a seaplane. From Calcutta to Australia, in particular, there were more options for landing on water than on a specially prepared aerodrome, especially in an emergency.

Cobham's trip had thus far been fraught with unexpected challenges. The plane had flown successfully through monsoons in India and Burma, but soon after leaving Baghdad a blinding sand storm had forced the plane to fly as low as fifty feet above the great swamp area of Basra. 'Suddenly there was a violent explosion,' Cobham recalled. A bullet, supposedly shot by so-called 'natives' on the ground, had gone through the cabin, hit the petrol pipe and ricocheted into Elliot, his on-board engineer. Cobham managed to land the plane on a muddy bank but, to his great distress, his good friend died from his wounds the next day.[16]

Cobham finally reached Port Darwin later than expected with a replacement engineer he hardly knew. There the Australian Navy, which assisted in removing the floats and preparing the plane for land travel, gave Cobham a 'rousing welcome', which somewhat lifted his spirits. At least he had made it to Australia in one piece.

The rest of Cobham's Australian trajectory saw him flying way above Alice and Jessie and the little Austin's ant crawl across the continent. Alongside news of the Austin's remarkable feat, it was the plane's arrival in Melbourne that drew the largest crowd and created the biggest headlines. When Cobham landed at Essendon Aerodrome on 15 August the attendance was overwhelming. One newspaper reported: 'Man Who Has Braved World Flight Ran From City's Wild Welcome: London to Melbourne; Famous flying ace is welcomed by over 100,000; Women faint when crowd stampedes'.[17] 'The moment our wheels touched the ground the crowds on all sides broke through the barriers and rushed at us,' Cobham recalled with alarm. He had to stop the propeller to avoid people being chopped in half. Cobham was then extracted from the cockpit by the police and air force and escorted to the safety of the nearby hangar rather than face the marauding hordes. The novelty and romance of a dashing young British aviator flying all the way from the mother country was irresistible to the people of what was then Australia's capital. Beyond the romance was the sense that long-distance flight promised a future where distance no longer mattered.

On 30 August Cobham visited Melbourne's Stock Exchange, housed in the same gothic building as the Lyceum Club. There, Cobham announced that 'Australia was on the eve of a big aviation boom', and advised members of the stock exchange to 'get in early and catch the windfalls'.[18] Cobham saw aviation as being on the brink of enormous civil and commercial possibilities, and he was right: four years later the jet engine was invented and it was only a further three years before the world's first modern airliner, the Boeing 247, graced the skies.

Cobham left Melbourne and flew north through the centre of Australia on his way back to Darwin. Once there he intended to refit the plane's floats for his return flight to London. As there were no maps sufficiently accurate, the overland telegraph was, according to Cobham, the only means of finding his way through the continent. The line itself could not be seen from the air; it was the passage of poles from which the bush had been cut away that provided the aerial guide. From the cockpit he saw the broad sweep of Australia's centre as nothing but 'one huge natural aerodrome', where severe weather was minimal and one could land 'practically anywhere'.[19] He took only hours to fly above the land Alice and Jessie had taken weeks to traverse, and on 31 August Cobham landed in Oodnadatta.

To fly all the way from England and descend into a tiny country town in the middle of nowhere was nothing short of miraculous to the people on the ground; just days earlier they had witnessed the smallest motorcar ever manufactured drive into town. For Cobham it was not just a matter of needing to fuel up: he was on a mission to promote aviation as a key to the future of remote communities. Little did he know that in only two years from this landing, Australian Reverend John Flynn would begin using aeroplanes for what was to become the Royal Flying Doctor Service. The RFDS was, and still is, an essential support to those requiring urgent medical attention in remote locations across Australia.

Cobham's plane began its descent towards the small crowd of people on the ground, their necks craned as the twin wings turned downwards and straightened for landing. Its tyres hit the dirt and a blast of wind and red dust drove the people back. Once stopped, they rushed forward, undeterred by the noise of the still rotating propeller. A couple of men climbed onto the wing to welcome Mr Cobham to their little town south of the border. Cobham extracted himself from the cockpit. He pulled up his goggles, produced a handkerchief from his breast pocket, dabbed the perspiration from his face and gave a wave. The crowd cheered and waved back. Alan Cobham was a small, dapper gentleman who, even after hours of flying, charmed all with his neatly moustached film-star good looks. He jumped lithely from the wing to the ground and exchanged quick meetings and greetings with the enthusiastic locals. It wasn't long before he and Alice, also a young, handsome, suntanned figure in shirt and breeches, were engaged in a deep discussion about their various adventures and the future of aviation.

It was a thrill for Alice to meet Cobham: not so much because of his celebrity status but because she was already in the first stages of studying for her own pilot's licence. Immediately before Alice left for Central Australia, she had attended the Aero Club and passed her medical test. For Alice it would be a hop and a skip from motorcars to aeroplanes. *She would get her pilot's licence and start her own flying school; she would lead passengers on air tours throughout Australia, taking as much time to fly from Melbourne to the outback as a motor tour from Melbourne to the Dandenong Ranges.* From the bush girl who ran with the wind and galloped on horseback, to the young woman who found freedom behind the wheel of a motorcar, Alice was ready to fly above the clouds.

19

A TRAGIC LOSS

'Acceleration is costly'

(1920s *Shell Motorists' Index*)

Alan Cobham was interested in Alice's own feat across the desert but he was understandably perturbed by her decision to sell the Austin in Oodnadatta. 'Don't you think you should have finished in Melbourne?' he queried. 'Oh no,' Alice replied cheerfully, as she looked across to her recently sold car, now empty of everything except for the new owner, a Mr Donnellard of Dalhousie Station, grinning behind its wheel. 'They do not have anything but American cars here, so I think it's wise to leave them a British built to prove up here over the years.' Cobham still appeared dubious.[1]

Alice had achieved her goal of driving to Alice Springs but why would she come all this way and not drive the Austin home? Perhaps it was because her sponsors were no longer involved. The true test of the Baby Austin was to reach Alice Springs; beyond that it was merely a matter of making one's way home by any chosen means, even though at the outset Alice declared she would be making a round trip in the little car over a period of six weeks. Perhaps Alice had had enough of driving; perhaps she sold the Austin on a whim and then regretted it, just as her father had done when he'd bought Alice's first motorcar. She certainly regretted not getting a good price for it: 'I was fool enough not to sell at a profit and so have been cursing myself for a fool ever since – however there you are', Alice wrote to her friend Elizabeth Lothian once she had left Oodnadatta.[2] However, Mr Donnellard, the local station owner who had persuaded Alice to part with her car, was very happy with the deal. The Austin did 40 miles to the gallon, which was a big consideration, he said, when local petrol cost around 5 shillings a gallon. Whatever Alice's reasoning, letting go of the Austin created a whole new set of 'adventures' for the journey home.

As Cobham made his way back to England to claim his record and a knighthood, Alice and Kath took the train east from Oodnadatta to Parachilna, a tiny town situated at the base of the Flinders Ranges in South Australia. Compared to the meandering journey in the Austin, the train was 286 miles (460 kilometres) of dull, unrelenting railway track. From Parachilna, Alice and Kath trekked on foot and hitched rides with a wool wagon, then a motor mail, making their way southeast through South Australia to Blinman and beyond. In all, they walked 40 miles over five days, with temperatures ranging from 13.8 to 30.6 degrees Celcius. They slept rough on open plains and in dry creek beds, and visited two more outback stations where they were warmly welcomed.

At Mullaloo Station, Alice and Kath were excited to listen to a wireless that gave them up-to-date news and stories from

Adelaide, Brisbane and Sydney. At Alpana Station, the lady of the house, Mrs Henry, timidly asked if Alice would have a go at cutting her hair in the 'modern style'. Alice took the scissors in hand and, though she was frightened she might make a hash of it, dived in with her usual aplomb. Kath looked on, finally announcing, 'Hooray, it's a good cut!'[3] Mrs Henry could not have been more thrilled nor Alice more relieved to have wielded the scissors with success. It was the least Alice could do in return for such wondrous hospitality.

In the last few days of her journey Alice also found time to write her monthly motor notes for the October edition of *Woman's World*. She chose to give tips on what to look for when choosing a car – a fitting topic in light of her recent experiences driving in all weathers and conditions. Her notes focused on the features best suited for optimum performance given the climatic and road conditions the car would be subjected to.

Alice arrived home on the morning of Saturday, 11 September 1926. Frankie caught up with her later that afternoon. 'No-one who was not hard and used to a Spartan life should undertake it as a pleasure trip,' Alice laughed, as she updated Frankie on her adventures in the desert. Alice also told her sister she was a little surprised when Jessie, who had travelled right through Central Africa, described Central Australia, with its heat, dust and flies, and lack of water as 'a new experience in hardship'. She added, 'I have never realised so much how my open air life in the bush as a child has hardened me to any kind of life as compared to the ordinary person – even Miss Webb who was an experienced traveller.'[4]

Alice quickly returned to the busyness of everyday life. On Monday 13 September she caught up with a journalist from *The*

Herald, who described Alice as 'sunburnt but happy'. The article appeared in the next day's edition. It conveyed some of Alice's recollections of the landscape: 'Central Australia is a land of enormous distances. In Victoria we simply have no idea of the land taken up by stations'; the challenges encountered, including 'fresh water – that is what we missed most'; and the people she had met along the way, especially the 'women settlers who are all cheerful, and take an interest in everything'.[5]

In the week following Alice's return, it was business as usual, with Alice catching up on all she had missed during her six weeks away. But things were about to take a tragic turn.

Just before 6 p.m. on Friday, 17 September, Alice was at the rear of her workshop. On the bench before her lay the rifle and small-bore shotgun she had borrowed from friend Geoff Gair as extra protection on her trip. The Gairs had invited her to dine with them that evening and, although Alice was running a little late for her hosts, she wanted to return the firearms thoroughly cleaned and oiled.

The two garage girls on duty that evening, Marie Edie, the petite eighteen-year-old and Heather Buchanan, her tall, skinny-limbed senior, were assigned to the front of the garage. A few minutes after Alice had moved to the back of the garage a sharp report rang out. Edie was first at the scene, followed by Buchanan, who saw Edie riveted to the spot, her face drained of colour. Alice lay on the floor near the workbench. There was blood pooling from a wound in her forehead and she was bleeding from the ears. Buchanan gasped. It seemed that only a minute ago Alice had been talking away in her usual bright, bubbly fashion and now here she was, collapsed and bleeding. They made an urgent call to the local medical practitioner, Dr

James Rowan, who was available if a car could pick him up. Buchanan fought her rising panic as she threw herself behind the wheel of the nearest vehicle. She pushed the starter button and stepped on the accelerator. Thankfully the engine kicked in without her needing to fiddle with the choke or – heaven forbid – get out the crank. She took off down Cotham Road and returned with Dr Rowan ten minutes later. The doctor wasted no time getting to Alice and checking for vital signs. He detected a faint pulse. There was only one thing to be done: take Alice to the nearest hospital.

Alice was rushed to Lancewood in Glenferrie Road – the private hospital run by Alice's close friend and supporter Jessie MacBeth. Now MacBeth and nurse Kate Griffiths were confronted with the sight of the woman they knew as young, vibrant and invincible, arriving through their door seemingly mortally wounded. They were used to taking charge in a crisis but utter shock momentarily rendered them helpless. All they could do was usher Alice's stretcher-bearers towards the first unoccupied room. MacBeth and Griffiths barely had time to view Alice's head wound before the coroner, Daniel Berriman, and Constable Malcolm McPhail arrived just before 6.30 p.m. The coroner examined the injury. He wet a finger and placed it above Alice's mouth. No sign of breath. He placed his fingers against Alice's neck. There was no perceivable pulse. He pulled back one eyelid then another and, with a tiny flashlight, shone it into her eyes. Her pupils did not react. Berriman gently pulled the sheet over Alice's face and pronounced her dead. She was twenty-nine years and three months old.

By the end of her first week back at the garage Alice was in the public eye again. This time every newspaper across the country carried her story. In Melbourne, newsboys shouted headings from *The Argus* and *The Herald* as they stood on street corners: 'Shot through head! Death of Miss Alice Anderson'; 'Miss Anderson's death! Widespread regret! First woman garage proprietor'.[6]

On hearing the news that there had been a second tragic death of an Anderson sibling, Katrine, the sister closest to Alice in so many ways, ran away from Melbourne in shock. She grabbed a few clothes, howled her way to the shops to buy a hat to shade her eyes, and took off to the ocean at Flinders on the Mornington Peninsula. There she 'bathed in the mad surf where you are not supposed to bathe' until she was utterly exhausted.[7]

Frankie had caught up with Alice on Thursday, 16 September. They had walked up the street together and chatted about a close friend who had recently married. Frankie recalled saying, 'Oh, well perhaps you'll get married some day if only for a rest.' She remembered Alice replying:

> A rest do you call it? I think it is only a change of work. Up there at Oodnadatta when I saw those women on the far-back stations suffering what we down here call privations cheerfully and happy I just felt that if any decent man up there asked me to bake his bread and darn his sox for him I would do it in spite of the dust, heat and flies.

Alice then teased Frankie by saying, 'If I have children they will be better brought up than yours!'[8] Frankie kissed her goodnight. It was the last time she saw Alice alive.

The following day, 17 September, Frankie pencilled in her diary, 'Alice. 6.10 p.m. Died.'[9] It was her only entry for that day.

Previous pages were filled with events, engagements and to-do lists but from this date on the diary remained virtually blank. For Frankie the world had stopped.

On hearing the news Frankie's husband, Alfred, who'd always had a particular fondness for his sister-in-law, immediately penned a poem.

Alice Anderson

> The gates of life have closed: I am beyond.
> That side is Spring, on this, Eternal quiet;
> But dim grey cars go on by well known roads,
> Towards tomorrow's dawn I shall not know.
> I have known other dawns, peaceful and grey,
> With long grey roads ahead, and wayside rest,
> But not this Peace, with sunny roads behind –
> Around me, and beyond, a new found love.[10]

How was a bullet lodged in Alice's forehead when she was so experienced with guns? Newspaper reports differed. *The Argus* wrote, 'Miss Anderson was preparing a rifle for return to its owner shortly before 7 o'clock last night. Apparently she failed to notice that a cartridge still remained in it, and in some manner it was discharged, the bullet penetrating Miss Anderson's forehead.'[11] However, *The Herald* wrote that it was an automatic pistol and that 'she [Alice] removed the magazine, unaware or forgetting that a bullet was still in the barrel. This by some means exploded.'[12] The Adelaide *Chronicle* reported similarly that Alice had 'met with a tragic death by accidental discharge of an automatic pistol while cleaning the weapon'.[13]

Would Alice really have been so reckless? And why did *The Herald* and *The Chronicle* mention an automatic pistol? The firearms Alice borrowed from Gair did not include an automatic pistol. Was this a' merely a mistake by the paper's reporters or was there a third gun involved? The circumstances under which Alice was fatally wounded would be teased out at the coroner's inquest to be held in two weeks' time. Meanwhile, Alice's body remained at Lancewood over the weekend until her funeral on the following Monday, 20 September, at the Boroondara Cemetery, Kew.

At the time of Alice's death the Melbourne morgue was located in Batman Avenue at the industrial end of town. It consisted of a series of buildings that provided post-mortem examinations, public viewings, inquests and coronial offices. The buildings stood between the Melbourne City Council storage site, full of rumbling trucks, and the Victorian Railways switchgear store that controlled the trains' electrical supply. Directly behind were the railway yards. On Batman Avenue cable trams clanged as they came round the corner. Beyond the railways lay the murky waters of the Yarra. The morgue was outdated and rundown: there had been scarcely any improvements since it was erected in 1881. Its walls were uninsulated and the inquest room in particular had very poor acoustics. The clamour outside was often so loud that those participating in proceedings had to yell in order to be heard. Water pipes leaked in the ceiling, a wall between the mortuary and an outside wall was falling down, and there was no separate room for female witnesses. The list went on. Even the attorney-general described the morgue as 'inconvenient, gloomy and generally obsolete'.[14] (Despite constant complaints and requests for remodelling and rehousing, Melbourne would have to wait decades for the situation to improve.)

At least Alice's family was spared the harrowing experience of having to view her body in the morgue's mortuary chapel. Generally, bodies were sent to the morgue for identification and examination prior to an inquest but Alice's remains had stayed at Lancewood Hospital until her funeral. Perhaps this was because the coroner had pronounced Alice dead at a hospital and the details of her obvious wound had been noted. The cause of death was clear even though the circumstances surrounding it were yet to be determined.

At Lancewood the family was at least able to view Alice's body and mourn with a degree of dignity. At the morgue family members and loved ones could be confronted by any number of bodies laid in rows without cubicles separating them. 'Feelings of grief-stricken relatives should not be further harrowed by their having other family tragedies forced on their attention, and being compelled to look upon other bodies, possibly mutilated, in the same room,' wrote the state attorney-general.[15] The mortuary was not even fly-proof.

Sequestered behind a tall, decorative redbrick wall, the cemetery's main entrance lies at the junction of High Street and Park Hill Road before fanning out across thirty-one acres to border the sports and leisure grounds of Victoria Park. On that Monday mourners from all over Australia passed through the cemetery's cast iron gates as the hands on the clock tower edged towards 3 p.m. It was a bright spring day with a warm north wind that fluttered women's skirts and threatened to make hats fly. Motorcars arrived, carrying hundreds of wreaths and tributes from friends and groups including the Lyceum Club, Boy Scouts, Old Grammarian Girls' Association, General Motors Limited, and staff at Lancewood Hospital. Barely more than a street away, Alice's garage stood still and padlocked for the first time since opening its doors.

Clusters of people made their way down the cemetery's main driveway. Ahead, through the exotic Victorian gardens dominated by towering cypresses, was the impressively columned memorial for David Syme, *The Age* newspaper magnate, and further on the even more elaborate Springthorpe Memorial erected by a grieving doctor for his wife. Along the winding path towards the rear of the Presbyterian section at the thick redbrick cemetery wall, a Reverend Deasey stood at the head of Alice's freshly dug grave, his robes flapping in the wind. On the other side of the wall, traffic drove along High Street, heedless of the ritual about to unfold. Alice's family huddled close to the gravesite, clutching handkerchiefs, their heads bowed. Beside them stood fourteen garage girls, red eyed and solemn in their chauffeur uniforms. Other mourners stood along the winding paths and between headstones right back to the main driveway.

For some, the huge crowd was an unexpected sight. One newspaper wrote that the funeral 'for a woman not in public life, was an amazingly big one, the number of flowers and expressions of regret being equally numerous and coming practically from all sections of the people'.[16] Alice was certainly not royalty (though her ancestry did include a distant and somewhat scandalous connection to the British monarchy) but her upper-middle-class heritage was not apparent to those who did not know her intimately; she might have made the motoring pages but Alice Anderson was never conventional enough to make the society pages. Understandably, the general public saw Alice as working class by the very act of her profession, and Alice had done nothing to dissuade this perception. The reporter's explanation for the turnout was the fact that 'Miss Anderson was a brave woman, and an attractive one, full of vitality and life, with a magnetism that drew people instinctively towards her.'[17]

A black hearse carrying Alice's body drove through the entrance, its tyres crunching on the gravel path as the crowd parted ways. The fourteen garage girls took their cue to move to the back of the hearse and divide into two rows. Each fought to contain their distress as they lifted the coffin together and moved slowly towards the grave. Alice was light, but carrying their boss to her final destination at that moment felt heavier than lifting the engine from a Chandler tourer.

At the end of the service, various mourners took the ceremonial shovel and tossed a clod of earth onto the coffin before stepping away. Alice was gone. But shock and disbelief were palpable and many questions remained. The public hoped the ensuing inquest to be held at the Melbourne morgue in ten days' time, on 30 September, would provide a clear explanation for her death.

───────

The day of the inquest, the air was cool and clouds obliterated the sun. Wind whistled round the buildings and rippled on the Yarra as attendees filed into the inquest room. Officiating at the proceedings were Coroner Berriman; Mr Maxwell, the lawyer representing sole executrix Jessie MacBeth; and Mr Brennan, the lawyer representing the Australian Mutual Life Insurance Society Ltd. Five witnesses sat ready to give evidence, together with an expert gun maker.

Plain-clothes constable William Penno, who had been called to Lancewood on 17 September to identify Alice's body, was first to be questioned. Penno had known Alice since she began her venture nine years before. Both Maxwell and Berriman wanted to know Penno's opinion of Alice's personality and temperament. 'I had seen her practically every day,' he said. 'She was a jolly girl of even temperament, a capable woman in every way.'[18] This sort of questioning continued throughout the inquest as the notion Alice might have deliberately taken her own life was explored.

Was this a real possibility? It was difficult to imagine Alice accidentally killing herself when she had such an intimate knowledge of guns. Had she intended to die by her own hand? Deliberately aiming a gun at one's forehead to this end seemed rather improbable. And wouldn't she have chosen a more private time and space if that was her intention? Had an intruder snuck into the garage, possibly by the side entrance, and used his or her own gun to shoot Alice? And if so, what would have been the motive?

The next person to be questioned was eighteen-year-old Marie Edie, the second-youngest garage girl in Alice's employ at the time. Standing in the witness box, she looked no bigger than a child. Edie was asked about the evening in question. What were she and Alice doing in the garage? Edie spoke quietly and the ongoing racket outside meant she was asked to speak up several times. 'She [Alice] had been very busy that day,' Edie said. 'She asked me to book, in the engagement book, that she would have to go out to tea that evening. She asked me would I be able to stay at the garage for tea, as she was going out and there would not be another driver on the premises.'[19] According to Edie, Alice then went to the rear workshop.

Shortly after I heard a report and about six or seven minutes after I went to the rear of the garage. I saw the deceased lying on her stomach with her face turned to the right. I found that there was a wound in her head and she was bleeding from the ears and there was a pool of blood on the floor . . . she was laying just about at the spot where she had been standing . . . in her hand was part of a gun and at her feet was her own revolver. I lifted her up and took the revolver and her tie off and rang for the doctor.[20]

What was Alice doing with her own revolver? This was the family's Colt pistol handed down from JT to Stewart and then to Alice. A revolver was shown in evidence. Was this the revolver Miss Edie saw? Edie nodded, then said, 'under her body was the handle part of the gun that she was cleaning. On a bench near the body was the remaining part of the gun she was cleaning and a bottle of cleaning oil. I picked up the revolver and handed it to the Police.'[21] Mr Brennan asked for clarification. Edie said:

she [Alice] went to clean the guns about five fifty p.m. I saw her at work on the guns. The revolver belonged to her and the gun she was cleaning she had borrowed. The stock of the gun was under her body and the barrel was on the bench. The revolver was at her feet lying on the floor.[22]

When the coroner then asked Edie to clarify which gun Alice had been cleaning prior to the gunshot, Edie was suddenly unsure: 'I do not know what she was cleaning when the shot was fired. She was cleaning the shotgun when I saw her about two minutes before.' The coroner then changed tack, asking Edie if she thought there was any reason that would lead Alice to take her own life. Edie replied, 'She had not at any time shown signs of depression. I know of no worries that she had. I know of no reason why she should take her own life.'[23]

At this point both witnesses agreed Alice was of sound mind and the idea that she might have committed suicide was unlikely. Apart from the stigma attached to suicide, such a finding would also render Alice's life insurance null and void.

However, not only was Edie unsure which firearm Alice was cleaning at the time, her testimony regarding timelines did not make sense. At first Edie said she went to the back of the garage about six or seven minutes after hearing the gunshot. Then she said she had seen Alice cleaning one of the borrowed guns only two minutes before. So when did Edie actually go to the back of the garage and what motivated her to do so? And what of the revolver? Why did Alice even have her revolver if she was cleaning the guns borrowed for her trip to Central Australia? Why was Edie confused as to which gun Alice had been cleaning? More importantly, from which firearm was the bullet discharged that killed Alice?

Heather Buchanan took the stand looking gaunt and thinner than usual. She too confirmed that shortly before 6 p.m. Alice went to the rear of the garage to clean Gair's guns. 'I did not see her [Alice] take anything with her. I was in the front of the garage with Miss Edie. I heard a report, which I thought was a stone on the roof. A few minutes later Miss Edie called to me as I went down the garage. She was at the workshop and I went to her.'[24] After seeing Alice on the floor Heather said she went and phoned for the doctor, and took a motorcar to pick him up.

Edie had also stated that she had made the call to the doctor. Was this a confusion of recall or was someone purposely not telling the truth? Coroner Berriman did not bother to query this or any other inconsistency in the two employees' statements; nor did Mr Maxwell or Mr Brennan.

In terms of the pistol, Buchanan also confirmed it was Alice's. 'The morning after the accident I found a magazine of cartridges in the right hand drawer of Miss Anderson's chest of drawers,' she declared. She also said she had previously seen Alice cleaning the revolver so was confident that Alice 'understood the cleaning of it'. In terms of Alice's state of mind at the time, Buchanan agreed with previous depositions that Alice appeared her usual self and did not show any signs of depression. 'She was always bright. She did not appear to be worried about the state of her business.' Buchanan, however, declared that Alice had said 'business had been very bad but that she had great hopes for the future'.[25]

It seemed from Buchanan's statement that Alice had taken her pistol to clean along with the other guns. This tended to refute any idea that an intruder had broken into the garage. But it begged several questions: Where did Alice store her gun? If it was in the chest of drawers in her office or den where Buchanan later discovered the magazine, how was it that Buchanan – who stated she'd been in the front of the garage prior to the gunshot – did not see Alice retrieve it? The office was at the front of the garage, where both Edie and Buchanan said they had been at the time, and the entrance to Alice's den was through a door in the office. Neither Edie nor Buchanan mentioned observing Alice carrying any guns to the rear workshop. It was probable that Alice had earlier stored Gair's guns in the workshop for cleaning and had rendered them safe by ensuring they were not loaded and there were no cartridges nearby. But what of her own revolver?

Second Constable Malcolm McPhail confirmed that the bullet that had fatally wounded Alice was indeed from Alice's own revolver. After viewing Alice's body at Lancewood Hospital, McPhail had gone to the garage. There Edie had handed him Alice's revolver, and he observed that:

> there was no magazine in the revolver. I looked down the barrel of the revolver and I saw that a bullet had been fired through it since it had been cleaned. I looked about the floor and about four feet from where the blood was on the floor I found the empty cartridge.[26]

McPhail said he was handed the missing magazine the following morning, which contained five bullets but was capable of holding six. Mr Maxwell asked if the gun could have shot a bullet without the magazine being in place. 'With this revolver, if the magazine is drawn, you may still have a bullet left in the chamber. It is possible for the explosion to take place apart from the magazine at all.' Mr Brennan asked if the revolver could have been broken. McPhail thought not. 'The barrel could not be oiled with a cartridge in it . . . The pistol is not defective as far as I know.'[27]

The last person to testify was expert gun maker Fredrick Clift from Moonee Ponds. On examination, Clift found several issues with Alice's revolver. 'I find that the pull of it is very light. It is an old model,' he told Coroner Berriman. Brennan then asked for clarification regarding the firing of a shot with the magazine out. Clift replied:

that is not usual. That should not be if the pistol is in good order. If the magazine was out and a live cartridge in the chamber, picking it up, it could accidentally be exploded. The trigger had a light pull. It could be picked up and pointed at the head and go off accidentally.[28]

This statement reinforced the idea that the gunshot had been accidental and not a deliberate act of suicide. But would Alice be so foolish as to point the gun towards her own head?

Despite inconsistencies that arose throughout the inquest, particularly in regard to Edie's and Buchanan's testimonies, there were no further questions. Coroner Berriman's findings concluded that Alice had died at Lancewood Hospital 'from a gunshot wound in the forehead accidentally inflicted at the Kew Motor Garage at Cotham Road, Kew, on 17th September 1926', the assumption being that Alice had accidentally shot herself while cleaning her own pistol. 'Evidence was given that a pistol which she [Alice] was cleaning exploded in the process.'[29] One newspaper even reported the coroner as stating, 'it [the revolver] was not a safe thing for a lady to be fooling with'.[30]

After the inquest findings had been made public, further articles appeared in newspapers and journals. The *RACV* journal wrote that Alice 'built a flourishing garage business at Kew', and 'died from a pistol accident in the heyday of her success, and when she had developed as a writer on motoring and touring subjects'.[31] Alice's friend and fellow Lyceum Club member Frances Taylor had left for Europe in May 1926, and was still abroad when Alice died. While Alice and Jessie Webb made their journey to Australia's remote desert centre, Frances was, due to the 'rapid development of the paper . . . securing new features and new services', as well as getting 'into personal touch with women's movements in England and Europe'.[32] Frances had chosen journalist and popular children's author Mary Grant Bruce as guest editor in her absence. How devastating it must have been for Frances to receive word of Alice's tragic death via telegram. The October edition of *Woman's World* published Alice's final column with the accompanying editor's note:

> A very poignant interest attaches to the publication of this article, the last written for 'Woman's World' by Alice E. F. Anderson, whose death from a gun accident took place just as we went to press. Aged only 29 years, Miss Anderson had made a high place for herself in the esteem of Melbourne, not only for her personal qualities, but through her business ability, her courage, and her enterprise . . . the complete confidence felt in her testified clearly to her high sense of business honour. She was a very popular member of the Lyceum Club, the members of which share the universal grief that so promising a life should be so tragically cut short.[33]

The article, 'Choosing a Car: A few points to note before buying', was written somewhere on Alice's journey through the desert. It was full of humour and practical advice:

> The average woman when purchasing a car is overwhelmed with the technical details which leave her so bewildered that she finally judges by its appearance, just as a man is attracted by a pretty girl, regardless of what is under the bonnet.
>
> Just as dancing slippers would not be suitable for a walking tour, so you will find that many cars will not stand up to rough country usage, although perfectly built . . .[34]

Alice's last article included requirements for particular road conditions and steep hill climbs: one needed a powerful engine,
though horsepower was not always a necessary component in
the hands of a skilled driver:

> A seven-horse-power engine may develop as much power as a
> twelve-horse-power if it is built to do so. So do not rely on horse-
> power – test the car out and see how she 'Revs up' when put to
> a steep hill. The writer recently went to Central Australia in a
> seven-horse-powered car, and had no trouble with sand that
> stopped cars of forty-horse-power . . .[35]

The inquest finding meant Alice's life insurance had to be paid
out. However, Alice's sudden death by her own gun set tongues
wagging. *She was experienced with guns. How could it have been an
accident? Perhaps her garage business had been going so badly she could
not see another way out! Perhaps she killed herself over a lesbian love
affair gone wrong!* Rumours of suicide were particularly upsetting
for Alice's grieving family. Not only was such an act socially
unacceptable, it was a crime. And unfortunately such rumours
would persist for decades to come.

The truth was that at least one person had lied at the inquest
and Alice's family knew it to be the case. Whenever anyone
asked the Anderson family questions regarding Alice's death, their
responses were fundamentally the same: Alice had accidentally
shot herself. In 1984 Frankie, who was then ninety years old,
was quoted as saying:

> She was cleaning his [Geoff Gair's] guns to take to him and
> she called one of the girls, 'bring me my Colt revolver and I'll

fix it, too.' Well, my husband told me that a Colt revolver has almost always got one bullet stuck in it. And by the damage done to her brain he said she must have been poking at that with a nail, without realising she could explode it that way.[36]

If this version of events sounded unrealistic, especially knowing how experienced Alice was with guns, then her sister Claire's explanation recorded in the same year came across as even more incredible:

> Gair lent Alice that revolver before she went . . . she was going to dinner at the Gairs' on the night that she died. And they'd asked her to dinner and to tell all about her trip and everything and she was going to, and she was running late, of course, because of all the rushing and getting out of uniform and everything and getting cleaned up to go nicely to dinner and then, 'Oh, I've got to take that revolver back.' Well she had a bullet in and the bullet was stuck. And she was in a hurry. And with all the knowledge she had of fire-arms and everything, what did she do in her hurry to try and get that bullet out, she tried to push it out from the wrong end with a knitting needle. Crazy![37]

When it was pointed out that Frankie had said Alice had kept the revolver only for security reasons in the garage and she wasn't familiar with it for that reason, Claire retorted, 'I don't think you need to mention who belonged to it or anything else, but I know she had to go to the Gairs'.'[38] The fact that the two sisters told similar but different stories, strongly suggested that neither were telling the truth, as they knew it. The fact that Claire said the revolver was not even Alice's and, when questioned, avoided answering altogether suggested that Claire was not a forgetful old woman but a poor liar. It would take exactly eight decades before what had remained a family secret was publicly revealed.

———

Not long after Alice's death, JT finally succumbed to bankruptcy, but he continued to work for the City of Richmond. Claire left for England where her engineering training qualified her as a draftsman/surveyor at a brickworks in Essex. Once married, she returned to Melbourne and lived next door to Katrine, who had also married, in Eltham. Joan, head gardener to Nellie Melba, took over The Hermitage guesthouse at Narbethong with the help of her mother. Ellen Mary died in 1945 aged eighty-one and JT, suffering from dementia, followed three years later, aged eighty-four. Frankie and Alfred had gone on to have more children, but Frankie never gave up her career and became well known as an artist and expert in early-childhood artistic expression. She out-lived Alfred (who served in both world wars) by twenty years, and was ninety-three when she died in 1987.

It was in her biography of her grandmother, *Frankie Derham: A Refuge Within*, written in 2006, that Penelope Alexander finally divulged that the family stories of Alice accidentally dying by her own hand were false. 'This was the story put out by the family,' she wrote, 'but it was not the truth. Alice was too well taught not to check for a spare cartridge before setting about cleaning her gun. In fact she was shot accidentally by a young employee at the garage who did not know that a cartridge had been left in the gun.'[39]

It made sense that Alice had asked either Marie Edie or Heather Buchanan to fetch her seldom-used revolver for a once-over while cleaning Gair's guns. The idea that one of the garage girls accidentally touched the trigger explained the inconsistencies in Edie's and Buchanan's depositions and perhaps why the two were never cross-examined further. Was it possible that those in the highest ranks of office colluded with Alice's family and her employees to determine the outcome of the inquest? The family certainly had its society connections. Perhaps even Geoff Gair, who was a solicitor, had been called in to give the family legal advice. The other possibility, of course, was that those leading the inquest were simply incompetent. In any case, it appeared both Edie and Buchanan decided, or were advised – with the consent of Alice's family – to cover up the details of the shooting at the hearing.

It was a terrible secret burden to carry, especially for the person directly responsible for Alice's death. And for anyone else who knew the details to never, ever speak of it again lest the truth should come out. There must have been a heavy strain on more than a few hearts. Without further forensic evidence it was impossible to say with absolute certainty what exactly happened in the moments before Alice's death. But based on Alice's relatives' more recent statements, it appeared the Anderson family had made a swift and perhaps noble decision to support a lie in order to protect a young garage girl from public scrutiny – despite it presenting Alice as either careless or suicidal. Their decision might have even prevented one of the garage girls from being charged with manslaughter or at least hounded by gossip and conjecture, though circumstances suggested that sheer ignorance in the proper handling of guns was possibly the culprit's greatest misdemeanour. One doubtless fact is that Alice was shot in the forehead, which meant the barrel of the gun was facing her when it went off.

Frankie never told her granddaughter Penelope the identity of the garage girl who had allegedly handed the loaded revolver to Alice. Penelope said she never wanted to know. Katrine's daughter, Jenny Ellis, also said she did not know the garage girl's identity but remembered clearly being told that the cover-up 'was to protect a sixteen-year-old girl'.[40] The only sixteen-year-old employed at the time was Edith Trebilcock, but she was not present in the garage when Alice died. Between Buchanan and Edie, who were present, Edie was the younger at eighteen while Buchanan was in her twenties and more experienced than Edie. More than likely the mistake in age was made because Edie was sixteen when she began working with Alice in 1924, or perhaps because she simply looked younger than her age. On this reckoning it could only have been Edie to whom Katrine's daughter was referring. Every photograph of Marie Edie at the garage prior to the tragic event shows a small, vulnerable-looking yet happy-go-lucky young woman laughing, teasing and being teased by her fellow garage girls. If Edie was directly involved in Alice's death, or at the very least was standing with Alice when the revolver went off, her life would have been irrevocably changed on the night of 17 September 1926, probably more so than Buchanan, who appeared not to be near Alice at the time and would therefore not have been present at the actual shooting.

As with most of Alice's employees, Edie held nothing but the highest regard for her boss. Edie's son, Maurice, said his mother 'admired Alice enormously because of Alice's irrepressible sense of adventure, and her supreme confidence in herself and her staff that they could do anything'.[41] Alice's discipline, along with a regular wage, also helped Edie escape the circumstances of her eccentric and financially unreliable family. The Kew Garage, she said, was the best job she'd ever had.

Did Edie ever tell anyone what really happened in the garage that night? She might well have confided in her husband after she resigned from the garage the following year to marry George Martin, who worked at the rival garage across the road, but otherwise no one appeared to ever know. Maurice had no idea his mother had even been in the garage at the time Alice died, let alone that she was possibly responsible for her demise. However, when presented with the most recent family revelations, Maurice came to the conclusion that the person responsible for the fatal shot, however accidental, could have been none other than his mother. Looking back over his childhood Maurice could not recall anything significant that suggested Edie's alleged dark secret, though he did remember she had a terrible aversion to guns and would never allow one in the house. Maurice recalled that her nature was generally sunny, that she never thought too deeply about things and always lived for the present, never wanting to look back. To what degree Edie was fundamentally affected by her experience in the garage that night can only be speculated upon. Only one thing can be sure: that Marie Edie was forever changed by the events of that night, as was Heather Buchanan.

In 1983, almost sixty years after Alice's death, Edie recalled a version of events that contradicted her evidence recorded at the inquest. By this time she was seventy-three years old and Alice was a faded local legend whose reputation was invariably bound up with the idea that she had committed suicide in her garage. In a letter to historian Mimi Colligan, Edie revealed, possibly unintentionally and somewhat vaguely, a more likely version of that fateful night in 1926:

*While cleaning the revolver or pistol (am never sure which is
which) after her trip she was telling me that now she would like
to open a flying school for women. She was sure aviation was
the coming thing. The next moment the gun went off and she
died instantly.*

*Her insurance company refused to pay saying it was suicide.
There was an inquiry and on my evidence and some other factors
it was proved to be an accident. One does not laugh and plan the
future then commit suicide in front of an eighteen year old . . .*[42]

In this letter Edie clearly put herself in the frame even though
she did not reveal whether it was she or Alice who held the
revolver at the critical moment. Was this the writing of a woman
whose memory had faded over time or had she merely forgotten
to hide elements of the truth? And why reveal so much yet fail
to disclose this vital piece of information? If it was Alice, why
not say so? If it was Edie, was she still afraid to admit what had
happened because it was something she had never shared with
anyone? Or had Edie been so traumatised by the event she had
simply blocked it out?

———

The past can throw up fragments that raise more questions than
they answer: pieces like a photograph or a letter that tell part
of a story, leaving us to guess at the rest. Alice's legacy has left
behind many such fragments but the most intimate of these was
discovered among Frankie's papers endowed to the University of
Melbourne Archives – papers that, until recently, had not been
catalogued. Inside a little plastic bag full of unrelated items was
a small square of folded papers, possibly unopened since Alice

had folded it more than ninety years ago. In Alice's unmistakable handwriting the outer piece bore the lines:

> If in this shadowland of life though hast
> Found one true heart to love then, hold it fast
> Love it again, give all to keep it thine
> For love like nothing in the world can last
> From Richard le Gallien's Omar Khayam[43]

Wrapped inside the quote from Omar Khayyam, the second piece of paper, again in Alice's handwriting but in the faintest pencil so that it seemed almost a whisper, she had written:

> Please God,
> That I may never look to you
> With the eyes of a stranger
> That this communion be ever
> Renewed in fresh ways
> That this flame of eternity
> That is ours be written
> In light[44]

From the centre of the two pieces of paper emerged a tiny, faded photograph of Alice in a car, a piece of herself wrapped in affairs of the heart. Somewhere, a lover, who may have never received Alice's offering, must have mourned in silence; a fledgling romance of such delicate intimacy, whose pain was wrapped in the longing Alice had taken to her grave. For whoever this lover was, their identity would forever remain a mystery.

If Alice had been involved with a man and it needed to be kept secret, what would that secret have been? That he was already married? Perhaps. Or had a woman stolen Alice's heart? There is nothing to prove the gender of the lover to whom Alice refers, but if one considers Alice's words carefully she speaks of a friendship that she hopes to acknowledge in public, that this relationship is deeply important to her: 'a flame of eternity', and one she hopes can be 'written in light' – a phrase inferring that Alice deeply wished their love could be publicly acknowledged.

EPILOGUE

GARAGE GIRLS CARRY ON

'If there is no spark . . .'

(1920s *Shell Motorists' Index*)

Seven-year-old Mary Houston woke in the middle of the night to the sound of muffled sobbing. Mary could not pull the covers over her head and pretend it away so she slid out of her warm bed and edged down the corridor towards the light emanating from beneath the kitchen door. Mary had overheard her mother crying before, usually following an argument with her father when he had drunk too much, but she had never heard her mother like this. Mary tentatively pushed the door open a crack and saw her leaning over the kitchen table, her head low. In her hands was a handkerchief wet with tears. Nancy looked up to see her pale-faced little girl peeping round the door. Before Mary had a chance to ask what was wrong – she had developed a pronounced stutter since starting school – Nancy said, 'Miss Anderson has died.'[1] Mary could barely comprehend what she was hearing. She stood riveted in the doorway. Her lip began to quiver. 'B-b-but I adore Miss Anderson!' she blurted, and ran to her mother's side.[2]

Nancy Houston had worked with Alice for the best part of nine years. She was an excellent mechanic but driving was something Nancy was finding increasingly difficult. She had a turned eye and her vision was deteriorating despite a new set of prescription spectacles. Nancy had been avoiding the inevitability that she needed to discontinue driving. She loved her job and didn't want to let her boss down. Alice's death was reason enough to never return to the garage.

———

It was the morning after Alice's funeral, the day the garage was to reopen, and Ruth Snell was covered in grief. The devoted second-in-charge no doubt arrived early to check everything was in order and to steel herself for the tasks at hand. For in the absence of Alice, Snell was the new 'boss'. Opening the garage door the first time since that fatal gunshot must have brought with it an overwhelming sense of Alice's presence and absence all at once. There was the corner opposite the office Alice had recently cloaked with oiled curtains to spray-paint car bodies – an added service she had been looking forward to offering her customers. There was the office, with notes and diary entries written in her boss's spirited hand; the windowless den where Alice slept. Snell and Alice were – had been – great mates. Snell felt her eyes stinging with tears she could barely hold back. Alice was gone and she, Ruth Snell, older and more experienced than most of the other garage girls, had to take charge. *But how on earth could she replace the irreplaceable? There had been no forewarning, no time to prepare!* Did she suddenly have an urge to find Alice to ask her advice? *Because Alice always knew what to do!* With Alice, Snell felt strong and capable, but as soon as her boss was called away and she was expected to take charge, she felt less sure of herself. Snell was an excellent driver and mechanic, and loyal to a fault; but she would never be comfortable walking in Alice's shoes.

The sun shone brightly that morning when the office manager, Maisey Rooney, and Ruth Snell opened The Kew Garage to the public once again. There was plenty of work to catch up on; in fact, they were dealing with a backlog. All went about their business as usual, but without Alice's cheery morning greeting it was as if the women were attempting to drive uphill with the parking brake on. The usual chatter, the hustle and bustle, gave way to grim silence. Every now and again one of the garage girls would catch another's eye and see a tear brimming from red eyelids puffy from too much crying.

When a man from *The Herald* arrived that first day, the garage girls were too intent on keeping a brave face to answer many questions. When talking of Miss Anderson, Snell's eyes fought unsuccessfully against tears. 'I know I am not so clever as Miss Anderson,' she said, 'but we are all going to pull together and do our best.'[3] The new boss then took a deep breath and managed to promote one core business strategy Alice had successfully instigated, which she assured would continue: the 'once-over' booking serviced a car every 500 miles and would be overhauled in eight hours. The cost to the customer was 30 shillings. The reporter complemented Snell on her efforts, noting 'a force of character', and 'a decision to do what the dead mistress would have wished'. As for the team as a whole, despite their grief there was still an 'efficient atmosphere. Everything is in its place. Everything completely shatters man's old conception of women. There is no one who would not wish them luck.'[4]

Snell also spoke with a reporter from the *Sun News-Pictorial* who described 'the new "boss"' as being 'the older of Miss Anderson's mechanics'. 'Miss Anderson taught her all she knows about cars, and what she doesn't know is not worth learning,' he noted.[5] Snell, like Alice, had no qualifications beyond garage work. She had started at the garage in 1921; driving and mechanics were all she had known her whole adult life. As with most of her colleagues, Snell was also a single woman who worked to maintain her independence as best she could. Of all the garage girls employed at the time, Snell was the most mannish in behaviour and appearance, but this exterior belied her inward timidity. She had relied on Alice for everything and her sense of loss was so crushing she was hardly in a position to manage herself, let alone the garage.

It was to everyone's relief – especially Snell's – when an older friend of Alice's came to the garage's rescue. On 29 October 1926, just five weeks after the garage reopened, *The Argus* announced that accountant Miss Ethel Bage would be taking over the business:

> Miss Bage had been a close friend of Miss Anderson for many years, and among university and professional women there are few with a wider circle of friends. Miss Anderson's tragic death when she was just enjoying the success of her plucky venture touched Miss Bage deeply, and her decision is based on her determination that Miss Anderson's work shall not be wasted, but her business carried on as, in a sense, a memorial to a woman pioneer. The pluck and determination associated with Miss Anderson's establishment of her business were recalled this week by Miss Bage when referring to her new venture . . . On every

side, among business men who had been associated with Miss Anderson, and among women who had been clients as well as friends, Miss Bage had been congratulated on her decision. And it has been interesting to find how many friends Miss Anderson had of different walks of life. An outstanding feature of her personality was the fact that people who only met her once had the clearest recollection of it, and those who knew her well had a vivid impression of the first time they met her. The girls who had been working with Miss Anderson are remaining on with Miss Bage, who in time hopes to have a complete working knowledge of every aspect of the business, so that she may consummate the success Miss Anderson began. It is her present proposal to carry on the garage under Miss Anderson's name.[6]

Ethel Bage was the perfect woman to take charge of Alice's business. Although she had never been on the payroll, Ethel had, on numerous occasions, assisted Alice in keeping the financial aspect of the business in good order. Ethel was reported as saying 'I am not taking up the work for the sole purpose of making money, but with the idea of making a memorial to my dear friend Alice Anderson.'[7] Another newspaper was more pointed, noting Ethel was 'prepared to risk her capital in an admittedly difficult enterprise, because of a sense of loyalty to other women'.[8] Such 'public spirit' displayed by Ethel was seen as being 'in line with her brother, Robert Bage, who went to the Antarctic with Mawson, and later was killed on Gallipoli, carrying out a task which he well knew meant certain death'.[9]

When Ethel took over the garage she also held several honorary positions. She knew she would have to stand down from some positions in order to take on her new venture, but hoped to at least maintain her roles as honorable treasurer of the Victorian Womens' Graduates Association and committee member of the Melbourne Lyceum Club. Commitment to civic duty is a marvellous thing, but it doesn't pay the bills or balance the books. So how well was The Kew Garage travelling prior to Alice's death? Heather Buchanan was quoted at the inquest as saying 'business had been very bad but that she had great hopes for the future'.[10] For details, one needs to look at the probate of Alice's will signed over to Jessie MacBeth on 20 October 1926. When considering all assets, the business looked quite healthy: her real estate at 88 Cotham Road, including the garage, was valued at £3000. Alice had also purchased some land down on the Mornington Peninsula, presumably for a potential beach house, for £50 and 8 shillings. Her personal estate included five motorcars (total worth £925), furniture and household effects (£33 and 16 shillings), a gold wristwatch (£5) and money in hand or house (a little over £14 and 14 shillings), but as an ongoing concern there was not a lot of money in the bank (just over £160 and 11 shillings). Then there was Alice's life insurance policy worth about £545, debts due to the estate (£241 and 1 shilling) and business stock (£219 and 1 shilling), bringing her total assets to £5195 and 11 shillings.

However, there was also a long list of clients who were listed as 'doubtful debts', which the business was unlikely to recoup.[11] It sounded like Alice would have done well to employ a bookkeeper rather than rely on Katrine or Ethel to come to the rescue. Alice was right to state before her death that business wasn't going so well financially. These doubtful debts added up to almost £163 across seventy-nine clients, including Robert Menzies, Fintona Girls' School, Penquite Hospital, Colonel Brinsmead, Victorian

Eye and Ear Hospital and Miss Enid Derham. The service Alice's garage provided to these clients is not listed and one can only guess as to why these debts were unlikely to be recovered. Had there been disputes over supply, delivery or condition of goods? Were some clients in financial stress? Whatever the reasons, they weighed heavily on the financial health of The Kew Garage.

Bage, Snell and Rooney, however, were in for the long haul. The Kew Garage continued to be promoted as Miss Anderson's Motor Service, and Bage continued to publicise it via the outlets Alice had always utilised. Business and tour cards were updated and advertisements continued to appear in the Melbourne and local newspapers as well as publications such as *Australian Motorist* and the *RACV* journal. On the surface the only visible change was a new proprietor, but everyone knew the spark had gone. The young, fresh-faced Alice with her brilliant, innovative mind and canny entrepreneurial skills was no more. Fewer interviews and articles appeared in newspapers and magazines; all that was left were regular advertisements advising that The Kew Garage was still running and offering the same services Alice had always promoted. Ethel Bage's business card for the garage was plain and simple, with no quotes and no advertising detail.

Alice's enterprise, once the darling of the press, quickly became a garage where the women were just as efficient but without the sort of public relations Alice had so effortlessly engendered. Local women, especially, continued to favour the female-run motor service, but by decade's end the optimism of the twenties had collapsed along with the stock market and the ensuing Great Depression saw Alice's dream fraying at the edges. People began to call 88 Cotham Road 'the tart's garage' – an apparent fond joke that replaced the almost reverent publicity Alice had received from the press despite, and perhaps because of, the under-lying currents that consistently threatened to give the garage a reputation of female incompetence and perversity.[12] Had Alice not died, she more than likely would have seen the writing on the wall and moved with the times towards some other new and exciting venture. In fact, none of the few all-female garages the world over survived much beyond the 1920s. The Great War that had fostered women ambulance drivers, mechanics, chauffeurs and tour operators quickly closed the door on women once men were back from the war and women were no longer required for 'the cause'.

Still, Ethel Bage persevered, eventually listing the enterprise as a company, 'The Alice Anderson Motor Service Pty. Ltd.', on 24 August 1931. By this time both Ethel and her sister Freda were listed as directors with business capital of £2500.[13]

However, a pall was falling across the industrial world and with it the opportunity for women to explore and express them-selves as they had done the previous decade. It was men who needed a working wage to support their families, whether they had families to support or not. As women were relegated back to the domestic realm along with those 'caring' pursuits society assumed women were born to embody, the garage girls them-selves were quickly becoming a relic of an aberrant past. At the same time the Depression, which weighed heavily on all busi-nesses, was changing the motoring landscape. People who could afford their own motorcars tended to drive their own vehicles; chauffeurs represented a different era of wealth and prosperity. Only the wealthiest of families continued hiring them.

Car manufacturing was also changing. Lathes for making spare parts were no longer required as car manufacturers began supplying commercially built spare parts. The garage girls were no longer fresh, innovative or as valued. By the end of the 1920s and into the 1930s the smart chauffeur uniforms once praised as a symbol of professional efficiency were perceived as frumpy and outdated. Marjorie Horne, one of Alice's apprentices in 1925, later remembered being viewed with hostility by some people in the streets: 'I suppose they thought I was some mannish old thing . . . a he-woman,' she said.[14]

The only articles regarding The Kew Garage that stood out from this time concerned a potentially fatal fire at the garage in 1935. According to *The Herald*, Ruth Snell

> had just returned with change after having served petrol, [when] she found that flames and clouds of thick black smoke were enveloping the pumps. Fed by the stream of petrol fumes the fire blasted fiercely. With another member, Miss Rooney, she fought desperately with fire extinguishers to quell the flames. Workmen passing in a truck laden with building materials stopped and threw off bags of sand. This was thrown around the base of the pumps and it effectively smothered the fire before the arrival of the brigade. Damage estimated at £50 was caused to the pumps and a nearby truck.[15]

The situation could have been so much worse. Snell and Rooney really were risking their lives attempting to put out such a fierce fire. All three pumps had been set alight and beneath the pumps were several hundred gallons of petrol stored in underground tanks. Had the bags of sand not miraculously arrived to dampen the fire, the two garage women might well have perished and, depending on how quickly the fire brigade could attend, the whole garage, side garden, and possibly the private residence next door could have been damaged beyond repair. Had this been the scenario, The Kew Garage would have been done and dusted then and there.

Ethel Bage was determined to keep the garage open as an all-women garage, even though times were changing. Some ten years after she had taken on the enterprise, however, Bage left the garage and Maisey Rooney – the office manager who had remained loyal to Alice and the garage for many years – took over the reins. It was a sentimental decision but also a business one: in order for the garage to survive, Rooney had to sell off the business to a local all-male engineering firm that continued with the same female management and staff. It is interesting to note that at this stage most of the customers keeping the enterprise afloat were men.

One newspaper might well have reflected current public sentiment when it wrote, '[The] Strangest memorial in Melbourne – possibly in Australia – maintained in memory of a resourceful and practical young woman is a garage and service station at Kew "manned" entirely by women.'[16] It spoke to times past. Those who still lived within the vicinity of the garage would recall Alice and her enterprise, but in reality eleven years had transpired since Alice had died and not much had appeared in the press since then. Gone were the numerous women's magazines that would champion women in motoring. Even *Woman's World*, which continued successfully into the 1950s, had lost its founder, Frances Taylor, to cancer in 1933 and the magazine gradually became more homely than adventurous. The rare acknowledgement of the 'all-women service station', as it was described by one newspaper, needed to assume there were those readers who might not 'know the entire circumstances' of the business.[17]

The language was changing as male journalists dominated the scene and articles aimed at women were relegated to magazines dedicated to women's fashions and domestic concerns. 'The feminist touch hits you in the eye as soon as you walk into the place,' wrote Max Evans of Melbourne's *Sun News-Pictorial* in November 1938.

> Everywhere there is conspicuous evidence of elbow grease and broom-work. Oil bottles are kept carefully wiped and their nozzles shined; the petrol pumps get a daily brightening up, and each tool is in its appointed place in the rack. Miss Rooney's office has an orderliness some couldn't stand and few could achieve. When I was out there this week there were several bowls of lily-of-the-valley on the shelves and other flowers here and there. 'The girls like to see flowers about the place,' she said.[18]

In other words, the 'girls' had matured into women and were represented as being as house proud as any wife. Even the garage kitchen got a mention in relation to each of the staff being 'pretty good cooks'. The article also commented on the only male at the garage, Michael the watchdog, which implied the women needed protecting. There had always been a garage cat and photos of Ruth in the 1920s with a dog, but it came across as a cute pet rather than a warning device. 'Michael is Cairn and the rest Australian terrier' and, as the only male 'staff member', he had 'been in several motor accidents and has had three legs and four ribs smashed up', supposedly in the line of duty.[19] In Alice's day no one in the press had openly questioned the safety of the garage girls but in this article Rooney was questioned along these lines. 'Miss Rooney thinks it's rather remarkable that her garage has never been the victim of hold-up men. She adds that it wouldn't do much good if it was, as their system of handling the takings provides against that sort of thing.'[20] Only then is there mention of a theft on Rooney's watch. 'A couple of men drove up and asked for some oil. While she was pouring it into the car, a third man who had been left off the car farther up the street, made a back entrance to the garage and took a money bag. But there were only a few shillings in it.'[21]

Rooney downplayed the idea of men breaking into the garage but the point had been made: the garage women were vulnerable to male attack just as they would be in any other public space or private domicile. On the one hand, the women were derided as she-men; on the other, they were vulnerable to violation. The garage was no longer the haven it was seen as in Alice's day. This gradual change in perception, particularly from a male perspective, was not helped by the fact that staff numbers at the garage had been reduced from eight to four, and that any 'heavy lifting work' was now 'sent round to the engineering shop'.[22]

In 1938 Pat Peterson was employed by Rooney to service cars. (Pat recalled a Mr Williams also supervising the garage at the time, but whether he was from the Williams garage round the corner is unclear.) Peterson recalled two other women already working there when she arrived – Frances Renny and Pauline Leggo. Peterson, who had no real qualifications except a driver's licence, started out doing 'mild servicing', which covered greasing and oiling for 3 shillings and sixpence. She went on to drive clients as well because, at this stage, the garage was still doing 'taxi work'.[23]

The word 'chauffeur' was no longer in the garage's lexicon. Apparently taxi work was what the supervising Mr Williams was mostly interested in, and he sometimes stepped in to take over the wheel. Peterson also recalled that by this time many of the clients were wealthy and elderly. However, just as the clients were ageing, so was the garage's original business model. Driving schools was where the competition was and where there was money to be made. Aside from general service station business, Rooney began teaching women to drive as the garage's main specialty. A new recruit to the garage while Peterson was there was a much younger woman called Roma, though she wasn't to stay for long. It was almost a statement of defiance when Rooney was quoted as saying in 1938 that 'The Alice Anderson tradition is here to stay'.[24] World War I had been raging when Alice began her fledgling enterprise. Would Miss Anderson's Motor Service survive the next world war that was rumbling towards the headlines when Rooney made this statement?

The first thing Rooney did once the war did break out was to align the garage with classes for woman transport drivers. Arranged by the Vacuum Oil Company under the auspices of the Women's Voluntary National Register, Rooney offered another opportunity for such women with a course of ten lectures that dealt with the mechanical side of motoring. The courses would take place Monday and Thursday evenings at The Kew Garage and, with the aid of a working model, all component parts of a motorcar would be explained and demonstrated. Whether the garage was continuing to offer such lectures as a matter of course, or whether Rooney had set them up specifically to attract those women who had enrolled for national service in class D as motor drivers, is unclear. But because over fifty women had applied to become transport drivers and each evening class was limited to fifteen, it was a good business move whatever the situation. However, not long after the war began the new girl, Roma, left the garage with Frances Renny to join the Australian Air Force, and Pauline Leggo went into the army. Pat Peterson stayed on until 1941 and then left to work in an aircraft factory. The Kew Garage was being dismantled piece by piece.

Who replaced these women is unknown. However difficult the situation, Maisey Rooney was determined to keep Alice Anderson's name alive. In 1940 she promoted the 'Alice Anderson Group' of garage women as a subsidiary branch of University of Melbourne women who provided homemade garments to assist child victims of World War II. The group was reported in December 1940 as having sent in 330 garments, the biggest lot from any group, and their third offering that year. Rooney continued the Alice Anderson Group into 1941. According to a newspaper report, the group this time had made:

> handknitted cot covers, warm clothing, and other articles needed by child victims of bombing in England, and to raise money for further work, and to show sympathisers what can be done to help will hold a sale of refreshments and exhibition of the goods already made up at the home of Miss M. Rooney, Burke rd. Deepdene on Saturday June 28, afternoon and evening.[25]

No doubt Alice would have heartily approved of any war effort, but it appears that her name, which in life was the 'brand' of a successful enterprise, had been somewhat relegated to domestic activities behind closed doors.

In 1942 the motor service was 'removed' to 322 High Street, Kew. This meant Alice's well-designed garage was no longer critical to the service. When a Mr REB Crosby took over as the new owner in 1946, he disposed of Alice's hire cars and reduced the business to a driving school. Still, it was advertised as 'Alice Anderson Motor School', despite many people not even recalling who Alice Anderson was. In 1949 the State Electricity Commission took over the ownership of 88 Cotham Road and it was this that ultimately sealed the fate of The Kew Garage.

In 1951 the Alice Anderson Motor School moved yet again, from High Street to 72 Charles Street, Kew. At this time the driving school consisted of two young women instructors: Miss Noleen Ferris, twenty-three, and Miss Julie Townsend, twenty-four. Ferris was described physically as 'fair, short-haired and slim'. She claimed she had 'dropped from ten stone to eight stone and a half since taking on the job'.[26] What losing weight had to do with teaching pupils to drive, particularly when one was mostly sitting on the job, was questionable. Such a comment regarding a woman's weight was very different to how earlier garage girls were portrayed and reflected the growing public pressure on women to look slim as part of their female attractiveness, no matter what their job responsibilities were.

Ferris had gained experience through driving several makes of cars owned by her father, and trucking cattle for him on his Gippsland property; Townsend, originally from Hobart, had been a chauffeur in Tasmania for about six years. With such work experience behind them, there is no doubt Alice would have also seriously considered employing Ferris and Townsend in her day. But the fact that the article written about the two staff was headed 'Woman Drivers No Joke Here' revealed how scarce women in the motor world had become since Alice's death. Thankfully a little echo of Alice could be heard when the two women said they had taken on the job because they both 'liked the outdoor life'. They also liked 'the feeling of "not having a boss looking over your shoulder while you work"'.[27]

The two were teaching with dual-control vehicles, which meant they could control the car from the front passenger seat – something not available in the 1920s. Alice might well have questioned whether this was actually an improvement for learner drivers. Dual controls could get a novice out of trouble, but so could Alice's boot coming down on a driver's foot.

In 1954 Bib Stillwell set up his used car sales business on the site of The Kew Garage. By now the car market had clearly divided itself into service stations, garage repairs, driving schools and car sales. It is unknown exactly which year The Kew Garage was demolished, but by the time Stillwell had set himself up at 88 Cotham Road, Alice's unique garage building was no more. Many locals recalled Stillwell's long, glass-windowed show-room on the corner of Cotham Road and Charles Street, which remained there for the next three decades. Stillwell never owned the land, however, and in 1967 the title was transferred from the State Electricity Commission to Trinity Grammar School. Meanwhile, Stillwell pressed on in a car sales market that was an exclusive male domain, aside from, perhaps, the reception and secretarial roles.

As Alice faded from public memory, the occasional article came along to highlight a lone woman who had dared to take on motor mechanics in the way Alice had done. In 1964 *The Australian Women's Weekly* featured an article written by a woman titled 'A Mechanic Called Miss'. The subject of the article was a 'red-headed eighteen-year-old' by the name of Lorraine Faulkner, who had become the 'first girl mechanic to be registered with the Victorian Apprenticeship Commission'.[28] While the article re-educated the public on Alice Anderson as a female motoring pioneer, it also revealed that this young woman struggled just as much as Alice had done in the early 1920s when it came to finding any employer who would take on a female apprentice mechanic. Apparently it was 'her refusal to take "no" for an answer' that finally garnered Miss Faulkner an apprenticeship after seven employers had knocked her back. Like Alice, Lorraine went against the grain. She'd dropped out of nursing school to chase her passion. Her interest in cars dated back to her teens, when 'she loved to get "inside" a vehicle with a spanner and screw-driver'.[29] Her apprenticeship salary at £6 a week was also not much more than Alice paid her own staff in the 1920s, though Alice would have most likely approved of the four-year appren-ticeship, which included going to technical school for two years.

Tragically, any gains Alice had delivered to women in motoring in the 1920s had more or less evaporated by the 1950s. Anything to do with cars, other than driving, was acknowledged strictly as a man's trade. Lorraine revealed she'd actually lost her boy-friend over her choice of career 'because he didn't consider my being a motor mechanic very ladylike'.[30] Many people also reacted strangely when she told them what her job was. Unlike Alice, many people outright refused to believe Lorraine was, indeed, a mechanic.

This article on Lorraine Faulkner was possibly the last to mention Alice Anderson until the early 1980s, when historian Mimi Colligan, who recalled that her mother had learnt to drive at the Alice Anderson Motor School, included Alice in her chapter of the book *Double Time: Women in Victoria* for the state's 150th anniversary in 1985.

Today, Alice Anderson and her garage have now largely been erased from Melbourne automobile histories. Even historian Georgine Clarsen, who initially trained as a mechanic in Melbourne in the 1970s, thought she was the first woman to do so until she discovered the existence of Alice. The only thread that continued through to the 1980s was written on the driving school cars that still bore Alice's name, operating locally in Kew and the surrounding eastern suburbs of Melbourne. In the mid 1990s, when Bib Stillwell was asked about his knowledge of Alice's business, he said, 'Alice Anderson Motors was, I understand, a hire-car service operated by the two Anderson sisters prior to World War Two and rumour has it that they committed suicide in the building.'[31]

Such is the confusion wrought by whispers passed down through the decades when the facts have been buried. This biography seeks to put the record straight and reinstate Alice Anderson as one of Australia's true pioneers, who deserves to be remembered, acknowledged and acclaimed as a national treasure.

NOTES

PROLOGUE: DESTINATION: ALICE SPRINGS

1   The clubrooms were originally the residence of the English, Scottish and Australian Bank's General Manager, Sir George Verdon. Today, the top floors are closed off to the public and the ground floor is home to the ANZ Bank.

2   'Woman's World: A woman's tribute to Alice Anderson', *The Herald* (Melbourne), 18 September 1926, p. 14.

3   Ibid.

4   See Alice E. F. Anderson, Lyceum Club application, 4 December 1918, Melbourne Lyceum Club Records, Box 9, SLV; 'New Lyceum Club Opened', *The Argus* (Melbourne), 30 June 1925, p. 1.

5   'Women Autoists', *The Mirror* (Perth), 7 August 1926, p. 5.

6   'Mrs. Marion Bell: The first woman motorist to attempt to encircle Australia reaches Adelaide on Plume and Mobil oil!' (advertisement), *The Register* (Adelaide), 19 February 1926, p. 16.

7   'Melbourne to Alice Springs', *Adelaide Mail*, 7 August 1926, p. 2.

8   Austin 7 advertisement, *The Car*, 5 February 1926, p. 22.

9   'Intrepid Women Motoring to Alice Springs', *Adelaide News*, 6 August 1926, p. 6.

10 Ibid.

11 'Melbourne Talk', *Western Mail*, 19 August 1926, p. 36.

CHAPTER 1: FAMILY PORTRAIT

1 E. Anderson to E. M. Anderson, 6 May 1897, Frances Derham Collection, University of Melbourne Archives (UMA) (ref. 1988.0061.0971).

2 E. Anderson to E. M. Anderson, 14 October 1897, Frances Derham Collection, UMA (ref. 1988.0061.0971).

3 J. Ellis, interview with the author, 29 May 2012, author's collection.

4 G. Serle, *John Monash: A Biography*, Melbourne University Press, Melbourne, 1982, p. 135.

5 K. Smith to E. M. Anderson, 1 November 1897, Frances Derham Collection, UMA (ref. 1988.0061.0971).

6 C. Fitzpatrick, interview with E. Shade, transcribed in 'Claire's Memories: Reflections on Childhood', 19 January 1994, p. 16, author's collection.

7 C. Fitzpatrick, interview with M. Colligan, 1984, audio transcript, pp. 3–4, sound recording courtesy M. Colligan, transcript by author.

8 F. Derham, interview with B. Blackman, 19 March 1984, NLA oral transcript 1792, 8:20 (sound recording), accessed 14 June 2011, http://nla.gov.au/nla.oh-vn2248904.

CHAPTER 2: LAND OF THE LONG WHITE CLOUD

1 F. Derham, interview with S. Lunney, 28 May 1975, NLA oral transcript 345, p. 24.

2 S. Murray to J. T. Anderson, 6 May 1909, Frances Derham Collection, UMA (ref. 1988.0061.0097).

3 C. Fitzpatrick, interview with G. Clarsen, 24 April 1994, audio transcript, p. 3, transcript courtesy G. Clarsen.

4 'Dunedin's Drainage: The board and their engineer: The scheme discussed', *The Evening Star* (Otago), 17 December 1902, p. 3.

5 *Bruce Herald* (Milton, NZ), 'Our Dunedin Letter', 23 December 1902, p. 3.

6 Derham, interview with Blackman, 19 March 1984, 29:17.

7 Derham, interview with Lunney, 1975, p. 17.

8 Ibid.

9 F. Derham biography and family history notes, Frances Derham Collection, UMA (ref. 1880.0061.0627).

10 K. Macmahon Ball, interview with M. Colligan, 1984, audio transcript, p. 6, sound recording courtesy M. Colligan, transcript by G. Clarsen.

11 Derham, interview with Lunney, 1975, p. 4.

12 Derham, interview with Lunney, 1975, pp. 8–9.

13 Derham, interview with Lunney, 1975, p. 7.

14 Fitzpatrick, interview with Clarsen, 15 May 1994, p. 5.

15 Ibid.

16 Ibid.

17 A. Anderson to J. Anderson, c. 20 December 1903, Frances Derham Collection, UMA (ref. 1988.0061.1482).

18 J. Anderson to E. M. Anderson, 2 March 1903, Frances Derham Collection, UMA (ref. 1988.0061.0977).

19 J. Anderson to J. T. Anderson, 10 February 1903, Frances Derham Collection, UMA (ref. 1988.0061.0977).

20 H. Anderson to J. T. Anderson, 6 April 1904, Frances Derham Collection, UMA (ref. 1988.0061.0978).

21 A. Anderson to J. Anderson, 4 September 1905, Frances Derham Collection, UMA (ref. 1988.0061.1482).

22 S. Anderson to E. M. Anderson, 9 September 1905, Frances Derham Collection, UMA (ref. 1988.0061.0227).

23 K. Anderson to J. Anderson, 30 November 1905, Frances Derham Collection, UMA (ref. 1988.0061.0103).

24 S. Anderson to J. T. and E. M. Anderson, 13 September 1905, Frances Derham Collection, UMA (ref. 1988.0061.0227).

25 Fitzpatrick, interview with Colligan, 1984, p. 1.

CHAPTER 3: TO THE MOTHERLAND

1 L. Anderson to E. M. Anderson, 8 September 1905, Frances Derham Collection, UMA (ref. 1988.0227).

2 Ibid.

3 Derham, interview with Blackman, 19 March 1984, 6:00.

4 Derham, interview with Lunney, 1975, p. 28.

5 Derham, interview with Colligan, 1984, p. 1.

6 M. Anderson to E. M. Anderson, 6 May 1897, Frances Derham
   Collection, UMA (ref. 1988.0061.0971).

7 M. Anderson to E. M. Anderson, 14 October 1897, Frances Derham
   Collection, UMA (ref. 1988.0061.0971).

8 Derham biography and family history notes, Frances Derham Collection,
   UMA (ref. 1988.0061.0627).

9 Derham, interview with Blackman, 19 March 1984, 41:46.

CHAPTER 4: A BUSH RETREAT

1 Fitzpatrick, interview with Shade, 17 June 1995, p. 29.

2 'Among the Pumps', *Mildura Cultivator*, 9 March 1907, p. 4.

3 J. T. Anderson to E. M. Anderson, 15 January 1908, Frances Derham
   Collection, UMA (ref. 1988.0061.1034).

4 J. T. Anderson to E. M. Anderson, 20 October 1908, Frances Derham
   Collection, UMA (ref. 1988.0061.1034).

5 J. T. Anderson to E. M. Anderson, 22 October 1908, Frances Derham
   Collection, UMA (ref. 1988.0061.1034).

6 J. T. Anderson to E. M. Anderson, 22 November 1908, Frances Derham
   Collection, UMA (ref. 1988.0061.1034).

7 Fitzpatrick, interview with Shade, 19 August 1995, p. 47.

8 Fitzpatrick, interview with Shade, 27 April 1996, p. 97.

9 Fitzpatrick, interview with Shade, 7 October 1995, p. 59.

10 Fitzpatrick, interview with Shade, 7 October 1995, p. 56.

CHAPTER 5: A EDUCATION OF SORTS

1 J. T. Anderson to A. Anderson, 17 November 1908, Frances Derham
   Collection, UMA (ref. 1988.0061.1034).

2 Fitzpatrick, interview with Clarsen, 24 April 1994, p. 5.

3 Fitzpatrick, interview with Clarsen, 24 April 1994, p. 4.

4 W.H. Cully to E. M. Anderson, 6 January 1909, Frances Derham
   Collection UMA (ref. 1988.0061.1034).

5 Fitzpatrick, interview with Shade, 19 August 1995, p. 51.

6 Ibid.

7 Derham, interview with Colligan, 1984, p. 2.

8 Fitzpatrick, interview with Colligan, 1984, p. 1.

9   Fitzpatrick, interview with Colligan, 1984, p. 28.

10 J. T. Anderson to E. M. Anderson, 21 November 1909, Frances Derham
    Collection, UMA (ref. 1988.0061.1035).

11 Fitzpatrick, interviews with Clarsen, 4 July 1995, p. 4; 24 April 1994, p. 5.

12 F. Derham, interview with K. Derham-Moore, 21 September 1986,
    Melbourne Lyceum Club Records, Boxes 64–6, SLV, audio transcript,
    p. 9.

13 S. Priestley, *The Crown of the Road: The Story of the RACV,* Macmillan,
    Melbourne, 1983, p. 6.

14 'Whirling Wheels of Europe: Growth of automobilism. Mr. J. P. Wallace's
    return', *Australian Motorist,* 15 October 1908, pp. 80–1.

15 Priestley, 1983, p. 6.

16 'Horse v Motor', *The Argus* (Melbourne), 12 December 1904, p. 4,
    as quoted in Keiran Tranter, 'The History of the Haste-Wagons: *The
    Motor Car Act 1909* (Vic), Emergent Technology and the Call for Law',
    Melbourne University Law Review, vol. 29, 2005, pp. 845–6.

CHAPTER 6: COMING OF AGE

1   J. T. Anderson to E. M. Anderson, 7 December 1908, Frances Derham
    Collection, UMA (ref. 1988.0061.1034).

2   Mcmahon Ball, interview with Colligan, 1984, p. 6.

3   J. Monash, 'The Motor Omnibus', *The Argus,* 23 March 1904, p. 4.

4   J. T. Anderson to E. M. Anderson, 19 April 1909, Frances Derham
    Collection, UMA (ref. 1988.0061.1035).

5   J. T. Anderson to E. M. Anderson, 3 November 1908, Frances Derham
    Collection, UMA (ref. 1988.0061.1034).

6   Derham, interview with Derham-Moore, 21 September 1986, p. 9.

7   Fitzpatrick, interview with Clarsen, 15 May 1994, p. 4.

8   Fitzpatrick, interview with Clarsen, 15 May 1994, p. 7.

9   J. T. Anderson to E. M. Anderson, 28 July 1910, Frances Derham
    Collection, UMA (ref. 1988.0061.1036).

10 Derham, interview with Derham-Moore, 21 September 1986, p. 1.

11 Fitzpatrick, interview with Colligan, 1984, p. 6.

12 Mcmahon Ball, interview with Colligan, 1984, pp. 4–5.

13 R. McCarthy and M. R. Theobald (eds.), *Melbourne Girls Grammar School Centenary Essays 1893–1993*, Hyland House Publishing, Sydney, 1993, p. 3.

14 Fitzpatrick, interview with Colligan, 1984, pp. 2, 6.

15 Joan was also known as Isabel, after her aunt Isabel.

16 A. Anderson to K. Anderson, undated (c. 1913), Frances Derham Collection, UMA (ref. 1988.0061.0210).

17 F. Anderson to E. M. Anderson, 3 June 1913, Frances Derham Collection, UMA (ref. 1988.0061.0096).

18 A. Anderson to E. M. Anderson, 24 August 1913, Frances Derham Collection, UMA (ref. 1988.0061.1454).

19 Francis Thompson (1859–1907), 'The Hound of Heaven', a 182-line poem first published in Thompson's first volume of poems in Britain, 1893.

20 Fitzpatrick, interview with Clarsen, 24 April 1994, p. 13.

CHAPTER 7: ANNUS HORRIBILIS

1 A. Anderson to E. M. Anderson, 24 August 1913, Frances Derham Collection, UMA (ref. 1988.0061.1454).

2 J. T. Anderson to E. M. Anderson, 12 November 1913, Frances Derham Collection, UMA (ref. 1988.0061.1039).

3 Lieutenant-Colonel Commanding RAGA to J. T. Anderson, 2 December 1913, Frances Derham Collection, UMA (ref. 1988.0061.0097).

4 Derham, interview with Lunney, 28 May 1975, pp. 50–2.

5 Fitzpatrick, interview with Shade, 1994–96, pp. 62, 84.

6 Derham, interview with Lunney, 28 May 1975, p. 50.

7 Fitzpatrick, interview with Colligan, 1984, p. 2.

8 Ibid.

9 J. T. Anderson to E. M. Anderson, 11 December 1913, Frances Derham Collection, UMA (ref. 1988.0061.1039).

10 C. Bean, *Official History of Australia in the War 1914–18, Vol 1, The Story of ANZAC: The First Phase*, Angus & Robertson, Sydney, 1921, pp. 46–7.

11 World War I propaganda postcard, SLV, accession no. H99.166/7.

12 Fitzpatrick, interview with Clarsen, 24 April 1994, p. 6.

13 Fitzpatrick, interview with Clarsen, 24 April 1994, p. 8.

14 E. M. Anderson to F. Anderson, 8 February 1915, Frances Derham Collection, UMA (ref. 1988.0061.0097).

15 Fitzpatrick, interview with Clarsen, 24 April 1994, p. 8.

16 Fitzpatrick, interview with Colligan, 1984, p. 6.

17 F. Anderson to A. Derham, 20 August 1915, Frances Derham Collection, UMA (ref. 1988.0061.1293).

18 Ibid.

19 A. Anderson to E. M. Anderson, 16 August 1915, Frances Derham Collection, UMA (ref. 1988.0061.0096).

20 F. Anderson to E. M. Anderson, undated, c. 1915, Frances Derham Collection, UMA (ref. 1988.0061.0096).

21 Fitzpatrick, interview with Clarsen, 24 April 1994, p. 9.

22 Ibid.

CHAPTER 8: OVER THE SPUR

1 'Hit or Miss Australian Methods of Road Building Compared to Scientific American Way', *Australian Motorist*, 1 June 1918, p. 865.

2 Fitzpatrick, interview with Colligan, 1984, p. 6.

3 Fitzpatrick, interview with Colligan, 1984, p. 8.

4 Fitzpatrick, interview with Colligan, 1984, p. 19.

5 Fitzpatrick, interview with Shade, 16 July 1995, p. 39.

6 J.T. Anderson to E.M. Anderson, undated, c. 1915, Frances Derham Collection, UMA (ref. 1988.0061.0101).

7 'Motor Service for Alexandra', *Alexandra and Yea Standard and Yarck, Gobur, Thornton and Acheron Express*, 14 April 1916, p. 2.

8 Mcmahon Ball, interview with Colligan, 1984, p. 1.

9 Ibid.

10 Fitzpatrick, interview with Clarsen, 24 April 1994, p. 6.

11 C. Hanson Towne, 'A Road that Leads to God Knows Where', *Australian Motorist*, 2 September 1918, p. 35.

12 Artemis, 'Women Awheel: The call of the open roads: One golden day', *Australian Motorist,* 1 January 1915, p. 433.

13 Fitzpatrick, interview with Clarsen, 24 April 1994, p. 8.

14 Ibid.

15 Alice Anderson, 'Her Wheel', *Woman's World*, 1 May 1926, p. 341.

16 'The New Motor Service: A great success', *Alexandra and Yea Standard and Yarck, Gobur, Thornton and Acheron Express*, 23 June 1916, p. 3.

17 'The Kew Garage: Founded and staffed by women', *Woman's World*, February 1922, p. 13.

18 Ibid.

19 Ibid.

20 Ibid.

21 'Motor Notes by Magneto Spark', *Punch*, 7 February 1918, Melbourne, p. 10.

22 'Women Awheel: The first woman to run a motor garage in Victoria', *Australian Motorist*, 1 August 1918, p. 972.

23 *The Argus,* 6 September 1916, p. 15.

24 F. Anderson to 'Mick', 26 October 1916, Frances Derham Collection, UMA (ref. 1988.0061.1210).

CHAPTER 9: HUPMOBILE TOURING

1 Fitzpatrick, interview with Clarsen, 24 April 1994, p. 9.

2 Fitzpatrick, interview with Clarsen, 27 July 1994, p. 2.

3 Fitzpatrick, interview with Colligan, 1984, p. 20.

4 Fitzpatrick, interview with Clarsen, 4 July 1995, p. 3.

5 Fitzpatrick, interview with Clarsen, 24 April 1994, p. 9.

6 Mcmahon Ball, interview with Colligan, 1984, p. 1.

7 Fitzpatrick, interview with Colligan, 1984, p. 20.

8 Fitzpatrick, interview with Colligan, 1984, p. 9.

9 *Healesville and Yarra Glen Guardian,* 27 January 1917, p. 2.

10 Fitzpatrick, interview with Colligan, 1984, p. 9.

11 Ibid.

12 Derham, interview with Blackman, 22 March 1984, 39:13.

13 E. M. Anderson to F. and A. Derham, 11 July 1917, Frances Derham Collection, UMA (ref. 1998.0061.0106).

14 *Healesville and Yarra Glen Guardian,* 8 September 1917, p. 2.

15 Fitzpatrick, interview with Clarsen, 24 April 1994, p. 11.

16 Ibid.

17 Mcmahon Ball, interview with Colligan, 1984, p. 1.

18 'Motor Sensations: Blacks' Spur coach overturns. Remarkable escapes', *The Argus*, 7 January 1918, p. 6.

CHAPTER 10: MISS ANDERSON'S MOTOR SERVICE

1 Alice so liked this poem that she cut it out of a magazine and saved it in her pocketbook. Copy with family note in author's possession.

2 'Motor Notes by Magneto Spark', *Punch*, 1918, p. 10.

3 'For the Home Circle: Between ourselves', *Brisbane Courier*, 26 March 1925, p. 11.

4 'Motoring Fashions for Winter Wear' (advertisement), *Australian Motorist*, 1 April 1918.

5 'Women Awheel', *Australian Motorist*, 1 January 1917, p. 541.

6 Ibid.

7 'Motor Notes by Magneto Spark', *Punch*, 7 February 1918, p. 9.

8 Artemis, 'Women Awheel: Indictment of women drivers brings sporting challenge', *Australian Motorist*, 1 September 1916, p. 79.

9 Ibid.

10 Advertisement, *Australian Motorist,* 2 April 1917, p. 887.

11 Advertisement, *Australian Motorist*, 1 January 1919, p. 39.

12 'Women Awheel: The approach of the professional chauffeuse', *Australian Motorist*, 1 December 1916, p. 381.

13 'Melbourne Woman's Chauffeur: Pioneer of industry', *The Register* (Adelaide), 24 March 1925, p. 5.

14 Mcmahon Ball, interview with Colligan, 1984, p. 1. (Katrine could not remember the manager's name.)

15 'Dodge the Hup' to Alice Anderson, 29 May 1918, Frances Derham Collection UMA (ref. 1988.0061.0097).

CHAPTER 11: A WOMEN'S CLUB

1 'The First Woman to Run a Motor Garage in Victoria', *Australian Motorist*, 1 August 1918, p. 972.

2 'Women Awheel', *Australian Motorist,* 2 September 1918, p. 14.

3 'Classifieds', *The Argus,* 25 September 1918, p. 2.

4 'The Kew Garage', *Woman's World*, February 1922, p. 13.

5 M. Lake, *Getting Equal: The History of Australian Feminism*, Allen & Unwin, New South Wales, 1999, pp. 12–13.

6 F. Kelly, 'Mrs. Smyth and the Body Politic: Health reform and birth control in Melbourne', in *Worth Her Salt: Women at Work in Australia*,

Margaret James, Margaret Bereg, Carmel Shute (eds.), Hale & Iremonger, Sydney, 1982.

7   'Women in Unconventional Callings', *Adam and Eve*, 1 June 1920, pp. 20–1.

8   Fitzpatrick, interview with Clarsen, 29 September 1996, p. 3.

9   G. Clarsen, *Eat My Dust: Early Women Motorists*, John Hopkins University Press, Baltimore, 2008, p. 115.

10   Ibid.

11   Clarsen, 2008, p. 32.

12   Minutes of General Committee Meeting, RACV Archives, 19 June 1918.

13   'Women Awheel: Proposed women's automobile club in Victoria', *Australian Motorist*, 1 July 1918, p. 946.

14   Priestley, 1983, p. 36.

15   'R.A.C.V at Home', *RACV*, September 1925, p. 1.

16   'Women's Interests: Pleasant afternoons at club' *RACV*, 15 April 1926, p. 48.

17   'Women Awheel: The proposed woman's club in Victoria', *Australian Motorist*, 1 August 1918, pp. 972–3.

18   'Return of the Wounded', Anzac Centenary, Victoria, accessed 10 December 2014, www.anzaccentenary.vic.gov.au/history/princes-pier.

19   Poem by Alice Anderson, undated, Frances Derham Collection, UMA (ref. 1988.0061.0751).

20   Artemis, 'Women Awheel: Motoriste dedicates herself and her automobile to the services of the Red Cross', *Australian Motorist*, 1 August 1916, p. 1457.

21   'Women Awheel: Women's Automobile Club of Australia', *Australian Motorist*, 1 November 1918, p. 112.

22   The first national Wattle Day occurred on 1 September 1910, promoting wattle as an emblem of national pride. Wattle took on particular significance during World War I as a potent symbol of home for military personnel serving overseas. Wattle Day then became a means of raising money for organisations such as the Red Cross. See Wattle Day Association: www.wattleday.asn.au.

23   J. Gillison, *A History of the Lyceum Club*, McKellar Press, Melbourne, 1975, pp. 24–8.

24 Derham, interview with Derham-Moore, 21 September 1986, p. 2.

25 Fitzpatrick, interview with Clarsen, 24 April 1994, pp. 33–4.

26 'Women Awheel: Women's Automobile Club of Australia', *Australian Motorist*, 1 October 1918, p. 69. Florence Young lent her Enfield car for Wattle Club Day as a member of the Women's Automobile Club of Australia; S. Cohn, interview with author, 7 August 2008.

27 'Woman's World: A woman's tribute to Alice Anderson', *The Herald* (Melbourne), 18 September 1926, p. 14.

CHAPTER 12: POSTWAR PRESSURES

1 A. Derham to F. Derham, 12 March 1919, Frances Derham Collection, UMA (ref. 1988.0061.0032).

2 J. Bell, 'Bage, Anna Frederika (Freda) (1883–1970)', *Australian Dictionary of Biography Online*, National Centre of Biography, ANU, accessed 10 November 2016, http://adb.anu.edu.au/biography/bage-anna-frederika-freda-5090/text8497.

3 A. Anderson to E. M. Anderson, 20 June 1919, author's collection.

4 'Women Awheel: An all-woman garage a success', *Australian Motorist*, 2 June 1919, p. 71.

5 'Miss Anderson's Death', *The Herald*, 18 September 1926, p. 41.

6 M. Billings, 'The Influenza Pandemic of 1918', accessed 8 September 2015, http://virus.stanford.edu/uda/.

7 A. Derham to F. Derham, 3 January 1919, Frances Derham Collection, UMA (ref. 1988.0061.0325).

8 Refers to Alfred's sister, Ruth Derham, who was now a qualified practising nurse and one of Frankie's closest friends.

9 A. Derham to F. Derham, 23 January 1919, Frances Derham Collection, UMA (ref. 1988.0061.0326).

10 A. Anderson to E. M. Anderson, 26 January 1919; Frances Derham Collection, UMA (ref. 1988.0061.0096).

CHAPTER 13: THE KEW GARAGE

1 *Sands & McDougall's Directory of Victoria for 1919*, p. 440.

2 A. Anderson to E. M. Anderson, 21 January 1919, Frances Derham Collection, UMA (ref. 1988.0061.0098). Curiously, this note from Alice

to her mother was written five months before the article in the *Australian Motorist,* which had outlined the garage's three storeys. What was Alice doing promoting her extravagant vision long after the garage's more modest construction had been realised? It is almost impossible to believe the garage had been built to lock-up stage without Alice being aware it would never house more than one level. Perhaps committing her dream to print, despite the reality, kept it alive that little bit longer and saved her ideas for posterity. It certainly made good copy even if her original plan was never going to see the light of day.

3 A. Anderson to E. M. Anderson, 26 January 1919, Frances Derham Collection, UMA (ref. 1988.0061.0098).

4 'Melbourne Notes', *Adelaide Chronicle*, 6 September 1924, p. 66.

5 Fitzpatrick, interview with Clarsen, 24 April 1994, p. 7.

6 'The Woman Who Does', *The Home*, 1 December 1920, p. 74.

7 Fitzpatrick, interviews with Clarsen, 24 April 1994, p. 22; 27 July 1994, p. 6.

8 'The Kew Garage', *Woman's World*, February 1922, p. 13.

9 'For the Home Circle', *Brisbane Courier*, 26 March 1925, p. 11.

CHAPTER 14: A THOROUGHLY MODERN GIRL

1 K. Holmes, *Spaces in Her Day: Australian Women's Diaries of the 1920s and 1930s*, Allen & Unwin, Sydney, 1995, p. 16.

2 'The Kew Garage', *Woman's World*, February 1922, p. 13.

3 'The Woman Who Does', *The Home*, 1 December 1920, p. 74.

4 Ibid.

5 Ibid.

6 '"Keb, Sir?" Melbourne Woman's Enterprise', *The Truth* (Brisbane), 3 May 1925, p. 14.

7 Ibid.

8 Fitzpatrick, interview with Clarsen, 24 April 1994, p. 18.

9 M. Martin (née Edie) to M. Colligan, 2 April 1983, author's collection.

10 Undated, unidentified newspaper cutting found in Monte Punshon's scrapbook, Australian Lesbian and Gay Archives, Melbourne.

11 A 'gasper' was 1920s popular slang for a cigarette.

12 M. Green, interview with author, 29 September 2015, p. 1.

13 H. Lawson, MLA, Jessica Millar reference, 13 May 1924. Courtesy Milton Green.

14 Green, interview with author, 29 September 2015, p. 2.

15 Claire dropped out of the engineering course after two years with poor marks. Many decades later she discovered the examiners had marked her differently to male students and she had in fact been one of the top students in the class. Claire believed this was because JT had an unresolved dispute with one of the lecturers but also that the lecturers were determined that a woman would not pass. (Fitzpatrick, interview with Colligan, 1984, pp. 22–3.)

16 Fitzpatrick, interview with Clarsen, 27 July 1994, p. 8.

17 Ibid.

18 *Dykes Automobile and Gasoline Engine Encyclopedia* by American Andrew Lee Dyke was a large, comprehensive automobile manual published annually from 1909 right through to the 1950s.

19 Fitzpatrick, interview with Clarsen, 27 July 1994, p.1.

20 'Melbourne's Woman Chauffeur: Pioneer of industry', *The Register,* 24 March 1925, p. 5.

21 Ibid.

22 M. Martin to M. Colligan, 2 April 1983, author's collection.

23 Ibid.

24 '"Keb, Sir?" Melbourne Woman's Enterprise', *The Truth*, 1925, p. 14.

CHAPTER 15: A VERY CLEVER INVENTION

1 This timeline is obviously incorrect. Alice was only thirteen years old in 1910.

2 'Women in Unconventional Callings', *Adam and Eve*, 1 June 1920, p. 20–1.

3 M. Horne, interview with G. Clarsen, 5 May 1996, p. 2.

4 Fitzpatrick, interview with Clarsen, 27 July 1994, p. 9.

5 'Miss Anderson's Death', *The Herald,* 18 September 1926, p. 1.

6 Advertisement, *RACV,* July 1926, p. 48; and subsequent editions 1926 onwards.

7 Fitzpatrick, interview with Clarsen, 24 April 1994, p. 18.

8 'Instructions for Lady Motorists', *Australian Automobile Trade Journal,* January 1920.

9 'The Care of Your Car' (advertisement), *RACV*, 15 June 1926, p. 21.

10 Clarsen, 2008, p. 113.

11 'The Kew Garage', *Woman's World*, February 1922, p. 13.

12 Fitzpatrick, interview with Clarsen, 24 April 1994, pp. 15–16.

13 M. Martin to M. Colligan, 2 April 1983, author's collection.

14 Fitzpatrick interview with Clarsen, 24 April 1984, pp. 15–16.

15 Ibid.

16 Now the Royal Melbourne Institute of Technology (RMIT), Melbourne.

17 'Women's Page: Melbourne's woman chauffeur: Pioneer of industry', *The Register* (Adelaide), 24 March 1925, p. 5.

18 'The Conquest of Housework', *The Home*, December 1920, p. 86.

19 'Women's Page: Melbourne's woman chauffeur', *The Register* (Adelaide), 24 March 1925, p. 5.

20 Ibid.

21 'For the Home Circle', *Brisbane Courier*, 26 March 1925, p. 11.

22 Warburton Franki (Ltd. Melbourne) advertisement, 'Give Her a Home Motor', *The Sun News-Pictorial*, 16 September 1922, p. 18.

23 'The Kew Garage', *Woman's World*, February 1922, p. 13.

24 'A Very Clever Invention', *Australian Motorist*, 1 September 1919, p. 20.

25 Fitzpatrick, interview with Clarsen, 27 July 1994, p. 8.

26 *The Australian Official Journal of Patents*, 19 September 1918, patent no. 8378/18:A37.D43 [patent lapsed 1919].

27 Fitzpatrick, interview with Clarsen, 27 July 1994, p.8

28 'The Kew Garage', *Woman's World*, February 1922, p. 13.

29 Fitzpatrick, interview with Clarsen, 27 July 1994, p. 8.

30 'For the Home Circle', *Brisbane Courier*, 26 March 1925, p. 11.

31 'He'd Have To Get Under – Get Out and Get Under', words by Grant Clark and Edgar Leslie, music by Maurice Abrahams, 1908. For lyrics see Jon W. Finson, *The Voices That are Gone*, Oxford University Press, New York, p. 155.

CHAPTER 16: DANGEROUS FREEDOMS

1 'The Social Swirl: Egeria's letter', *The Call* (Perth), 12 November 1926, p. 5.

2 'Order of the Garter', *Sun News-Pictorial*, 6 January 1923, p. 7.

3   Clarsen, 2008, p. 112.

4   'The Woman Who Does', *The Home*, 1 December 1920, p. 74.

5   Fitzpatrick, interview with Colligan, 1984, p. 9.

6   Mcmahon Ball, interview with Colligan, 1984, p. 4.

7   Mcmahon Ball, interview with Colligan, 1984, p. 3–4.

8   Fitzpatrick, interview with Clarsen, 15 May 1994, p. 8.

9   Fitzpatrick, interview with Clarsen, 15 May 1994, p. 1.

10 A. Anderson to E. M. Anderson, 26 June 1919, Frances Derham Collection, UMA (ref. 1988.0061.0098).

11 A. Anderson to E. M. Anderson, undated, author's collection.

12 Fitzpatrick, interview with Clarsen, 4 July 1995, p. 5.

13 Fitzpatrick, interview with Clarsen, 4 July 1995, p. 4.

14 'Miss Anderson's Death', *The Herald*, 18 September 1926, p. 1.

15 M. Cohn (née Houston) interview with author, 13 August 2008.

16 L. Johnston (née Garlick) to M. Colligan, 1 April 1983, author's collection.

17 Fitzpatrick, interview with Clarsen, 15 May 1994, p. 1.

18 Horne, interview with Clarsen, 5 May 1996, p.1.

19 Though it is not recorded in the transcript of Colligan's interview with Katrine, Colligan stated to the author several times that Katrine had used 'walked with the girls' to describe Alice.

20 Cohn, interview with author, 3 March 2009.

21 Cohn, interview with author, 13 August 2008.

22 Cohn, interview with author, 3 March 2009.

23 'Garage Girls: Miss Anderson's team to carry on', *The Herald*, 21 September 1926, p. 1.

24 'A Jeanne d'Arc in Khaki', *Australian Motorist*, 1 October 1917, p. 159.

25 Mcmahon Ball, interview with Colligan, 1984, pp. 2–3.

26 Ibid.

27 Ibid.

CHAPTER 17: BEYOND THE GARAGE

1   Derham, interview with Blackman, 19 March 1984, 21:35.

2   A. Anderson to E. M. Anderson, undated, author's collection.

3   Fitzpatrick, interview with Clarsen, 27 July 1994, p. 6.

4   *The Argus,* 27 June 1924, p. 5.

5   *The Age* (Melbourne), 9 October 1925, p. 9.

6   *Riverine Herald,* 26 April 1928, p. 2.

7   *Weekly Times* (Melbourne), 8 June 1918, p. 32.

8   *The Argus,* 22 January 1925, p. 13.

9   *Motor Car Act 1915,* Victoria, section 10.

10 'Motor Accidents', Alice Anderson letter to the editor, *The Argus,* 8 April 1925, p. 20.

11 'Horse Killed in Collision', *The Age,* 13 April 1921, p. 13; 'Equestrienne Sued: Court awards damages', *The Argus,* 13 April 1921, p. 5.

12 Fitzpatrick, interview with Colligan, 1984, pp. 21–2.

13 'Woman and the Car', *Australian Woman's Mirror,* 20 October 1925, p. 9.

14 Ibid.

15 Ibid.

16 Peter Fitzsimons, 'Foreword', *The Old Hume Highway,* 2nd edition, NSW Roads and Maritime Services, Sydney, 2018, p. 2.

17 'Melbourne's Woman Chauffeur: Pioneer of industry', *The Register* (Adelaide), 24 March 1925, p. 5.

18 'Maya V. Tucker, Irene Frances, (1890–1933)', *Australian Dictionary of Biography Online,* ANU, accessed 27 November 2012, http://adb.anu.edu. au/biography/taylor-irene-frances-8761/text15353.

19 A. Anderson, 'Her Wheel', *Woman's World,* 1 May 1926, p. 341.

20 Ibid.

21 A. Anderson, 'Her Wheel', *Woman's World,* 1 June 1926, p. 411.

22 K. Summerscale, *The Queen of Whale Cay,* Harper Perennial, London, 2008, unmarked page in endmatter.

CHAPTER 18: TO THE NEVER-NEVER

1   G. R. Broadbent, 'Motoring', *The Argus,* 24 March 1925, p. 4.

2   *Broadbent's Motor Route: Melbourne to Adelaide (and Back): The grand overland tour,* Melbourne, F.W. Niven Pty. Ltd. Printers, 1915.

3   'The Long Long Trail!' (advertisement) *Adelaide Mail,* 14 August 1926, p. 9.

4   'Women Motorists to Alice Springs', *The Advertiser* (Adelaide), 24 August 1926, p. 19.

5   'Intrepid Women Motoring to Alice Springs', *Adelaide News,* 6 August 1926, p. 6.

6 'Women Overlanders', *The Mail* (Adelaide), 21 August 1926, p. 30.

7 V. E. Turner, *Pearls From the Deep*, United Aborigines' Mission, Adelaide, 1936, p. 8.

8 Ibid.

9 J. Nicholls, 'Woman's life in Central Australia', *Woman's World*, 1 January 1923, p. 1.

10 Details are based on Alice's reports of women she met in Central Australia at the time and provided in the newspaper interview 'Women in Central Australia: Never complain of being lonely', *The Herald*, 14 September 1926, p. 14.

11 Ibid.

12 Ibid.

13 'Venturesome Lady Motorists', *The Register* (Adelaide), 25 August 1926, p. 10; 'Overlander at Alice Springs', *Adelaide News*, 24 August 1926, p. 9.

14 'Death of Miss Anderson', *The News* (Adelaide), 22 September 1926, p. 4.

15 A. Anderson to E. Lothian, 9 September 1926, Frances Derham Collection, UMA (ref. 1988.0061.0101).

16 Sir A. Cobham, KBE, *Australia and Back*, A. & C. Black Ltd, London, 1926, pp. 20–7.

17 *Sun News-Pictorial*, 16 August 1926, p. 3.

18 'Aviation Boom', *Northern Territory Times and Gazette*, 31 August 1926, p. 1.

19 Cobham, 1926, pp. 89, 100.

CHAPTER 19: A TRAGIC LOSS

1 A. Anderson to E. Lothian, 9 September 1926, Frances Derham Collection, UMA (ref. 1988.0061.0101)

2 Ibid.

3 Ibid.

4 F. Derham's typed statement about Alice's death, undated, Frances Derham Collection, UMA (ref. 1988.0061.0270).

5 'Women in Central Australia: Never complain of being lonely', p. 14.

6 'Shot Through Head: Death of Miss Alice Anderson', *The Argus*, 18 September 1926, p. 41; 'Miss Anderson's Death', *The Herald*, 18 September 1926, p. 1.

7 Mcmahon Ball, interview with Colligan, 1984, p. 7.

8   F. Derham's statement about Alice's death, undated.

9   F. Derham's 1926 diary, Frances Derham Collection, UMA
    (1988.0061.0270).

10 A. Derham, 'Alice Anderson' poem, penned on the night of Alice's
    death, 17 September 1926, Frances Derham Collection, UMA
    (ref.1988.0061.0751).

11 'Shot Through Head', *The Argus*, 18 September 1926, p. 41.

12 'Miss Anderson's Death', *The Herald* (Melbourne), 18 September 1926,
    p. 1.

13 'A Tragic Death', *The Chronicle* (Adelaide), 16 October 1926, p. 68.

14 'An Obsolete Morgue', *The Age*, 9 March 1928, p. 8.

15 'The City Morgue: Attorney General's opinion. Present buildings
    unsatisfactory', *The Age*, 27 October 1927, p. 12.

16 'A Tragic Death', *The Chronicle* (Adelaide), 16 October 1926, p. 68.

17 Ibid.

18 Proceedings of Inquest, 30 September 1926, VPRS 24/P/0 Unit 1099,
    File 1926/1034.

19 Ibid.

20 Ibid.

21 Ibid.

22 Ibid.

23 Ibid.

24 Ibid.

25 Ibid.

26 Ibid.

27 Ibid.

28 Ibid.

29 'A Woman's Death: Accidentally shot', *Western Argus*, 5 October 1926,
    p. 14.

30 'Miss Anderson's Death: Accidental says coroner', *Geelong Advertiser*,
    1 October 1926, p. 5.

31 'Mainly About Members', *RACV*, 15 October 1926, p. 9.

32 'Our Good Fortune and Yours: Mary Grant Bruce, author and journalist,
    to edit "Woman's World"', *Woman's World*, 1 April 1926, p. 242.

33 'Choosing a Car: A few points to note before buying. Written for *Woman's World* by Alice E. F. Anderson', *Woman's World,* 1 October 1926, p. 653.

34 Ibid.

35 Ibid.

36 Derham, interview with Colligan, 1984, p. 4.

37 Fitzpatrick, interview with Colligan, 1984, p. 30.

38 Fitzpatrick, interview with Colligan, p. 1984, p. 31.

39 P. Alexander, *Frances Derham: A Refuge Within*, Grey Thrush Publishing, Melbourne, 2006, p. 173.

40 Ellis, interview with author, 2 May 2013.

41 E. M. Martin to G. Clarsen, 17 July 1995, author's collection.

42 E. M. Martin to M. Colligan, 2 April 1983, author's collection.

43 Alice quotes the words of Omar Khayyam, the eleventh-century astronomer and poet, as translated by Richard le Gallienne (1886–1947) in *Rubaiyat of Omar Khayyam*, The Philosopher Press, Wausau, Wisconsin, 1901.

44 Poem penned by Alice, undated, Frances Derham Collection, UMA (ref. 1988.0061.0751).

EPILOGUE: GARAGE GIRLS CARRY ON

1 Cohn, interview with author, 3 March 2009.

2 Every time the author mentioned Alice Anderson to the elderly Mary Cohn (née Houston) her eyes lit up and she said with great conviction, 'Oh, I adored Miss Anderson!'

3 'Garage Girls: Miss Anderson's team to carry on', *The Herald*, 21 September 1926, p. 1.

4 Ibid.

5 'Will Carry On Miss Anderson's garage: Her girls decide', *Sun News-Pictorial* (Melbourne), 22 September 1926, p. 10.

6 'A Friend's Memorial', *The Argus*, 29 October 1926, p. 14.

7 'Woman in Motor Business', *The News* (Adelaide), 3 November 1926, p. 6.

8 Ibid.

9 'Women's Work', *Hobart Mercury*, 28 October 1926, p. 6.

10 Proceedings of Inquest, VPRS 24/P/O Unit 1099, File 1926/1034.

11 Supreme Court of Victoria (Probate Jurisdiction), 'Inventory of Assets in the Will of Alice Anderson Foley, late of Cotham Road Kew in the State of Victoria, Spinster deceased', 20 October 1926, VPRS 28/P/3, Unit 1704, File 211/726.

12 L. Wells, telephone interview with author, 18 November 2017. Lenis is the daughter of garage girl Linda Hotham.

13 'New Companies Registered', *Daily Commercial News and Shipping List* (Sydney), 4 September 1931, p. 4.

14 Clarsen, 2008, p. 115.

15 'Women Put Out Fire: Brave danger of explosion', *The Herald*, 3 September 1935, p. 1.

16 'Woman's Garage: Melbourne enterprise', *Daily Mercury* (Mackay, Queensland), 7 November 1938, p. 6. The *Daily Mercury* acknowledges Max Evans of Melbourne's *Sun News-Pictorial* as the article's source.

17 Ibid.

18 Ibid.

19 Ibid.

20 Ibid.

21 Ibid.

22 Ibid.

23 P. Peterson interviewed by G. Clarsen, 1 August 1995, pp. 2–4, transcript courtesy G. Clarsen.

24 'Woman's Garage', *Daily Mercury*, 7 November 1938, p. 6.

25 'Life of Melbourne: Alice Anderson group', *The Argus* (Melbourne), 17 June 1941, p. 6.

26 'Woman Drivers No Joke Here', *The Age* (Melbourne), 6 February 1951, p. 5.

27 Ibid.

28 'A Mechanic Called Miss', *The Australian Women's Weekly*, 23 December 1964, p. 7.

29 Ibid.

30 Ibid.

31 B. Stillwell to G. Clarsen, 7 May 1996, author's collection.

BIBLIOGRAPHY

BOOKS

Alexander, Penelope, *Frances Derham: A Refuge Within*, Grey Thrush Publishing, Melbourne, 2006

Allen, Grant, *The Woman Who Did*, Jon Lane for Bodley Head, London, 1895

Anderson, Joshua Thomas Noble, *A Twentieth Century City* (paper presented by J.T. Noble Anderson, Proceedings at the Conference of Engineers, Architects, Surveyors and Others Interested in the Building of the Federal Capital, May 1901, Melbourne), accessed 19 September 2017, http://urbanplanning.library.cornell.edu/DOCS/anderson.htm

Bean, Charles, *Official History of Australia in the War 1914–18, Vol 1, The Story of ANZAC: The First Phase*, Angus & Robertson, Sydney, 1921

Bridges, Philippa, 'The Account of an Englishwoman's Epic Camel Journey in 1924' in Frank Shanahan *Oodnadatta Walkabout: Reminiscences of Oodnadatta and Beyond in the 1920s*, Melbourne, 1996

Bruce, Mary Grant, *A Little Bush Maid*, Ward, Lock and Co. Limited, London and Melbourne, 1910

Caroll, Brian, *Getting Around Town: A History of Urban Transport in Australia*, Cassell Australia, Sydney, 1980

Clarsen, Georgine, *Eat My Dust: Early Women Motorists*, John Hopkins University Press, Baltimore, 2008

Cobham KBE, Sir Alan, *Australia and Back,* A. & C. Black Ltd, London, 1926

Country Roads Board Victoria, *Fifty Years of Progress 1913–1963,* Melbourne,
    Meteor Press, 1964

Dyke, A. L., *Dykes Automobile and Gasoline Engine Encylopedia*, 12th ed.,
    Goodheart-Wilcox company inc., Chicago, 1921

Fitzsimons, Peter, 'Foreword' in *The Old Hume Highway,* 2nd edition, NSW
    Roads and Maritime Services, Sydney, 2018, pp. 2–3

Gillison, Joan, *A History of the Lyceum Club,* McKellar Press, Melbourne, 1975

Holmes, Katie, *Spaces in Her Day: Australian Women's Diaries of the 1920s and
    1930s,* Allen & Unwin, Sydney, 1995

Kelly, Farley, 'Mrs. Smyth and the Body Politic: Health Reform and Birth
    Control in Melbourne', in *Worth Her Salt: Women at Work in Australia,*
    Margaret James, Margaret Bereg, Carmel Shute (eds.), Hale & Iremonger,
    Sydney, 1982

Khayyam, Omar, *Rubaiyat of Omar Khayyam* (trans. Richard le Gallienne),
    Grant Richards, London, 1901

Knibbs, Sir George, Commonwealth Bureau of Census and Statistics (Australia),
    1925 Official Year Book of the Commonwealth of Australia, Commonwealth
    Bureau of Census and Statistics Melbourne, Victoria, 1925

Lake, Marilyn, *Getting Equal: The History of Australian Feminism,* Allen &
    Unwin, Sydney, 1999

Lay, Dr Maxwell, *Melbourne Miles: The Story of Melbourne's Roads,* Australian
    Scholarly Publishing, Melbourne, 2003

Lloyd, Prof. Brian E., *Joshua Thomas Noble Anderson (1865–1949), Engineer:
    A Biographical Sketch,* Volume GE23, Transaction of Multidisciplinary
    Engineering, Deakin University, Melbourne 1999

Macintyre, Stuart and Shelleck, R. J. W., *A Short History of the University of
    Melbourne,* Melbourne University Press, Melbourne, 2003

Mackrell, Judith, *Flappers: Six Women of a Dangerous Generation,* Macmillan,
    London, 2013

McCarthy, Rosslyn and Theobald, Marjorie R. (eds.), *Melbourne Girls Grammar
    School Centenary Essays 1893–1993,* Hyland House Publishing, Sydney, 1993

Piscitelli, Barbara Ann, *The Life of Frances Derham: Process, Product and Reflections,*
    Ph.D. thesis, James Cook University of North Queensland, 1994

Priestley, Susan, *The Crown of the Road: The Story of the RACV*, Macmillan, Melbourne, 1983

Ridley, Ronald T., *Jessie Webb: A Memoir*, History Department, University of Melbourne, 1994

Royal Automobile Club of Australia, *50 Years: The Jubilee Book of the Royal Automobile Club of Australia*, 1953

Sands & McDougall's Directory of Victoria for 1919, Sands & McDougall, Melbourne, 1919

Scharff, Virginia, *Taking the Wheel: Women and the Coming of the Motor Age*, The Free Press, A Division of Macmillan Inc., New York, 1991

Serle, Geoffrey, *John Monash: A Biography*, Melbourne University Press, Melbourne, 1982

Shanahan, Frank, *Oodnadatta Walkabout: Reminiscences of Oodnadatta and Beyond in the 1920s*, Melbourne, 1996

Shell Company of Australia, *Shell Motorists' Index*, Shell Company, Australia, n.d., c. 1928

Summerscale, Kate, *Queen of Whale Cay*, Harper Perennial, London, 2008

Thompson, Francis, *The Hound of Heaven*, 1st edition, Chatto & Windus, London, 1914

Tranter, Keiran, 'The History of the Haste-Wagons: *The Motor Car Act 1909* (Vic), Emergent Technology and the Call for Law', *Melbourne University Law Review*, vol. 29, 2005, pp. 845–6

Turner, Violet, *Pearls From the Deep*, United Aborigines' Mission, Adelaide, 1936

Wyatt, Horace, *The Motor Industry, Its Growth, Its Methods, Its Prospects, and Its Products; with an Indication of the Uses to Which Motor Vehicles of All Kinds Are, or Could Be, Advantageously Applied*, Sir Isaac Pitman & Sons, Ltd., London, 1917

ARTICLES

MAGAZINES AND JOURNALS

Adam and Eve: 'Women in Unconventional Callings', 1 June 1920, pp. 20–1

Australian Automobile Trade Journal, 'Instructions for Lady Motorists', VACC Melbourne, January 1920

Australian Motorist: 'Whirling Wheels of Europe: Growth of automobilism. Mr. J. P. Wallace's return', 15 October 1908, pp. 80–1; Artemis, 'Women Awheel: The call of the open roads: One golden day', 1 January 1915, p. 433; 'Women A-wheel: Motoriste dedicates herself and her automobile to the services of the Red Cross', 1 August 1916, p. 1457; Artemis, 'Women A-wheel: Indictment of women drivers brings sporting challenge', 1 September 1916, p. 79; D. Mary, 'Women Awheel: The approach of the professional chauffeuse', 1 December 1916, p. 381; 'Women Awheel', 1 January 1917, p. 541; CAV Car Lighting and Steering (advertisement), 2 April 1917, p. 887; 'A Jeanne d'Arc in Khaki', 1 October 1917, p. 159; 'Motoring Fashions for Winter Wear' (advertisement) 1 April 1918; 'Hit or Miss: Australian methods of road building compared to scientific American way', 1 June 1918, p. 865; 'Women Awheel: Proposed women's automobile club in Victoria', 1 July 1918, p. 946; 'Women Awheel: The first woman to run a motor garage in Victoria', 1 August 1918, pp. 972–3; 'Women Awheel: The proposed woman's club in Victoria,' 1 August 1918, pp. 972–3; 'Women Awheel,' 2 September 1918, p. 14; Towne, C. Hanson, 'A Road that Leads to God Knows Where', 2 September 1918, p. 35; 'Women Awheel: Women's Automobile Club of Australia', 1 October 1918, p. 69; 'Women Awheel: Women's Automobile Club of Australia', 1 November 1918, p. 112; 'Women Awheel: An all-woman garage success', 2 June 1919, p. 71; 'A Very Clever Invention', 1 September 1919, p. 20

The Australian Official Journal of Patents, Volume 28, patent no. 8378/18:A37. D43, 19 September 1918

Australian Woman's Mirror, 'Woman and the Car', Vol. 1 No. 48, 20 October 1925, p. 9

The Australian Women's Weekly, 'A Mechanic Called Miss', 23 December 1964, p. 7

RACV: 'R.A.C.V at Home', September 1925, p. 1; 'Women's Interests: Pleasant afternoon at club', 15 April 1926, p. 48; 'The Kew Garage Kew: A "once-over"' (advertisement), July 1926, p. 48; 'The Care of Your Car' (advertisement) 15 June 1926, p. 21; 'Mainly About Members', 15 October 1926, p. 9

The Car, Austin 7 advertisement, 5 February 1926, p. 22

The Home: 'The Woman Who Does', 1 December 1920, p. 74; 'The Conquest of Housework', December 1920, p. 86

Pointers magazine, 'Striking Some Notes – New or Old – in Used Car Ads', Vol. XXVI, No. 9, General Motors-Holden's publication, October 1962, p. 10

Punch, 'Motor Notes by Magneto Spark', 7 February 1918, Melbourne, pp. 9–10

Woman's World: 'The Kew Garage: Founded and staffed by women', February 1922, p. 13; Nicholls, J. 'Woman's Life in Central Australia', 1 January 1923, p. 1; 'Our Good Fortune and Yours: Mary Grant Bruce, author and journalist, to edit "Woman's World"', 1 April 1926, p. 242; Anderson, A., 'Her Wheel', 1 May 1926, p. 341; Anderson, A., 'Her Wheel', 1 June 1926, p. 411; 'Choosing a Car: A few points to note before buying. Written for *Woman's World* by Alice E. F. Anderson', 1 October 1926, p. 653

NEWSPAPERS

Adelaide Chronicle, 'Melbourne Notes', 6 September 1924, p. 66

Adelaide Mail, 'Melbourne to Alice Springs', 7 August 1926, p. 2; 'The Long, Long Trail!' (advertisement) 14 August 1926, p. 9

Adelaide News: 'Intrepid Women Motoring to Alice Springs', 6 August 1926, p. 6; 'Overlander at Alice Springs', 24 August 1926, p. 9; 'Venturesome Lady Motorists', 25 Aug 1926, p. 10

The Advertiser (Adelaide), 'Women Motorists to Alice Springs', 24 August 1926, p. 19

The Age (Melbourne): 'Horse Killed in Collision', 13 April 1921, p. 13; 'Sensational Collision. Tram and lorry. Motorman injured', 9 October 1925, p. 9; 'The City Morgue: Attorney General's opinion. Present buildings unsatisfactory', 27 October 1927, p. 12; 'An Obsolete Morgue', 9 March 1928, p. 8; 'Women Drivers No Joke Here', 6 February 1951, p. 5

Alexandra and Yea Standard and Yarck, Gobur, Thornton and Acheron Express: 'The New Motor Service: A great success', 23 June 1916, p. 3; 'Motor Service for Alexandra', 14 April 1916, p. 2

The Argus (Melbourne): Monash, J., 'The Motor Omnibus', 23 March 1904, p. 4; 'Horse v Motor', 12 December 1904, p. 4; 'Motor Manager, Black Spur Motor Service Company Limited' (advertisement), 6 September 1916, p. 15; 'Motor Sensations: Blacks' Spur coach overturns. Remarkable

escapes', 7 January 1918, p. 6; 'Classifieds', 25 September 1918, p. 2;
'Equestrienne Sued: Court awards damages', 13 April 1921, p. 5; 'Horse
Bolts with Lorry: Collision with tram. Driver's skull fractured', 27
June 1924, p. 5; 'Motor-cyclist killed. Accident at Brighton. Struck by
motor-car,' 22 January 1925, p. 13; 'Fatal Motor Accident', 13 February
1925, p. 11; Broadbent, G. R., 'Motoring', 24 March 1925, p. 4; Anderson,
A., 'Motor Accidents', 8 April 1925, p. 20; 'New Lyceum Club Opened',
30 June 1925, p. 1; 'Shot Through Head', 18 September 1926, p. 41;
'A Friend's Memorial', 29 October 1926, p. 14; 'Life of Melbourne:
Alice Anderson group', 17 June 1941, p. 6

Brisbane Courier: 'For the Home Circle: Between ourselves', 26 March 1925,
p. 11; 'Miss Ethel Bage's venture', 8 November 1926, p. 19

Bruce Herald (Milton, New Zealand), 'Our Dunedin Letter', 23 December
1902, p. 3

The Call (Perth), 'The Social Swirl: Egeria's letter', 12 November 1926, p. 5

The Chronicle (Adelaide), 'A Tragic Death' in 'Melbourne Notes', 16 October
1926, p. 68

Daily Commercial News and Shipping List (Sydney), 'New Companies
Registered', 4 September 1931, p. 4

Daily Mercury (Mackay, Queensland), 'Woman's Garage: Melbourne enterprise',
7 November 1938, p. 6

The Evening Star (Otago), 'Dunedin's Drainage: The board and their engineer:
The scheme discussed', 17 December 1902, p. 3

Geelong Advertiser, 'Miss Anderson's Death: Accidental says coroner', 1 October
1926, p. 5

Healesville and Yarra Glen Guardian: Noble Anderson, J.T. , 'Correspondence: to
the editor,' 27 January 1917, p. 2; 'Motor to Melbourne' (advertisement),
8 September 1917, p. 2

The Herald (Melbourne): 'Ready to Set Out for Alice Springs', 7 August 1926,
p. 12; 'Women in Central Australia: Never complain of being lonely', 14
September 1926, p. 14; 'Miss Anderson's Death', 18 September 1926,
pp. 1, 41; 'Woman's World: A woman's tribute to Alice Anderson', 18
September 1926, p. 14; 'Garage Girls: Miss Anderson's team to carry on.
Pals pull together', 21 September 1926, p. 1; 'Women Put Out Fire: Brave
danger of explosion', 3 September 1935, p. 1

Hobart Mercury, 'Women's Work', 28 October 1926, p. 6

The Mail (Adelaide), 'Women Overlanders', 21 August 1926, p. 30

Mildura Cultivator, 'Among the Pumps', 9 March 1907, p. 4

The Mirror (Perth), 'Women Autoists', 7 August 1926, p. 5

The News (Adelaide): 'Death of Miss Anderson', 22 September 1926, p. 4; 'Woman in Motor Business', 3 November 1926, p. 6

Northern Territory Times and Gazette, 'Aviation Boom', 31 August 1926, p. 1

The Register (Adelaide): 'Women's Page: Melbourne's woman chauffeur: Pioneer of industry', 24 March 1925, p. 5; 'Mrs Marion Bell: The first woman motorist to attempt to encircle Australia reaches Adelaide on Plume and Mobil oil!' (advertisement), 19 February 1926, p. 16; 'Venturesome Lady Motorists', 25 August 1926, p. 10

Riverine Herald, 'Fatal Collision: Bolting horse dashes into motorcar', 26 April 1928, p. 2

Sun News-Pictorial (Melbourne): 'Give Her a Home Motor', (Warburton Franki Ltd. Melbourne advertisement), 16 September 1922, p. 18; Fifty-Fifty, Public Views of Public Questions: 'Order of the Garter', 6 January 1923, p. 7; 'Man Who Has Braved World Flight Ran From City's Wild Welcome', 16 August 1926, p. 3; 'Will Carry On: Miss Anderson's garage: Her girls decide', 22 September 1926, p. 10

The Truth (Brisbane), '"Keb, Sir?" Melbourne Woman's Enterprise', 3 May 1925, p. 14

Weekly Times (Melbourne), 'Fatal Road Collision: Motorcar strikes horse', 8 June 1918, p. 32

Western Argus, 'A Woman's Death: Accidentally shot', 5 October 1926, p. 14

Western Mail, 'Melbourne Talk', 19 August 1926, p. 36

ONLINE ARTICLES

Australian Dictionary of Biography Online, National Centre of Biography, Australian National University, accessed online 10 November 2016, http://adb.anu.edu.au/

Billings, M. 'The Influenza Pandemic of 1918', accessed 8 September 2015, http://virus.stanford.edu/uda/

'Return of the Wounded', Anzac Centenary, Victoria, accessed 10 December 2014, www.anzaccentenary.vic.gov.au/history/princes-pier

MAPS

AIATSIS Map of Indigenous Australia (ed. David R. Horton), Aboriginal
Studies Press, AIATSIS, 1996, accessed 17 November 2018, https://aiatsis.
gov.au/explore/articles/aiatsis-map-indigenous-australia

Broadbent, George. R., *Special Motor Route: Melbourne to Adelaide (and Back):
The Grand Overland Tour*, Melbourne, F. W. Niven Pty. Ltd. Printers, 1915

ARCHIVAL MATERIAL

LETTERS

FRANCES DERHAM COLLECTION, UNIVERSITY OF MELBOURNE ARCHIVES

Alfred Derham to Frances Derham, 3 January 1919 (ref. 1988.0061.0325); 23
January 1919 (ref. 1988.0061.0326); 12 March 1919 (ref. 1988.0061.0032

Alice Anderson to Elizabeth Lothian, 9 September 1926 (ref. 1988.0061.0101)

Alice Anderson to Ellen Mary Anderson, 24 August 1913 (ref.
1988.0061.0102); 24 August 1913 (ref. 1988.0061.1454); 16 August 1915
(ref. 1988.0061.0096); 21 January 1919 (ref. 1988.0061.0098); 26 January
1919 (ref. 1988.0061.0098); 26 June 1919 (ref. 1988.0061.0098)

Alice Anderson to Jack Anderson, c. 20 December 1903 (ref. 1988.0061.1482);
4 September 1905 (ref. 1988.0061.1482)

Alice Anderson to Katrine Anderson, undated (c. 1913) (ref. 1988.0061.0210)

'Dodge the Hup' to Alice Anderson, 29 May 1918 (ref. 1988.0061.0097)

Eliza Anderson to Ellen Mary Anderson, 6 May 1897 (ref. 1988.0061.0971);
14 October 1897 (ref. 1988.0061.0971)

Ellen Mary Anderson to Frances Anderson, 8 February 1915 (ref.
1988.0061.0097)

Ellen Mary Anderson to Frances and Alfred Derham, 11 July 1917 (ref.
1998.0061.0106)

Frances Anderson to Alfred Derham, 20 August 1915 (ref. 1988.0061.1293); 24
July 1916 (ref. 1988.0067.0210)

Frances Anderson to Ellen Mary Anderson, 3 June 1913 (ref. 1988.0061.0096);
undated (c. 1915) (ref. 1988.0061.0096)

Frances Anderson to 'Mick', 26 October 1916 (ref. 1988.0061.1210)

Henry Anderson to J. T. Anderson, 6 April 1904 (ref. 1988.0061.0978)

Jack Anderson to Ellen Mary Anderson, 23 December 1902 (ref. 1988.0061.0976); 2 March 1903 (ref. 1988.0061.0977)

Jack Anderson to J. T. Anderson, 23 December 1902 (ref. 1988.0061.0976); 10 February 1903 (ref. 1988.0061.0977); 2 March 1903 (ref. 1988.0061.0977)

J. T. Anderson to Alice Anderson, 17 November 1908 (ref. 1988.0061.1034)

J. T. Anderson to Ellen Mary Anderson, 15 January 1908 (ref. 1988.0061.1034); 20 October 1908 (ref. 1988.0061.1034); 22 October 1908 (ref. 1988.0061.1034); 3 November 1908 (ref. 1988.0061.1034); 22 November 1908 (ref. 1988.0061.1034); 7 December 1908 (ref. 1988.0061.1034); 19 April 1909 (ref. 1988.0061.1035); 21 November 1909 (ref. 1988.0061.1035); 28 July 1910 (ref. 1988.0061.1036); 12 November 1913 (ref. 1988.0061.1039); 11 December 1913 (ref. 1988.0061.1039)

Katie Smith to Ellen Mary Anderson, 1 November 1897 (ref. 1988.0061.0971)

Katrine Anderson to Jack Anderson, 30 November 1905 (ref. 1988.0061.0103)

Lettie Anderson to Ellen Mary Anderson, 8 September 1905 (ref. 1988.0227)

Lieutenant-Colonel Commanding RAGA to J. T. Anderson, 2 December 1913 (ref. 1988.0061.0097)

Mater Anderson to Ellen Mary Anderson, 6 May 1897 (ref. 1988.0061.0971); 14 October 1897, (ref. 1988.0061.0971)

Stewart Anderson to Ellen Mary Anderson, 9 September 1905 (ref. 1988.0061.0227)

Stewart Anderson to J. T. and Ellen Mary Anderson, 13 September 1905 (ref. 1988.0061.0227)

Stuart Murray to J. T. Anderson, 6 May 1909 (ref. 1988.0061.0097)

W. H. Cully to Ellen Mary Anderson, 6 January 1909 (ref. 1988.0061.0100)

LETTERS IN OTHER COLLECTIONS

Alice Anderson to Ellen Mary Anderson, 20 June 1919, author's collection

Alice Anderson to Ellen Mary Anderson, undated, author's collection

Bib Stillwell to Georgine Clarsen, 7 May 1996, author's collection

Edward Maurice Martin to Georgine Clarsen, 17 July 1995, author's collection

Edward Maurice Martin to Mimi Colligan, 2 April 1983, author's collection

Frances Derham to Kathie Derham-Moore, 20 November 1986, Melbourne
 Lyceum Club Records, boxes 64–6, p. 2, State Library of Victoria
Lucy Johnston (née Garlick) to Mimi Colligan, 1 April 1983, author's collection
Marie Martin (née Edie) to Mimi Colligan, 2 April 1983, author's collection

INTERVIEWS AND AUDIO TRANSCRIPTS

Claire Fitzpatrick interviews with Elizabeth Shade, recorded and transcribed
 in 'Claire's Memories: Reflections on Childhood', 1994–96, author's
 collection
Claire Fitzpatrick interviews with Georgine Clarsen, 24 April 1994; 15 May
 1994; 27 July 1994; 4 July 1995; 29 September 1996, transcripts courtesy
 Georgine Clarsen
Claire Fitzpatrick interviews with Mimi Colligan, 1984, sound recording
 courtesy Mimi Colligan, transcript by author
Frances Derham interview with Barbara Blackman, 19–29 March 1984, NLA
 Oral History Collection 1792, sound recording accessed 14 June 2011,
 http://nla.gov.au/nla.oh-vn2248904
Frances Derham interview with Kathie Derham-Moore, 21 September 1986,
 Melbourne Lyceum Club Records, State Library of Victoria, Boxes 64–6
Frances Derham interview with Mimi Colligan, 1984, sound recording
 courtesy Mimi Colligan, transcript by author
Frances Derham interview with Suzanne Lunney, 28 May 1975, NLA Oral
 History Collection, oral transcript 345
Jenny Ellis interview with the author, 29 May 2012; 2 May 2013
Katrine Macmahon Ball interview with Mimi Colligan, 1984, sound recording
 courtesy Mimi Colligan, transcipt by Georgine Clarsen
Lenis Wells telephone interview with author, 18 November 2017
Majorie Horne interview with Georgine Clarsen, 5 May 1996; 20 September
 1996, transcript courtesy Georgine Clarsen
Mary Cohn (née Houston) interview with author, 13 August 2008; 3 March
 2009
Milton Green interview with author, 29 September 2015
Pat Peterson interview with Georgine Clarsen, 1 August 1995, transcript
 courtesy Georgine Clarsen
Simon Cohn telephone interview with author, 7 August 2008

OTHER ARCHIVAL MATERIAL

PRIVATE COLLECTION, MILTON GREEN

Harry Lawson, MLA, Jessica Millar reference, 13 May 1924, photocopy of
original

FRANCES DERHAM COLLECTION, UNIVERSITY OF MELBOURNE ARCHIVES

Alfred Derham, 'Alice Anderson' poem, 17 September 1926 (ref.
1988.0061.0751)

Alice Anderson poem, undated (ref. 1988.0061.0751)

Frances Derham biography and family history notes (ref. 1988.0061.0627)

Frances Derham's 1926 diary (ref. 1988.0061.0270)

Frances Derham's typed statement about Alice's death, undated (ref.
1988.0061.0270)

MELBOURNE LYCEUM CLUB RECORDS

A. E. F. Anderson, Melbourne Lyceum Club application, 4 December 1918,
Box 9, State Library of Victoria

PUBLIC RECORDS OF VICTORIA

Proceedings of Inquest, VPRS 24/P/0, Unit 1099, File 1926/1034

Supreme Court of Victoria (Probate Jurisdiction), 'Inventory of Assets in the
Will of Alice Anderson Foley, late of Cotham Road Kew in the State of
Victoria, Spinster deceased', 20 October 1926, VPRS 28/P/3, Unit 1704,
File 211/726

RACV ARCHIVES

Minutes of General Committee Meeting, 19 June 1918

ACKNOWLEDGEMENTS

One doesn't begin or end a journey like this without scampering down lots of rabbit holes and discovering some very helpful and generous people along the way. Firstly, if not for the productive criticism and camaraderie of my emerging writer's group, The Cartridge Family, I wouldn't have had a halfway quality manuscript to offer anyone. So, to 'family' members past and present, a big warm hug: Phillip Siggins, Suzanne McCourt, Patsy Poppenbeek, Lea Weaver, Geoffrey Dobbs, Robert King, Ranee Mischlewski, Terry Hastings and Greg Every. Thanks to Danielle Clode, who opened my eyes to the possibilities when she led a group of would-be authors through her Writers Victoria Year of Non-Fiction class. And I couldn't have reached publishing stage without the wonderful advocacy of my agent Jacinta di Mase and her trusty sidekick Danielle Binks, and the terrific team at Hachette Australia, especially Sophie Hamley, who showed as much passion for Alice's story as I did, and Rebecca Allen, for her meticulous editing.

If not for historian Dr Mimi Colligan chasing down material in the early 1980s when Alice's sisters and many garage girls were still alive, much of this story would never have come to light, and would have died along with the further passing of time. Historian Dr Georgine Clarsen added to those materials when, for her PhD thesis on early women motorists, she conducted further interviews with Alice's sisters and some garage girls in the mid 1990s. Both Mimi and Georgine have championed me from the beginning and, in the process, become valued friends.

Staff from organisations that have been particularly helpful on my 'how and where to research' learning curve: National Library of Australia, State Library of Victoria (SLV), Public Records Office Victoria. Staff from the Australian Lesbian and Gay Archives who were there from the beginning and continue to donate their time and skills to not only getting the book going but helping with exhibition ideas and launching places: Angela Bailey, Gary Jaynes, Liz Ross and Nick Henderson. Helen Stitt at the RACV Archives has been particularly helpful in seeking out sources as well as giving me the opportunity co-present with her on early women motorists at the RACV Club. David Russell at the Victorian Automobile Chamber of Commerce has been equally generous in helping me access valuable source material. Thank you also to the Melbourne Lyceum for allowing me access to their archives at the SLV. And special thanks to Katie Wood at the University of Melbourne Archives, whose enthusiasm for Alice's story was apparent from the beginning.

Many thanks also go to my medical 'team', who have kept me alive and mobile: Dr Vagif Soultanov, Professor Richard de Steiger, Mr Michael Johnson and Dr Walter Plehwe.

Then there are relatives of Alice Anderson: Penelope Alexander and Mark Derham (Frankie's grandchildren); Peto Beal (Claire's daughter) and Jenny Ellis (Katrine's daughter). All have shared their family histories with deep and abiding trust in my ability to get this biography off the ground. Likewise, family members of garage girls: Simon Cohn (grandson of Nancy Houston and son of Mary Cohn); Maurice Martin (recently deceased, son of Marie Edie).

Thanks to *The Age* journalist Carolyn Webb who approached me back in 2015 for a feature article on Alice Anderson that reached out to more relatives of garage girls, who then made contact to tell me their stories, and share valuable photographs and memorabilia, namely Anna Louise Nolan (great niece of Peggy Bunt) and Milton Green (son of Jessie Millar). Thanks also goes out to staff at the National Motor Museum, South Australia, for realising the dream of a stand-alone semi-permanent exhibition of Alice Anderson's garage.

And last, but certainly not least, those individuals who have donated their time and expertise in various ways: Peter and Julie Langford, for teaching me all there is to know about the 1926 model Austin 7. I shall never forget that thrilling ride in the passenger seat down Riversdale Road, terrified the narrow-width tyres were going to get stuck in the tram tracks; John Streeter, for his knowledge of guns; Ros Walker, for her invaluable knowledge of the film production world; Kerry Greenwood, Graeme Davison and Miriam Margoyles, thank you; Dennis Woodley for enlightening me on the 'Get Out and Get Under' song; Dr Helen Lunt and Petrina Dakin, for their enthusiasm in lending their own research skills to the project; and to Carolyn Lunt, for her response to impromptu requests for feedback and patience for the time it has taken to get to this point.

INDEX